THE COMPLETE BREAD BAKING COOKBOOK

1000 Days Homemade Bread Baking Recipes with the Beginner-friendly Crash Course to Achieve Bakery-Quality Results At Home

MARIAN D. BENNETT

Copyright© 2022 By Marian D. Bennett All Rights Reserved

This book is copyright protected. It is only for personal use. You cannot amend, distribute, sell, use, quote or paraphrase any part of the content within this book, without the consent of the author or publisher.

Under no circumstances will any blame or legal responsibility be held against the publisher, or author, for any damages, reparation, or monetary loss due to the information contained within this book, either directly or indirectly.

Disclaimer Notice:

Please note the information contained within this document is for educational and entertainment purposes only. All effort has been executed to present accurate, up to date, reliable, complete information. No warranties of any kind are declared or implied. Readers acknowledge that the author is not engaged in the rendering of legal, financial, medical or professional advice. The content within this book has been derived from various sources. Please consult a licensed professional before attempting any techniques outlined in this book.

By reading this document, the reader agrees that under no circumstances is the author responsible for any losses, direct or indirect, that are incurred as a result of the use of the information contained within this document, including, but not limited to, errors, omissions, or inaccuracies.

Table of Contents

Introduction	1
Chapter 1	
Basics of Bread Baking	2
What is Bread Baking?	3
Key Terminology	3
Know your Bread-making Methods	3
Steps to Making Great Bread	5
Pro Tips for Bread Baking	6
Chapter 2	
Yeast Breads	8
Pita	9
Ursa Baguette	10
Red Onion Focaccia	11
Artichoke Fougasse	12
Spelt Pretzels	13
Hoagie Rolls	14
Bagel	15
Olive Filone	16
Oven-Dried-Tomato Stecca	17
Chapter 3	
Sourdough Breads	18
Sourdough Starter	19
Simple Sourdough Table Bread	20
Sesame Durum Bread	21
Pane Di Genzano	22
Spelt Sourdough Boule	23
100% Sonora Slab	24
Buckwheat Buttermilk Bread	25
Omni Bread	26
Ciabatta Grano Arso With Einkorn	27
Sourdough Baguette	28
Blueberry-Lemon Sourdough Country Bread	29
Chapter 4	
All-Purpose Breads	30
Master No-Knead Rustic Boule	31
Fougasse	32
Bountiful Bagels	32
Pizza Dough	33
Sesame-Coated Bâtard	33
Sub Rolls	34
Pita Pockets	34
Foolproof Focaccia	35
Olive Oil Sandwich Loaf	35
Herbed Muffin Pan Peasant Rolls	35
Rosemary Bread Sticks	36
Easiest English Muffins	36
Chapter 5	
Enriched Breads	37
Brioche	38
Chocolate Babka	39
Challah	40
Springtime Challah Snails	40
Cinnamon Wreath Bread	41
Sorghum Whole Wheat Bread (Vegan)	42
Zucchini Spice Quick Bread	42
Star Bread	43
Berry Scones	44
Potato Burger Buns	45
Cheese-Filled Challah	46
Rosemary-Tomato Focaccia	47
Chapter 6	
Keto Breads	48
Low Carb Bun For One	49
Low Carb Vanilla Bread	49
Keto Blueberry Lemon Bread	49
Grain Free Cashew Sourdough Bread	50
Easy Low Carb Baked Bread	50
Keto Pumpkin Bread	50
Keto Baked French Toast Bread	51
Keto Pumpkin Bread Loaf	51
Keto Bun And Roll Recipe	52
Best Keto Bread	52
Keto Mummy Dogs	52
Chapter 7	
French Breads	53
Fougasse	54
Pain Complet	55
Le Cramique	56
French Baguette	57
Fouée	57
Croissants	58
Buckwheat French Bread	59
La Charbonée De Boulanger	59
Croque Monsieur	60
Oysters with Mignonette	60
Chapter 8	
Pan Loaves	61
Sandwich Bread	62
Light Wheat Bread	62
Whole Wheat Pan Loaf	63
Cinnamon Raisin Light Wheat Pan Bread	63
Multiseed Light Wheat Pan Bread	64
New York Deli Rye Pan Bread	64
Turmeric Fennel Pan Loaf	65
Buckwheat Pan Bread	66
Einkorn Pan Loaf	66
Flaxseed Pan Bread	67
Whole Wheat Chocolate Babka	67
Kamut Cinnamon-Raisin Swirl Bread	68
New York Deli Rye	69
Millet Hamburger Buns	69
Chapter 9	
Sandwich Breads and Pizza	70
Sandwich Loaf Bread	71
Pizza Crust	71
Sesame Sandwich Bread Squares	72
Cinnamon-Raisin Sandwich Bread	72

Honey, Nuts, And Oats Sandwich Bread	73
Garlic Butter Focaccia Bread	73
Chicago Deep-Dish Pepperoni Pan Pizza	74
Parmesan Pull-Apart Pizza Breadsticks	74
Einkorn Sandwich Bread	75
Whole Wheat Sandwich Bread	75
Focaccia Picnic Sandwiches	76
Marbled Rye Sandwich Bread	77
Sesame Spelt Sandwich Bread	78
Oatmeal Sandwich Bread	78
Honey Kamut Sandwich Bread	79
Muffaletta-Style Pizza	79
Grilled Pizzas	80

Chapter 10
Sweets and Treats for Leftover Starter — 81

Coconut Sourdough Pancakes	82
Pecan Waffles	82
Sourdough Chocolate Chip Cookies with Several Flavor Variations	83
Sourdough Tropical Carrot Cake	84
Flavorful Focaccia Bread	85
Sourdough Breadstick Twists	86
Sourdough Pizza Dough	86
Double Piecrust	87
Southern Sourdough Biscuits	88
Sourdough Pretzels	89
Sourdough Cinnamon-Sugar Doughnuts	90
Roasted Garlic and Cheddar Cheese Bialys	91
Holiday Fruited Loaf	92

Chapter 11
Cookies, Brownies, and Bars — 93

Blondies	94
Chewy Fudgy Brownies	94
Salted Caramel Brownies	95
Coconut Macaroons	95
Pumpkin Everything Squares	96
Zesty Lemon Squares	96
Red Velvet Whoopie Pies	97
S'mores Cookies	97
The Softest Peanut Butter Cookies	98
Dunkable Chocolate Chip Cookies	98
Thin Mint Copycat Cookies	99
Blackberry Shortbread Thumbprints	99
Easy Frosted Sugar Cookies	100
Cranberry Oatmeal Cookies	100
Sensational Snickerdoodles	101
Biscotti	101

Chapter 12
Cakes and Cupcakes — 102

Vanilla Cupcakes	103
Pumpkin Pie Cupcakes	103
Thin Mint Cupcakes	104
Super Moist Cream Cheese Pound Cake	104
Gingerbread Cupcakes	105
Gooey Butter Cake	105
Very Strawberry Cupcakes	106
Angel Food Cake	106
Fudgy Chocolate Cupcakes	107
Death-by-Chocolate Cake	107
Carrot Cake	108
Lemon Lover's Bundt Cake	109
Classic Cheesecake	110
Triple-Layer Birthday Cake with Buttercream Frosting	111

Chapter 13
Holidays — 112

Sweet Levain Rolls Master Recipe	113
Red, White, and Blueberry Bread	114
Sourdough Rustic Bread Master Recipe	115
Olive Oil Rolls	116
Brioche Cinnamon Rolls	117
Red Velvet Chocolate Chip Bread	117
Cranberry Orange Hot Cross Buns	118
Apple Spice Sourdough Bread	119
Ciabatta Sandwich Rolls	119
Bavarian-Inspired Pretzel Rolls	120
Pumpkin Rolls	121
Molasses Spice Cinnamon Swirl Bread	122
Caramel Pecan Sticky Buns	123

Appendix 1 Measurement Conversion Chart — 124
Appendix 2 The Dirty Dozen and Clean Fifteen — 125
Appendix 3 Index — 126

Introduction

The art of baking bread goes back to Egyptian times, but the principles are still the same. Bread has always been a staple, bringing families together and providing nourishment. Do you think of your grandmother's kitchen when those delicious sweet aromas fill the air? What fond memories come to mind when baking bread? Finding this book means you are longing for that experience of making bread in the comfort of your home. Welcome! This is the right place to be. Our bread baking cookbook will guide you through the whole process. We understand that bread baking might seem challenging, and you may find it impossible to spend hours in your kitchen preparing the dough instead of ordering it from a nearby supermarket and getting it delivered in minutes, thinking bread is just bread! The good news is that bread is not just bread. We understand your needs and have prepared a list of super-easy recipes to shine a light on your kitchen. After trying your first recipe, you will start to find your answers. A new hobby like baking homemade bread will bring more warmth and coziness to your home. We do not want to take too much of your time but first, let us help you understand:

What is Bread Baking?

Bread baking is preparing and making bread with dry heat without exposure to a flame. Bread is the product of a mixture of flour, water, yeast, and other ingredients to the baker's preference. Bread baking involves mixing the ingredients into a stiff dough and then baking it into a loaf. No matter the process you use in your dough preparation, the dough must be able to stretch out when pulled, hold the gases produced during rising and be stable enough to hold its cell structure. As a new baker, it's important to understand that your flour contains two proteins (gliadin and glutenin). The two proteins form gluten when mixed with water. Gluten influences the baking properties of your dough and its mixing and kneading properties. To successfully walk through this journey, you must first understand how to mix your ingredients. Unlike other forms of cooking, where you can randomly mix ingredients and still have a properly cooked dish, baking starts right from preparation. You lose your bread right from the start if the mixing goes wrong. We want you to enjoy the journey right from the beginning. The primary goal of why we have prepared this cookbook is to make your bread-making process easy by achieving dough that will rise easily and cook good bread for your family. Your family will appreciate being woken up by the aroma of freshly baked homemade bread. What a gift!

Key Terminology

Proofing. This step in the yeast or other baking process allows the dough to rest and rise for the final time before baking.
Fermentation. An anaerobic process changes sugars and starches into carbon dioxide and other simple substances.
Kneading. This is the process of massaging dough before baking it.
Yeast. It is a leavening agent that causes the dough to rise. It converts fermentable sugars into carbon dioxide and ethanol.
Oven spring. This is how the dough expands and grows in the oven before the crust hardens.
Rest. It is the process of letting the dough set for some time before baking to prevent shrinkage.
Shaping. This means molding the dough into a shape of your preference.
Leaven. A substance that causes the dough to expand.
Gluten. This is a protein found in wheat products.
Hydration. This is the ratio of liquid to flour in your dough. The liquid could be water or milk.
Folding. This is the process of carefully adding a light mixture to a heavier mixture. It develops gluten and the strength of the dough.

Know your Bread-making Methods

With the diversity of bread-making methods, you can easily get confused. Therefore, we have prepared some recipes to save you from all the hard work and confusion. Choose your method today!

- **Straight dough method.** This is a technique that is commonly used. It is also known as direct dough. The common white bread, milk, and brown bread are baked through this method. It is the easiest and most basic to prepare. First, you have to directly mix the ingredients and then knead until the dough is ready, which you'll have to leave for about an hour to proof, followed by a second proofing before baking it. The ingredients used in this method include flour, yeast, sugar, salt, butter, and water. You should also note that if you use dry yeast, add warm water and a small amount of sugar.
- **No time dough method.** This technique takes less time to prepare compared to other bread baking methods. The dough takes less time because the fermentation period is lesser than in other methods. Unlike the straight dough method, the dough is proofed once and shaped. Ingredients to use in this method include flour, yeast, sugar, salt, butter and water. This method is suitable for products with fewer sponges (hard loaves of bread). It is important to note that in this method, the mixing process should be faster so that gluten formation happens more quickly. Although this method is faster, it will compromise the taste of your bread due to the increased amount of yeast added.
- **Delayed salt method.** The delayed method is similar to the straight dough method, but the difference is that in the delayed salt method, the salt is added later on to enable the dough to continue with fermentation. Salt stops yeast action. Oil is also added later on, along with salt. Ingredients used in this method include flour, yeast, sugar, salt, butter and water.
- **Sponge and dough method.** In this method, the sponge and dough are prepared in two stages. Pre-fermentation for sponge mixing and dough final mixing. The aim is to get a better aroma and flavor. Fermentation helps produce alcohol, carbon dioxide and enzymes, which improve aroma and flavor. The dough also has enough time to rest. Therefore the bread is softer.

PRE-FERMENT DOUGH METHODS

We would like to walk you through some of the pre-ferment dough methods. Please stay with us.

- **Biga Method**

Biga is a low hydration method used in Italian baking. Fermentation takes longer if compared to the poolish method. How much do you love a ciabatta? Did you know it is made through this method? Biga's technique adds flavor and texture. This method is used for pieces of bread that need an open texture with holes. It also helps by preserving the bread.

- **Poolish Method**

As the name suggests, Poolish was developed by the polish bakers, which the French bakers later adopted. Unlike biga, poolish is highly hydrated. It comprises equal amounts of water and flour, hence the high hydration. Using a whisk when mixing is recommended to ensure no lumps of dry flour. Fermentation time will depend on the yeast used and the environment temperature. As a baker, you should understand how the environment's temperature affects pre-fermentation. During winter, use more yeast and less in summer. High hydration results in a dough that will rise better in your oven and one that is difficult to handle. Ready to make a baguette?

- **Sponge Method**

Unlike other methods, the sponge contains all the yeast of the recipe and, most times, all the liquid. It is a quick and explosive method taking less than forty-five mins to prepare, unlike the other slow methods. This method is mostly used in doughs that do not require much acidity and complexity, such as enriched dough. It gives the bread more character and preserves it longer. This type of pre-ferment acts as the leavening agent and shouldn't over ferment it. If you are longing for that cinnamon bun or butter rolls, you should consider this method.

- **Pate Fermented/Old Dough Method**

Pate fermented is a French term meaning, "fermented dough". It being a French term doesn't mean it is only used in France, but that it is a method used all over the world. Unlike other methods, pate fermentation does not impart a sour flavor. It is a convenient method for often bakers. After you have finished baking for the day, you can put the remaining in the refrigerator to slow ferment and use it straight from the fridge the next time you want to bake. This method is best used with lean doughs as they do not contain many ingredients. Do not use dairy products or eggs in your dough if you use this method. Dried nuts and fruits are not recommended. If you still want to use them, make sure you pinch the dough you need before adding them.

Steps to Making Great Bread

Bread baking is a critical process, therefore, you should be careful and follow all the predictable steps. Bread baking shouldn't be challenging anymore. We would like you to enjoy the experience and the bread itself. Every step affects the final result, and we will help you understand how. Here is the bread baking process overview:

- **Scaling**. This is the first step in successful baking. It involves weighing all ingredients and ensuring you have the right water temperature and baking equipment. A good plan baking process ensures everything runs smoothly. Mistakes during scaling risk the intended result, and it will be difficult to determine what went wrong during the process. A good baker will ensure consistency right from the beginning. You should not miss your favorite bread due to poor scaling skills, do you?
- **Mixing**. This process has two main functions, to distribute ingredients evenly and to allow the development of gluten to bake the best bread possible. Mixing hydrates the dough as it combines all the ingredients. Each type of dough has a mixing time depending on the type of flour and the preferred method of use. Mixing is an act of balance. You shouldn't overdo it as the dough will reduce its elasticity, and if underdone, there could be some unmixed patches that will not rise, giving the bread a poor final appearance.
- **Rising (fermentation)**. After properly mixing your dough, you should give it time to ferment. The process will enable the rough dough to change into a smooth dough with better gas holding properties. Carbon dioxide and alcohol are formed during this process from carbohydrate breakdown. Starch and sugars are naturally found in flour. Yeast requires much oxygen to complete fermentation. The dough has a limited oxygen supply; therefore, the yeast achieves partial fermentation producing carbon dioxide and alcohol.. This is well known as alcohol fermentation. Carbon dioxide produced is essential as it enables the dough to rise as the alcohol evaporates during the process.
- **Kneading and folding**. This is a technique that involves stretching and folding your dough in a uniform manner that helps develop gluten and release excess gas. All gas holes formed during the rising process are released through this process. Stretching and folding give better results. Doughs without proper gluten become difficult to shape and may refuse to rise. If you decide to go for homemade bread, make sure you knead your dough properly as it will develop great gluten, which means it will be strong enough, stretchy, rise and hold its shape in the oven. You'll have your bread as you imagined it. What fun!
- **Shaping**. At this stage, you determine the shape of your bread.
- **Proofing or second rising**. This is the final rising before baking your bread. Again the dough is left to form more gas bubbles. As soon as the dough has formed enough gas bubbles, the dough is put in the oven to bake. Make sure you follow the recipe to the letter. If the rise is not enough, your bread will lack flavor and be as heavy as a brick.
- **Baking**. This process transforms dough into a readily digestible product which, in our case, is bread. The product is light and flavorful. As the heat in the oven penetrates the dough, the gases in it expand, increasing in

size. The process is known as oven spring. As the heat increases, the carbon dioxide in the solution transforms into a gas and moves to existing gas cells. It also transforms the liquids into gases; the produced alcohol evaporates. High temperature means a high fermentation rate. The yeast dies at approximately 46 degrees Celsius. Different enzymes die at different temperatures during the process. As the process continues, the internal temperature goes up to 98 degrees Celsius. Your bread is not baked until this internal temperature is reached. Browning occurs at a rate above 160 degrees Celsius.

- **Cooling**. Bread cools quickly after leaving the oven. It is cooled at 35 degrees Celsius, which you later slice and wrap. Cooling is enabled through evaporation which is affected by air temperature and movement around the loaf.

Pro Tips for Bread Baking

- **Weigh your ingredients**. Scaling is key in bread baking, and if you go wrong in this stage, it's most likely that your baking will go wrong.
- **Temperature is critical**. This includes both water and air temperatures. The temperature of your baking water is important as it creates the temperature of the dough, which determines how long it will take for your dough to rise. The temperature of your room or environment is also important in fermentation. In summer, you should use water with a lower temperature, and vice versa during winter.
- **Time.** As with temperature, time is important! It unlocks the flavor in the bread. You should understand how long you need to ferment and bake your bread. If you get the wrong time, everything goes wrong. Our cookbook will help you with this. We've included baking times in all our recipes.
- **Use the right yeast**. Yeast has three types: fresh, active dried and fast-acting dried yeast. Your recipe will guide you in choosing the type of yeast to use.
- **Store yeast properly**. If you want your yeast to go for a few days, store it in a fridge, and if you want it to go for months, you can decide to freeze it.
- **Be careful with salt**. Too much salt prevents yeast action and may lead to high blood pressure. Follow the recipe closely to avoid this.
- **Practice.** You will get better at baking if you keep practicing.

SUPER-EASY RECIPES

Sourdough bread. This is one of the oldest breads. Unlike other slices of bread, it uses wild yeast that occurs naturally. Sourdough bread originated in Egypt. It is produced as a result of a long fermentation process. This process creates lactic acid, which gives the dough a tangy and sour flavor. A longer fermentation period improves the flavor of the bread. This bread is nutritious and has many health benefits, such as blood sugar control and helping with indigestion. It's time to make a bomb-grilled cheese!

WHOLE WHEAT BREAD

Whole wheat bread is different from the common white bread. The whole wheat makes it different. To bake this bread, you use whole wheat flour; this means the flour still has its germ, bran, and endosperm intact. Unlike white bread, it is healthier as it contains more fiber. Besides this bread being very nutritious, it also has a richer aroma. You'll be able to differentiate whole wheat bread from a piece of white bread as it has a darker color, rough texture, and a better taste. For a healthy sandwich, go for this bread.

NO-KNEAD BREAD

This technique involves a longer fermentation period instead of kneading. Your dough should be given enough time to rise, preferably 12 to 18 hours. Once the rising time is over, the dough will have doubled in size and bubbles. Fold, shape, and give it another hour (to rise again), then bake. It has a lower yeast content than other recipes and wet dough.

ENRICHED BREAD

Enriched bread had added ingredients such as eggs, milk, and butter. It has a high-fat percentage and is sweeter than other lean loaves of bread. Do you remember that brioche you had last? What did it taste like? Our cookbook will help you prepare this in the comfort of your home.

WHY HOMEMADE BREAD?

You may ask yourself why you must prepare your bread instead of walking to a nearby bakery and buying one. We have combined a list of reasons homemade bread will always be your all-time bread. The benefits include:

- The choice of ingredients is in your hands. You do not have to eat additives that you are not comfortable with.
- You enjoy fresh bread straight from the oven.
- Homemade bread tastes better than commercial bread. You may decide to add ingredients that suit you, unlike commercially made bread which tastes the same as it has to meet a certain standard.
- You can cater to food allergies. In case of any allergic reaction, you can do away with the ingredient.
- Sourdough bread will reduce the chances of getting diabetes.
- Homemade bread has no preservatives.
- Home baking can be a fun activity or hobby.
- You can prepare homemade bread gifts for the people you love.

Bread baking shouldn't be a challenging task anymore. This should be a smooth journey with the basics we have provided. It is important to note that some common mistakes people make cost them a lot. The common mistakes include the following: not baking in a preheated oven, opening the oven when it's not necessary, wrong ingredient temperatures, being uncomfortable with a sticky consistency which makes them tempted to add more flour which spoils the dough, not buying or using a digital scale, avoiding to prepare baking notes and even switching the type of flour to use. No matter if you have all the ingredients and equipment, if you make these mistakes, that is the end of a proper bread baking process. The results will be disappointing. The time has come for us to wish you all the best in your kitchen, follow our recipes to the letter, avoid these common mistakes, and you will not regret buying this book. A journey of a thousand miles begins with a single step. Make yours now. It's baking time, enjoy!

Chapter 2
Yeast Breads

Pita

They're easy, quick, and foolproof. Fun! In the oven, they puff up like balloons. Pita are easy to make with kids because you roll out the dough with a pin. I didn't want to complicate things by using yogurt or ghee. A little oil makes the dough tender.

Prep time: 55 minutes | Cook time: 45 minutes | Serves about 20 pita, about 7-inch diameter

- 719 g (5¾ cups) bolted hard wheat flour
- 475 g (2 cups) water
- 48 g (3½ tablespoons) extra-virgin olive oil
- 4 g (1¼ teaspoons) dry yeast
- 21 g (3½ teaspoons) salt

1. Mix. Measure the flour and set aside. Combine the water, oil, yeast, flour, and salt in the bowl of a stand mixer. Mix with the dough hook on low speed for 1 minute, then switch to medium speed and mix until the bread clings to the hook and clears the sides of the bowl, about another 6 minutes. The mixer will really get rocking and rolling, so do not leave it unattended or it might just walk off your countertop. A damp towel placed under the mixer will minimize this scooting around. (This trick works well to keep cutting boards in place, too.)
2. Bulk ferment. Transfer the dough to an oiled bowl and cover with a tea towel or slip a plastic grocery bag, plastic wrap, or beeswax wrap over the bowl if the room is very dry. Leave to rise at room temperature (65° to 75°F) for 1½ hours. The dough should nearly double in size.
3. Shape. After bulk fermentation, place a baking stone on a rack set about two-thirds of the way to the top of the oven. Preheat your oven to 500°F.
4. Turn the dough out onto a floured countertop and divide it into 60-gram pieces. Keep in mind that making too many unnecessary cuts will make the dough tougher to shape, so get a sense of the amount of dough you need with the first few pieces and then try to get close to the correct size for the rest of the pieces in one or two tries. They certainly don't need to be exact.
5. Round each piece by patting out gently and tucking four sides in toward the center. Then tighten it into a ball by turning it over onto a dry part of the countertop, cupping your hand over it, applying gentle pressure, and rotating your hand in a circle, kind of dragging the seam against the counter to seal the seam and tighten the surface. The seam should roll around but stay in contact with the countertop as you drag the dough in a circle, increasing the surface tension and rolling it into a ball. With practice you'll get a perfectly round ball, but if you're having a hard time, balls for pita bread don't need to be perfectly round. Cover all the balls with a tea towel.
6. Gather some flour for dusting, a rolling pin, a timer, tongs or hot pads, another tea towel, and a plate for stacking the baked pita on as they cool. I prefer to alternate between rolling and baking for a few reasons, but mostly because I'm impatient and I like to bounce around. But if you have a different temperament, you could do all the rolling, then all the baking. Either way, dust a small area on the counter liberally with flour. Take the first dough ball and flatten it with the pin. Flip it and roll it out more. Keep flipping, rotating, and rolling until you get a circle about 7 inches in diameter, dusting it with flour as needed to prevent sticking. The circle should be very thin, about ⅛ inch. Set it aside and repeat with a second dough ball. If your baking stone can comfortably hold three 7-inch circles, you could roll out a third dough. The pita will be baked in batches, and every few rounds, turn your broiler on and wait a few minutes to blast more heat to the top of the oven. Then turn the broiler off and turn the oven back to 500°F and continue to bake. You open the oven a lot in this recipe because of all the batches, and the broiler helps recover the heat that gets delivered to the top of the pita. If you don't have a broiler, expect your oven to cool more as you bake, so later rounds may take longer than the first ones. Try not to open the oven unnecessarily.
7. Bake. I hope this goes without saying, but this part of the recipe—the oven work—is not kid-friendly. Set your timer to 45 seconds. Open your oven, pull out the rack, and quickly but carefully lay each rolled pita on the hot stone. I make this a bit more efficient by draping two or three pita rounds over my forearm; this leaves my hands free to open the oven and pull out the rack. Then the pita rounds are right there to lay one at a time on the hot stone. Quickly push the rack back, close the oven, and start your timer. The pita will be done in about a minute, give or take, depending on your oven, so start checking at 45 seconds. In a perfect world, the pita will fully inflate like a balloon with one large bubble, it will have singed in a spot or two, and it will still be soft and just barely done inside, so when you put it under a towel, it will steam itself. My ideal flavor comes when the pita bake really quickly and burn just a touch, but not all ovens get hot enough. Know that pita can go from soft and perfect to crispy crackers quickly, so get them out of the oven before they dry out. When they come out of the oven, they are full of hot steam. Use tongs or hot pads to grab them and transfer them to a plate. Cover with a tea towel to allow the baked pita to steam and soften.
8. Roll out another set of pita and bake them off. To keep the pita warm and soft, I like to bury the freshly baked pita in the middle of the stack and cover the whole stack in a tea towel. That way the new hot pita steams itself and its neighbors. Once you have the hang of things, you can roll while you bake and minimize down time. Troubleshooting tip: if your pita aren't fully puffing, they probably aren't being rolled thin enough or don't have enough top heat.
9. Pita are best super fresh, but they do keep for several days in an airtight container at room temperature.

Ursa Baguette

For years, I thought baguettes were a baker's mark of skill. Then I saw them as sad industrial baking products. I've rediscovered Ursa Bakery since they returned to farmers' markets. They're my best sellers at the market, and it's satisfying to see a customer tuck her baguette under her arm, rip off the end, and eat it. My favorite flour is bolted Redeemer, but any hard wheat flour will work.

Prep time: 55 minutes | Cook time: 55 minutes | Serves 4 baguettes, 16 to 18 inches long

POOLISH
- 194 g (1½ cups) bolted hard wheat flour
- 194 g (¾ cup + 1⅛ tablespoons) water
- 0.27 g (⅛ teaspoon) dry yeast

DOUGH
- 579 g (4⅔ cups) bolted hard wheat flour
- 377 g (1⅔ cups) water
- 1 g (⅓ teaspoon) dry yeast
- 388 g (2½ cups) poolish (from above)
- 15 g (2½ teaspoons) salt

1. Day 1: mix poolish. Measure the flour and set aside. Choose a container with a tight-fitting lid and enough space for the poolish to triple in volume. Pour in the water and sprinkle in the yeast. Then mix in the flour, stirring just long enough to make sure all the flour is wet. Scrape the bottom of the container to get any stray clumps. Cover with the lid and leave at room temperature (65° to 75°F) to rest overnight, 8 to 16 hours. On the short end of that time, you may get a stiff dough. On the long end, you may get a very extensible dough due to the extra enzyme activity.
2. Day 2: mix dough. Measure the flour and set aside. Combine the water, yeast, poolish, and flour in the bowl of a stand mixer, then mix with the dough hook on low speed for 4 minutes. Cover the bowl with a tea towel and rest at room temperature for 30 minutes.
3. Sprinkle in the salt and mix on low speed for another 4 minutes. Then switch to medium speed and mix for 3 minutes. At the end of mixing, the dough should look shinier than at the beginning. Tug on the dough with your fingertips. When pulled, it should feel cohesive, moderately elastic, and moderately extensible. If it feels super extensible, the dough may be a little overmixed. In that case, skip the first couple of folds in the next step. If it tears before stretching, give it another minute in the mixer. After mixing, test the dough temperature with an instant-read thermometer. It should be around 78°F. If it's lower than that, put the dough in a warm spot. If it's higher, pop it in the fridge for a few minutes. If it's both warm and feeling stiff, mix in about 17 grams cold water. During the winter or in a cold room, you may want to use warm water.
4. Bulk ferment. After mixing, transfer the dough to a lightly oiled bowl, cover with a tea towel, and rest in a draft-free place for 1½ hours total, with folds after 30 and 60 minutes. With each fold, you should notice that the dough has become increasingly active, with bubbles of gas showing under the surface. If it doesn't, the dough may need a little more fermentation time.
5. Preshape. After bulk fermentation, scrape the dough onto a lightly floured countertop. Divide the dough into four equal pieces, each around 340 grams. A very simple preshape is sufficient: take what looks like a short end, then tuck and roll the dough up into a thick tube like a fat jelly roll. Seal the seam with a couple pinches and repeat with the other pieces. Place them seam-side up on a floured surface. Normally we rest doughs seam-side down. But the next shape is intensive, and we don't want to have a bunch of flour on the inside (the seam side). If the room is dry, cover the pieces with a tea towel. Leave them for 20 minutes.
6. Shape. Place a large baking stone and hotel pan on the highest oven rack they will fit on. Preheat the oven to 500°F.
7. To get the final loaf shape, have a couche or a well-floured tea towel ready. Very lightly flour your countertop. A baguette is a fairly dry bread to begin with, so I use a minimal amount of flour on an as-needed basis. In particular, minimize flour along the seam side. To begin stretching, lightly pat out the dough to a rectangle about 8 inches long. Then, gently lift the long edge closest to you, tuck it into the dough, and gently roll forward to the opposite edge. Use your palms to roll the dough back and forth from the center to the ends, but don't squish it down too much. Continue gently rolling the dough back and forth from the center outward until the baguette reaches its full length of 16 to 18 inches, pressing down just on the last inch or so to taper the ends slightly. Since these are home-oven baguettes, they can only be stretched to the length of your stone, so keep that in mind: aim for 16 to 18 inches long. After resting, the loaves will ideally stretch out to their full length right away, but if you're feeling a lot of resistance from the dough (tearing skin or springing back), just stretch each piece partway out, let it relax for a few minutes, and then take it out the rest of the way. Once the baguette reaches its full length, if the seam hasn't sealed well, use your fingers to gently press and seal the seam along the length of the dough.
8. Set the baguette seam-side up on the couche or tea towel and repeat with the remaining pieces. Set each baguette down about an inch from the one before and then slide it right up next to its neighbor with the towel folded between them. This nesting system supports the final shape of the baguettes while regulating the temperature and moisture of the dough. It lets a little moisture

out to form a thin skin. If the room is dry, cover the baguettes with another tea towel or the remainder of the couche. Leave the baguettes to rise at room temperature for 30 to 45 minutes. When ready, the baguettes will have plumped up to about 1½ times their original size.

9. Bake. Baguettes get their signature, crusty "ears" from their oven spring. To get them, the dough must be active (gaining volume and showing bubbles) when the baguettes go in.
10. Cut a sheet of parchment paper that will fit over the back side of a half sheet pan to use as a peel (or line a large cutting board with parchment). Then gently lift and transfer two baguettes to the parchment, flipping them over so they are seam-side down. Adjust them so they are straight and evenly spaced from each other. Re-cover the remaining baguettes with the couche or a tea towel. Working quickly, score each baguette three to five times with a few almost perfectly centered lines from end to end.
11. Quickly, but carefully, open your oven, pull the rack that you are baking on partway out, and move the hot hotel pan to the stovetop or side of the oven. Slide the parchment paper with the baguettes onto the stone. Still working quickly, but without burning yourself or smooshing the baguettes, rest one side of the hotel pan on the back of the stone, spray water into the pan, then set the pan onto the stone over the baguettes to trap steam. Close the oven and bake for 8 minutes. Remove the hotel pan completely and then rotate the loaves from side to side and front to back to ensure even color. At this point, the baguettes will be full size, and some spots will have turned golden in color. Ideally, you'll have a nice crisp ear on every cut, and those will color first, along with the ends. Bake (without the hotel pan) until the predominant color all over the baguettes is a light terra-cotta, slightly darker than the skin of butternut squash, an additional 8 to 10 minutes. Remove the baguettes to a rack to cool and repeat the scoring and baking with the remaining baguettes.
12. Try to eat them within 36 hours; baguettes are not for long keeping.

Red Onion Focaccia

Mastering Pizza has the recipe. This traditional focaccia is about an inch thick, airy, light, and made with baguette dough. This recipe compares baguettes and focaccia based on their baking traditions. Baguettes and focaccia have different shapes, but similar doughs.

Prep time: 55 minutes | Cook time: 55 minutes | Serves 1 half sheet pan focaccia, 18 by 13 inches

DOUGH
1,360 g (2 quarts) ursa baguette dough

TOPPING
¼ cup extra-virgin olive oil, plus some for shaping
2 teaspoons balsamic vinegar
1 small red onion, sliced lengthwise about ¼ inch thick
1 tablespoon coarse salt, such as maldon
½ teaspoon freshly ground black pepper

1. Day 1: mix poolish. Follow the instructions for mixing the baguette dough poolish.
2. Day 2: mix dough. Continue making the baguette dough through the bulk fermentation.
3. Preshape. Drizzle a little water on your countertop and spread it around so the surface is wet but not puddled. Turn the dough out onto the countertop, then give it a loose preshape by folding all four edges in toward the center and rolling it over so it is seam-side down. Spread a teaspoon or two of oil on the top of the dough, cover with a tea towel, and leave to rest for 30 minutes.
4. Make topping. While the dough rests, heat a sauté pan over medium-low heat. Add 2 tablespoons of the oil and the balsamic vinegar. Add the onion slices and sauté until they sweat down a bit and soften, 8 to 10 minutes, stirring occasionally. Transfer the onion to a plate and spread out to cool.
5. Shape. Now, I hope you don't mind a bit of a mess. Line a half sheet pan with parchment paper. Spread a couple tablespoons of olive oil over a section of your countertop and use a bench knife to pick up the dough and transfer it to the oiled area. Stretch the dough from left to right by lifting a section of it and letting it lengthen under its own weight, kind of like stretching a section of pizza dough. Coax it out farther by using your fingers to dock the dough, pressing your fingers deep in all over the dough. Try to work the edges first, then the center to get an even thickness throughout. You ultimately want a rectangular shape. Continue going all around the dough, lifting and tugging sections to work the dough to about the size of your half sheet pan. It is better to have the dough a little overstretched and crumpled in the pan than understretched and dull looking. Now carefully and quickly lift the dough under your hands and forearms and transfer it to the pan. This will stretch it farther. Coax and tug it gently to evenly fill the pan. Scatter the onion evenly over the focaccia so there are no large clumps. Leave the dough to rise in a draft-free place until it is puffy, about 1 hour.
6. Bake. Place a large baking stone on the middle rack of the oven. Preheat the oven to 450°F. Drizzle the focaccia with the remaining 2 tablespoons olive oil. Dock it all over by poking your fingers deep into the dough. Sprinkle the top with the salt and pepper, then load the pan into the oven on the stone. Bake for 15 minutes, then rotate the pan and bake until lightly browned, another 5 to 10 minutes. Depan by sliding the focaccia to a rack to cool.
7. Focaccia tastes best on the day it is baked.

Artichoke Fougasse

Provençal fougasse is similar to Italian focaccia. I learned it at Seattle's Tall Grass Bakery. The fun shape makes fougasse popular at farmers' markets. "That giant pretzel thing" or "fugazi" Fougasse is traditionally shaped like an oval leaf or sheaf of wheat. You cut the dough with scissors to make leaf veins. My fougasse resembles an inverted peace sign. As with the Red Onion Foccacia, I like to start with Ursa Baguette dough to simplify things. Here, you can add anything. I love poached artichokes.

Prep time: 55 minutes | Cook time: 65 minutes| Serves 4 fougasses, about 12-inch diameter

- 1,360 g (2 quarts) ursa baguette dough
- 203 g (¾ cup) poached artichoke hearts
- 23 g (1¾ tablespoons) extra-virgin olive oil
- 3 g (½ teaspoon) salt

1. Day 1: mix poolish. Follow the instructions for mixing the baguette dough poolish.
2. Day 2: mix dough. Chop the artichoke hearts into pieces between ¼ and ½ inch.
3. Continue making the baguette dough through the mixing stage. After mixing on medium speed for 3 minutes, add the oil, artichokes, and salt and mix on low speed until mostly incorporated, just a minute or so.
4. Bulk ferment. Transfer the dough to a lightly oiled bowl, cover with a tea towel, and rest in a draft-free place for 1½ hours total, giving the dough a four-fold after 30 and 60 minutes. With each fold, the dough should become increasingly active with bubbles of gas showing under the surface. It should also feel somewhat stretchy and smooth. Make sure the oil and artichokes are evenly incorporated.
5. Preshape. Place a large baking stone on the middle rack of the oven. Preheat the oven to 500°F.
6. Turn the dough out onto a lightly floured countertop and gently pat it out. Divide the dough into four equal pieces, each about 400 grams. Loosely preshape each piece by patting it down and folding all four edges in toward the center. Set the pieces seam-side down on the countertop, cover with a tea towel, and let rest for 30 minutes.
7. Shape. You will shape and bake these one at a time, so be prepared to spend about an hour mostly in the kitchen. Cut a sheet of parchment paper that will fit over the back side of a half sheet pan to use as a peel. Have plenty of flour at hand to keep the fougasse from sticking. For each piece of dough, pat out to an oval about 1½ inches thick and dust with flour. Grab a pair of scissors. Starting and ending about an inch from the edge, make four slightly fanned cuts all the way through the fougasse. Immediately dust flour into the holes you cut to keep them from sticking. You could also make other shapes and decorative cuts if you prefer.
8. Either way, stretch the dough from the holes out to its final size by pulling and stretching from the thickest parts with your fingers in the holes. If your dough is stiff enough to pick up, you can lift it, allowing gravity to pull down the "branches" of dough between the holes, so each branch is about an inch in diameter. It's okay if some branches get slightly thinner but try to pull and work out the thickest ones. Stretch out the dough more than you might expect to: it will puff and partially fill the holes, and you don't want them to close completely. The final diameter of the whole fougasse should be about 12 inches. Slide the fougasse onto the parchment-lined peel, adjusting to ensure the shape is artful, with big spaces between the branches. The shape should be somewhat like a triangular leaf; my fougasse tends to have two larger holes on the bottom of the leaf and two slightly smaller holes on top, like a peace sign.
9. Bake. Slide the fougasse and parchment paper directly onto the preheated stone. Bake for about 15 minutes. The fougasse is finished when the crust reaches a corn-flake color, ideally with some singed bubbles, like a good pizza crust. Unlike many breads in this book, when in doubt, err on the side of underbaking rather than overbaking. With such thin segments, the finished fougasse texture can go from crispy crust and chewy interior to thoroughly crunchy rather quickly. Repeat shaping and baking the remaining dough.
10. Like a baguette, fougasse tastes best eaten within a day or so.

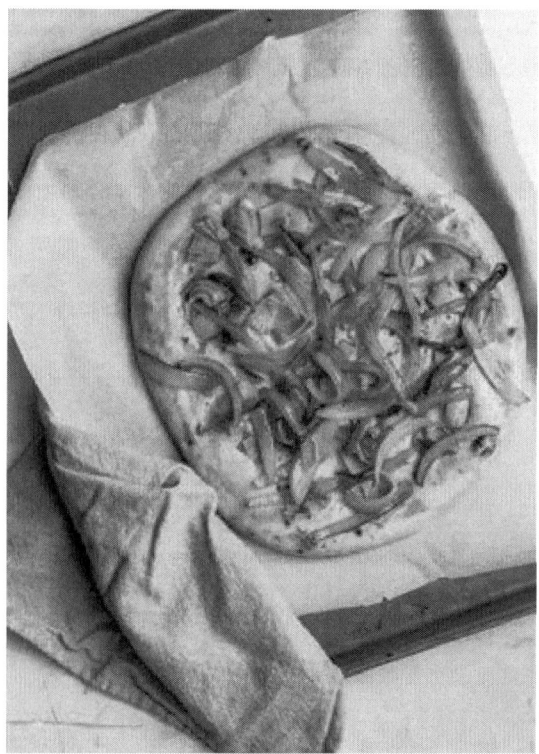

Spelt Pretzels

Spelt flour makes pretzel dough easy to shape and stretch. Spelt adds a mild, sweet wheat flavor. A dip in lye (a strong alkaline) gives Bavarian-style pretzels their dark, shiny crust. Find lye in baking stores or online. Caustic lye requires gloves and eye protection.

Prep time: 55 minutes | Cook time: 55 minutes | Serves 10 large pretzels, 4- to 5-inch diameter, or 30 mini pretzels, 1½- to 2-inch diameter

BIGA
- 91 g (¾ cup) bolted hard wheat flour
- 61 g (¼ cup) water
- 0.06 g (1/64 teaspoon) dry yeast

DOUGH
- 375 g (3 cups) bolted hard wheat flour
- 125 g (1 cup) whole-grain spelt flour
- 300 g (1¼ cups) water
- 30 g (2¼ tablespoons) extra-virgin olive oil
- 5 g (1⅔ teaspoons) dry yeast
- 150 g (¾ cup) biga (from above)
- 10 g (4 teaspoons) barley malt flour or powder
- 11 g (1¾ teaspoons) salt
- 1½ tablespoons food-grade lye (sodium hydroxide) for lye solution
- 2¼ cups water for lye solution
- pretzel salt (coarse, large-grain white salt) for sprinkling

1. Day 1: mix biga. Measure the flour and set aside. Combine the water, yeast, and flour in a container with a lid, stirring them together with a spoon. Cover and let sit at room temperature (65° to 75°F) to rest overnight, 12 to 16 hours.
2. Day 2: mix dough. Measure the hard wheat and spelt flours and set aside. Combine the water, oil, yeast, biga, reserved flours, malt flour or powder, and salt in the bowl of a stand mixer. Mix with the dough hook on low speed for 3 minutes. Switch to medium speed and mix until the gluten develops and the dough comes together, another 3 minutes.
3. Transfer to an oiled bowl, cover with a tea towel, and let rest for 45 minutes. Give the dough a four-fold, then cover and let rest for another 45 minutes.
4. Preshape. Divide the dough into ten 100-gram pieces for large pretzels or about thirty 30-gram pieces for mini pretzels. Preshape each piece on a dry surface by folding and rolling it into a short log, then rolling with a little more pressure under your palm to make a fat log for large pretzels, about 1½ inches wide by 4 inches long. Make a thinner log for mini pretzels, about ½ inch wide by 2 inches long. Let the logs rest for 10 minutes.
5. Shape. Line two sheet pans with parchment and coat the parchment with cooking spray. Pat the dough with your palms to start lengthening the log. Then roll it out under your palms, from the center outward, lengthening the dough as you go, until the rope is about 16 inches long and ½ inch thick for large pretzels, or 6 inches long and ⅛ inch thick for mini pretzels. To make the classic Bavarian pretzel shape, pick up the ends of the rope, leaving a semicircle of dough on the countertop, then cross the strands of dough, twist them once, and press the two ends you are holding onto the semicircle of dough. Carefully transfer the pretzels to the parchment. The dough will be soft.
6. After shaping, you can either cover and refrigerate the pretzels for at least 2 hours or freeze them for up to 3 days. Either way, they must be firm before dipping in the lye solution. If frozen, defrost the pretzels in the refrigerator for 1 hour before dipping.
7. Dip in lye. Preheat the oven to 375°F.
8. The lye solution is caustic, so put on gloves, eye protection, and a face mask or bandana. Protect your countertop with parchment paper and coat two cooling racks with cooking spray, placing them over the parchment. Line a sheet pan with parchment paper and coat the parchment with cooking spray. Then carefully mix the lye and water in a medium stainless-steel or glass mixing bowl until the lye dissolves.
9. Dip each pretzel into the solution for about 30 seconds, turning to coat it completely, then transfer to the cooling rack to dry a bit. The dough will be soft, so handle it carefully. When the pretzels appear dry on the surface, after about 1 minute, transfer back to the oiled, parchment-lined sheet. The lye solution can be stored in a covered container and reused up to four times. This quantity of solution can also be safely poured down the drain.
10. Bake. Score the dough if you like: it helps the pretzels split in the oven, so they look nicer. Just give each one a straight score where the ends of the ropes meet the base of the pretzel. Then sprinkle the pretzels with the salt. Bake until the pretzels are dark brown and shiny. Mini ones will take 8 to 10 minutes, and large ones 20 to 25 minutes.
11. Pretzels are best eaten warm, but they will last a day or two in an airtight container at room temperature. They can also be frozen for a few weeks and thawed/rewarmed in a 350°F oven for 10 minutes.

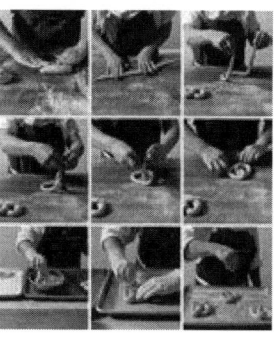

Hoagie Rolls

Easy, adaptable recipe. Oil helps soften the rolls. Because, let's be honest, sandwich greatness is all about dancing the line between quality and trash, feel free to use all-purpose flour.

Prep time: 3 hours| Cook time: 55 minutes| Serves 12 rolls, about 6 inches long

- 844 g (6¾ cups) bolted hard wheat flour
- 558 g (2⅓ cups) water
- 25 g (1¾ tablespoons) extra-virgin olive oil
- 5 g (1⅔ teaspoons) dry yeast
- 17 g (2¾ teaspoons) salt

1. Mix. Measure the flour and set aside. Combine the water, oil, yeast, flour, and salt in the bowl of a stand mixer. Mix with the dough hook on low speed for 4 minutes. Switch to medium speed and mix for another 5 minutes. After mixing, the dough should feel moderately developed—elastic and cohesive but still a little sticky.
2. Bulk ferment. Transfer the dough to an oiled bowl and cover with a tea towel. Leave to rise at room temperature (65° to 75°F) for 45 minutes. Then give the dough a four-fold. At this point, there should be definite signs of activity: the volume should have increased by about 30%, and there should be visible bubbles. If you do not see this level of activity, move the bowl to a warmer place and give it an extra 15 minutes before portioning and shaping. If everything is progressing as it ought to at the fold, then just leave it for another 45 minutes of bulk fermentation. Ideally, the total rising time will be about 1½ hours (plus 15 minutes if you need to goose up the activity).
3. Shape. Line two sheet pans with parchment paper. Turn the dough out onto a lightly floured countertop, then divide the dough into twelve equal pieces, each about 120 grams. To shape each piece, start on one of the short sides and roll/crimp the edge in toward the center. Keep rolling and crimping until you have a cylinder about 3 inches long. Even out and extend the cylinder to about 6 inches by placing one palm in the center and gently compressing the cylinder, then starting to roll the piece of dough while moving your hand outward toward the end. Add your second hand once you have moved the first from the center and press/roll that hand in the opposite direction. For the ends, roll harder with the outside edge of your palm to round them off and blunt the point, enclosing the seal at the rounded end. Place the roll seam-side down on the parchment. You should be able to fit six rolls on each half sheet pan. Repeat with the remaining pieces and cover the rolls loosely with a plastic grocery bag, plastic wrap, or beeswax wrap. Leave to rise for about 1 hour at room temperature, until the rolls have almost doubled in diameter.
4. Bake. Halfway into the rising time, preheat the oven without a stone to 400°F. You'll need two oven racks to bake all the rolls at once. Quickly score the rolls all the way down the center in a straight line, then load them into the oven. Bake for 10 minutes, then turn the pans and bake for an additional 5 minutes. When done, the rolls will be puffed but still somewhat pale, like the color of straw.
5. Hoagie rolls don't keep particularly well. Eat or freeze them within a couple days.

Bagel

People have strong opinions about bagels, so the breads are a touchy thing to mess with. We're here. Traditional bagels are made with 100% refined white flour, lightly fermented, dense, and huge. By changing just one factor—the flour—we can make something healthier and chewier.

Prep time: 40 minutes | Cook time: 2 hours | Serves 12 small bagels, about 4-inch diameter

DOUGH

- 756 g (6 cups) bolted hard wheat flour
- 416 g (1¾ cups) water
- 4 g (1¼ teaspoons) dry yeast
- 8 g (3¼ teaspoons) barley malt flour or powder
- 17 g (2¾ teaspoons) salt
- 3 tablespoons malt syrup or honey for boiling
- 1 cup sesame seeds, poppy seeds, or other seeds (optional) for topping
- ½ cup coarse salt for topping (optional)

1. Day 1: mix. Measure the hard wheat flour and set aside. Combine the water, yeast, reserved flour, malt flour or powder, and salt in the bowl of a stand mixer, then mix with the dough hook on low speed for 6 minutes. Let the dough and machine rest for 10 minutes, then mix on low speed for another 3 minutes. The dough should come together in a smooth ball and feel elastic. Alternatively, or if you have a less-powerful mixer, this dough is a good candidate for good old-fashioned hand kneading. As you knead, the dough should go from dry and shaggy to smooth and elastic. It is a low-hydration dough, so expect it to be firmer and drier than just about every other dough in this book. Once it's looking smooth and feeling elastic, work the dough into a ball and set it in a lightly oiled bowl. Cover and let rest for 1 hour at room temperature (65° to 75°F).
2. Shape. After an hour, the dough should have risen by about 75%. If it hasn't, give it a little more time. Turn the dough out onto a dry countertop and press out the gas until the dough is about 1 inch thick. Cut a 2-inch-wide strip off the dough and then cut a 3-inch-wide piece off.
3. For each bagel, press a dough piece out nearly flat with your fingers, then fold and roll it up along the longer side to make a blunt rope. Roll the rope on the countertop, starting with your palms at the center and moving outward until the rope is about 9 inches long. Wrap the rope around your hand, overlap the ends in your palm to connect them (the bagel will be wrapped around your hand), then gently press and roll the connected ends on the countertop to smooth out the seam. The dough should have some elasticity and shrink back a bit. When you remove it from your hand, the bagel should be near its final diameter (about 4 inches) with a fairly big hole. The hole will fill in some as the bagels rise overnight.
4. Bulk ferment. Set the bagels on a lightly floured baking sheet with about a ½-inch space between them. Cover loosely with a plastic grocery bag, plastic wrap, or beeswax wrap and let rest at room temperature for 20 minutes. Then transfer to the refrigerator to rest overnight.
5. Day 2: boil, then bake. The next morning, the bagels should have risen slightly. Fill a wide, deep pan with water to a depth of 5 inches, then add the malt syrup or honey and bring everything to a boil. Meanwhile, place a large baking stone on the middle rack of the oven. A rectangular stone is clutch here but make do with what you have. Preheat the oven to 450°F. Soak two bagel boards in a pan of water.
6. If you haven't realized it yet, this operation is going to take over your kitchen, so make some space and get organized. If you are topping your bagels with seeds, fill the bottom of a wide shallow bowl with a generous layer of whatever flavoring you've chosen. For a mixed batch, have one bowl for each topping ready to go. Next to that, lay out a towel to briefly dry the bagels after their bath. And get out a spider or other skimming tool for pulling the bagels from their bath. Have a timer that measures seconds ready to go (most smartphones work fine). Nearby (or wherever you can find room!), set up a rack for cooling the bagels.
7. Once the oven and water are ready, pull the bagel boards out and set them on the cooling rack to drain a bit. Pull the pan of bagels from the fridge and set it somewhere near the pot of boiling water.
8. At the end of the 45-second timer, flip the bagels and boil for another 45 seconds. The bagels should have puffed a bit in the bath. Skim them out of the pot and set on the towel to dry briefly. Once all the bagels have been boiled and pulled, the first bagel out will probably be ready to transfer to the topping bowl or, if you're skipping the toppings, straight to your bagel board for baking. If topping, just lift and set each bagel into the seeds, then lift and set it seed-side down on the bagel board. For salted bagels, sprinkle with the coarse salt and then set salt-side down on the bagel boards with at least 1 inch between each. Once the bagel boards are full, transfer to the oven, setting them directly onto the baking stone.
9. Bake for 4 minutes, then use two towels or hot pads to lift and tip each board, inverting the bagels onto the stone and removing the bagel boards from the oven. Bake the bagels directly on the stone until they are slightly puffed, shiny, and a few shades darker than when they originally went in, an additional 11 to 14 minutes. Check the bottoms, too: they should be browned but not scorched. Meanwhile, resoak the boards for the next rounds of bagels. Transfer the baked bagels to the rack to cool. Then repeat the boil-drain-top-bake cycle, until all the bagels are finished.
10. Allow the bagels to cool for a few minutes before digging in. Bagels are best fresh but will keep in an airtight container at room temperature for up to 3 days.

Olive Filone

This bread is like a short, chunky baguette or a smaller Italian loaf. The bread's name comes from the Italian word filo, which means "line." Table bread, sandwich bread, and bruschetta base. Olives add texture and saltiness. Gaeta and Kalamata olives are best because their flavor mellows during baking.

Prep time: 60 minutes | Cook time: 2 hours | Serves 3 narrow loaves, about 3 by 12 inches

- 577 g (4⅔ cups) bolted hard wheat flour
- 404 g (1⅔ cups) water
- 29 g (2 tablespoons) extra-virgin olive oil
- 9 g (1 tablespoon) dry yeast
- 9 g (1½ teaspoons) salt
- 173 g (¾ cup) chopped briny olives

1. Day 1: mix. Measure the flour and set aside. Combine the water, oil, yeast, flour, and salt in a medium mixing bowl. With clean hands, mix everything by hand until it comes together in a shaggy mass, then mix it in the bowl for a few minutes more, alternately breaking the dough up and folding it back onto itself. At this point, the dough will still look shaggy and feel sticky and weak. Cover the bowl with a tea towel and let rest for 15 minutes.
2. Repeat the hand-mixing process in the bowl. By now, you'll notice that the dough feels a bit firmer; it will stretch some instead of tearing, and while it's still shaggy, it will look somewhat smoother. Cover and let rest for 15 minutes more. Then add the olives and hand-mix it again. It will still be a little sticky, but more gluten should be developed; this will make the dough feel more supple and allow it to stretch more easily without tearing. The dough should also look shinier. Finally, give the dough another 15-minute rest, then transfer to an airtight container, cover, and refrigerate it overnight.
3. Day 2: preshape. Pull the dough from the refrigerator and allow it to warm up for 30 minutes. By now, the dough should be elastic and strong, and you should see some bubbles in the dough: signs of fermentation. Place the dough on a lightly floured countertop and divide it into three pieces, each about 400 grams. For each piece, pat the dough down, then fold all four edges in toward the center, until the dough is somewhat rounded. Place the pieces seam-side down on the countertop and let rest for 15 minutes.
4. Shape. Dust the top of each dough piece lightly with flour. To shape each loaf, flip it over, pat it down a bit, and roll it under your palms from the center outward to a rough cylinder about 3 inches in diameter in the center and 11 to 12 inches long. Keep the edges blunt so the loaf looks like a pudgy baguette. Place the loaves seam-side up on a lightly floured couche or tea towel, with small folds between the loaves to give each some support. Cover with another tea towel and let rest for about 1 hour at room temperature (65° to 75°F).
5. Bake. Place a large baking stone and hotel pan on the middle rack of the oven. Preheat the oven to 500°F. Have a spray bottle and razor within reach.
6. Cut a sheet of parchment paper that will fit over the back side of a half sheet pan to use as a peel, then place two loaves seam-side down on the parchment. Quickly score the top of each loaf in a single line down the center from end to end, less than ½ inch deep. Immediately slide the scored loaves and parchment onto the stone, cover with the hotel pan while spraying water into the top of the pan, and close the oven door.
7. Bake until the loaves are fully puffed and the score marks are filled in, about 9 minutes. This is not a baguette, so you won't get dramatic "ears" from the scoring. Remove the hotel pan and bake for an additional 10 to 12 minutes. These guys will color like baguettes, with a shade similar to corn flakes. Pull the loaves out and allow them to cool on a rack.
8. The loaves will last for about 3 days at room temperature in a paper bag, bread box, or cupboard.

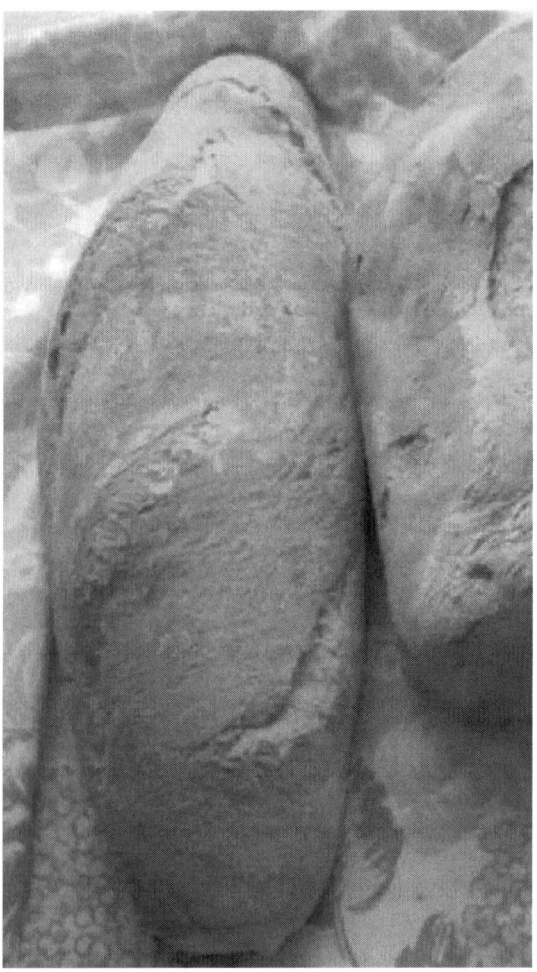

Oven-Dried-Tomato Stecca

My mom sun-dried tomatoes, fruits, and herbs on her car's dashboard when I was a kid. I was horrified to be seen in that car. it worked Later, I started putting semi-dried tomatoes in bread. I dry tomatoes differently. This bread is perfect for summer when fresh tomatoes abound. I made it at Philadelphia's Avance. Local farmers sent us B-grade heirloom tomatoes that were too imperfect to sell but still delicious. We saved money, reduced waste, and made incredible bread. Tomato guts (juice, seeds, pulp) replace some dough water.

Prep time: 60 minutes | Cook time: 2 hours | Serves 4 narrow loaves, about 3 by 10 inches

POOLISH
- 138 g (1⅛ cups) bolted hard wheat flour
- 138 g (½ cup) water
- 0.19 g (1/16 teaspoon) dry yeast

DOUGH
- 413 g (3½ cups) bolted hard wheat flour
- 165 g (1 cup) tomato guts
- 103 g (½ cup) water
- 25 g (1¾ tablespoons) extra-virgin olive oil
- 0.66 g (¼ teaspoon) dry yeast
- 276.19 g (1⅓ cups) poolish (from above)
- 11 g (1¾ teaspoons) salt
- 206 g (1⅛ cups) oven-dried tomatoes (from above)
- extra-virgin olive oil for drizzling
- coarse salt for topping
- 1 pound fresh tomatoes, any kind

1. Day 1: dry tomatoes. If your tomatoes are medium or large, cut away the stem, cut them in half, and scoop or squeeze out the juice and seeds, reserving the tomato guts for the dough. Then cut the tomatoes into bite-size pieces about ¼ inch thick. If you are using cherry tomatoes, you can just nick them to squeeze out the guts, then cut them in half. Drying is easiest with a dehydrator. If you have one, set it to medium (about 150°F) and dehydrate the tomatoes for several hours until semi-dry but still flexible. Or place the tomatoes on wire racks in an oven set as low as it goes and dry for several hours. You could also go old-school and place the tomatoes on a wire rack, cover them with cheesecloth, then allow them to air-dry outside on a warm, sunny day or in a sunny window until ready to use. This method will take several days. You don't want them leathery like fully dehydrated tomatoes, just more concentrated and less watery than fresh tomatoes.
2. Mix poolish. Measure the flour and set aside. Combine the water, yeast, and flour in a container large enough for the poolish to triple in volume. Cover with a lid, plastic grocery bag, plastic wrap, or beeswax wrap and leave at room temperature (65° to 75°F) to rest overnight.
3. Day 2: mix dough. Weigh the flour and the remaining ingredients, including the tomato guts. If you're short on tomato guts, make up the difference with water. We'll be hand-mixing, so everything will go into a mixing bowl. If you prefer to mix the dough in a machine, follow the mixing instructions for Ursa Baguette, adding the oven-dried tomatoes with the salt.
4. Combine the tomato guts, water, oil, yeast, poolish, and flour in a large mixing bowl. Mix with a spoon, dough scraper, or your hands, scraping the bottom of the bowl to hydrate all the flour. Keep mixing by stirring, folding, and breaking up the dough for another 3 minutes. Cover with a tea towel and let rest for 15 minutes. Add the salt and repeat hand-mixing (breaking up and folding the dough) for 3 minutes. Cover and let rest for 15 minutes. Add the oven-dried tomatoes and mix again for 3 minutes. Cover the bowl and let the dough rest at room temperature for 1 hour. Transfer the dough to a lightly oiled container with a lid and room for the dough to double in volume. Put on the lid and refrigerate for 30 minutes. Then pull the dough and give it a four-fold. Finally, return the container to the fridge for 8 to 24 hours. On the short end of that range, the dough will be bubbly and well risen, and on the long end, it may be more wobbly and on the brink of collapse. Try not to let it go too long.
5. Day 3: shape. Pull the dough from the fridge. At this point, it should be very bubbly and inflated. Place a large baking stone on a rack, preferably near the top of the oven. Preheat the oven to 400°F. Have a couche, sheet pan or large cutting board, and a bench knife ready. Dust a section of countertop liberally with flour and turn the dough out onto it. Dust the top of the dough with more flour. This is a sticky dough, so be prepared to handle it lightly. Coax the dough from an oval into a loose rectangle, then divide the dough in half, bisecting the long sides. Divide each piece again to make four strips of dough, about 3 by 10 inches. Dust all the cut edges with flour. Roll each strip over once to ensure it is evenly coated with flour, then gently lift it onto the couche.
6. Assemble your toppings, in this case, the olive oil and salt. Cut a sheet of parchment paper that will fit over the back side of a half sheet pan to use as a peel, then gently transfer two of the loaves to the parchment. If the dough has been very active, put the remaining two loaves in the fridge to slow the fermentation down a bit. Dock the stecca all over by poking your fingers down into the dough, almost all the way through. Drizzle the stecca with the oil, then sprinkle with the salt.
7. Bake: Load the stecca into the oven by sliding the parchment paper onto the stone. Bake for 12 minutes. Rotate the loaves as necessary for even browning, then bake for an additional 5 minutes. When done, the crust color should be medium tan. Pull the stecca out and transfer to a rack to cool. Give the oven 5 minutes to rebound, then begin assembling your second round to bake.
8. Stecca are great fresh, but they'll keep all right for a few days in a paper bag or a bread box at room temperature. After day one, refresh them in a 350°F oven for a few minutes for the best flavor and texture.

Chapter 3
Sourdough Breads

Sourdough Starter

It's amazing how flour and water can create life when combined. When you "feed" the starter with flour and water, it becomes more stable. You can feed the starter to maintain it or to bake with it. Some bakers start from scratch, and that's fine. As you'll see below, starter maintenance involves a lot of discarding, so find a local baker to share. You'll have a baking partner.

Prep time: 20 minutes | Cook time: 50 minutes | Serves 250 grams

INITIAL MIX
- 100 g (1 cup) whole-grain rye flour
- 100 g (½ cup) water

REGULAR FEEDING
- 100 g (1 cup) whole-grain rye flour
- 100 g (½ cup) water
- 50 g (¼ cup) old starter

1. Mix. Choose a 1-quart container, preferably clear and with a lid. For the initial mix, measure the rye flour and water into the container and stir it up. Cover with a cloth (not the lid) and leave it alone for 24 to 36 hours at room temperature (65° to 75°F). It's not strictly necessary to use rye flour, but rye's high starch and enzyme levels help to establish a starter culture from scratch. If you use another flour, it will still work, but it may take more time to obtain vigorous activity.
2. Establish. To help establish the starter, use the "Regular Feeding" amounts listed above: Discard all but 50 grams of the starter, leaving that amount in the same unwashed container. Then add 100 grams each of fresh flour and water to the container and stir it up. Give the starter this regular feeding twice a day, covering it with a cloth and keeping it at room temperature. When establishing a starter, it helps to reuse the same container because it gives you the best chance of capturing lots of the target microorganisms. Just wipe any messes from the outside of the container.
3. After 4 to 8 days of regular feeding twice a day, you should see signs of activity such as bubbles at the top or through the sides of the container and catch an aroma just before feeding that could range from a yogurtlike tang to a whiff from a vodka bottle. The starter should also begin to visibly rise in the container. At this point, the concentration of yeast and bacteria in the starter is sufficient to change containers and start using a lid.
4. After 7 to 14 days of regular feeding twice a day, the starter should approximately double in volume, bubble, and develop a tart tang between feedings. These are signs that the starter is ready to build up for baking. Congratulations, you did it!
5. Maintain. Once your starter is established, or you were smart and acquired one from someone else, you need to maintain it to keep it alive. Once a day, give it a regular feeding, mixing 50 grams of old starter with 100 grams each of fresh flour and water. At this point, you can use any flour you want. A vigorous starter kept at room temperature (65° to 75°F) needs to be fed only once a day to keep it healthy. And if you bake often, you will never be more than a few hours away from starting any recipe. But if you plan on baking only once a week or less, you can keep your starter in the refrigerator so it doesn't need to be fed as often. In that case, to keep it alive, remove the starter from the fridge at least once a week, give it a regular feeding, and leave it out for a few hours before putting it back. There should be definite signs of activity, such as bubbles on the surface, before you return the starter to the fridge. If the starter appears to be flagging and doesn't show signs of activity, leave it out for a day at room temperature, then feed it again to help it get going.
6. Build and ripen. Building your starter is similar to feeding it, but now you are feeding it for a specific baking recipe. This feeding may involve increasing the starter's total amount, changing its base flour, and/or changing its hydration. When you build a starter, you are also controlling its ripeness, or readiness for baking. To build up an established starter, about 3 hours before you plan to bake with it, give the starter a regular feeding at room temperature (65° to 75°F), using the flour specified in your recipe. After 3 hours or so, the starter should be on the upswing of fermentation activity, gaining in volume, and developing a lightly tangy aroma. It may not be fully aerated with bubbles everywhere, but it should have some bubbles. That's what we mean by "ripe sourdough starter," which is called for in most of our recipes. Although some of our recipes have different instructions for building the starter, including Pain Normand, Ciabatta Grano Arso with Einkorn, and Malted Grain Sourdough. For those recipes, establish and maintain your starter as described here and then follow the instructions in the recipe to build and ripen it. In this book, we wanted to show you several different starter styles, so that as you grow as a baker, you can choose the starters that best fit your palate and your baking schedule.

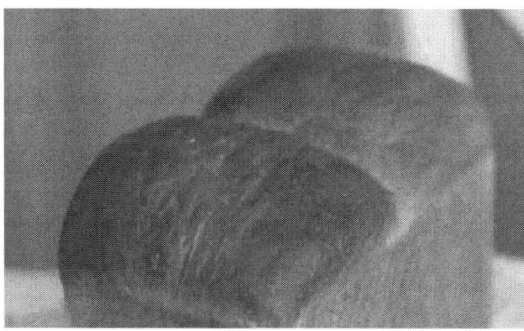

Simple Sourdough Table Bread

This is a family staple. The dough only requires 10 to 15 minutes of hands-on time over two days. Choose any flour! There is no right way to make this bread because not all flours behave the same. 100% whole-wheat, bolted wheat, or half whole-wheat and half bolted are good options. Try 10% rye flour, cornmeal, or oat flour.

Prep time: 20 minutes | Cook time: 30 minutes | Serves 2 batards, about 8 by 10 inches

- 710 g (5⅔ cups) bolted hard wheat flour
- 532 g (2¼ cups) water
- 142 g (¾ cup) ripe whole-wheat Sourdough Starter
- 16 g (2⅔ teaspoons) salt

1. Day 1: mix. Measure the flour and set aside. Combine the water, starter, flour, and salt in a mixing bowl. With clean hands, mix until it comes together in a shaggy mass, then mix it in the bowl for a few minutes more, alternately breaking the dough up and folding it back onto itself. At this point, the dough will still look shaggy and feel sticky and weak. Get as much dough from your hands back into the bowl as possible, scraping down your hands and the bowl. A dough scraper is handy here. Cover the bowl with a tea towel and leave to rise at room temperature (65° to 75°F) for 3 hours, giving the dough a four-fold every 30 minutes.
2. Preshape. After the final 30-minute rest, dampen your countertop with water. Pour the dough out onto the damp countertop and divide it into two 700-gram pieces. For each loaf, give it a four-fold, then turn it over, so it is seam-side down. The loaves will look like square-ish pouches. Cover them with a tea towel and leave them to rest at room temperature for 20 to 30 minutes.
3. Shape. Generously flour the bottom and sides of two medium oval bannetons or towel-lined bowls (you'll get round loaves if using the latter). Drizzle a little more water on your countertop and spread it around so the surface is wet but not puddled. Use a bench knife to flip a loaf over onto the wet surface, then stretch and fold the left and right sides in toward the center, patting them into place. Now you should have a somewhat rectangular piece of dough. Starting from one of the short sides, roll the dough up, increasing the surface tension as you go. Roll firmly but try not to knock all of the gas out of the dough. Repeat with the other loaf, then let the loaves rest seam-side down on the countertop for a minute or two to help seal the seam shut. Lightly dust the loaves with flour, then gently slip your hand beneath each loaf, pick it up, and invert it into the floured banneton, seam-side up. (The seam will eventually become the bottom of the bread.)
4. Place the filled bannetons in plastic grocery bags or loosely cover with plastic wrap or beeswax wrap and leave at room temperature for 30 minutes. Then move the covered loaves to the refrigerator to rest overnight.
5. Day 2: bake. Place a 6-quart or larger Dutch oven (a round or oval Dutch oven will do) and its lid into the oven. Preheat the oven to 475°F. Have kitchen towels or hot pads, dusting flour, and a razor within reach, as well as space to place the hot Dutch oven and its lid.
6. When the oven is hot, pull one loaf from the refrigerator and dust the side facing up with flour. Using towels or hot pads, pull out the hot Dutch oven and place it on the stovetop or a trivet. Carefully remove the lid, setting it down on the stovetop or another trivet. Gently but confidently invert the banneton over the Dutch oven to set the loaf inside. Score the top of the loaf (I like one straight line down the center), quickly replace the lid, and return the Dutch oven to the oven shelf.
7. Bake for 20 minutes. Then remove the lid (leave the lid in the oven if there is space) and bake for an additional 10 minutes. When the loaf is deeply browned and singed in spots, carefully pull out the Dutch oven, then remove the loaf with kitchen towels or hot pads, or tip it out. Cool the loaf on a rack. Carefully replace the lid on the Dutch oven and return it to the oven shelf to reheat for 5 to 10 minutes. Repeat with the second loaf.
8. This bread keeps for almost a week in a paper bag, bread box, or cupboard at room temperature.

20 | The Complete Cosori Air Fryer Cookbook

Sesame Durum Bread

It's a favorite, and I make it with different grains often. Whole-grain durum flour adds pasta's mellow flavor. It's delicious dipped in olive oil. Antipasti-style. As toast. Anytime. Good-tasting, versatile bread.

Prep time: 20 minutes | Cook time: 50 minutes | Serves 2 skinny batards, about 4 by 10 inches

- 401 g (3¼ cups) bolted hard wheat flour
- 134 g (¾ cup) whole-grain durum flour
- 401 g (1⅔ cups) water
- 107 g (½ cup) ripe whole durum Sourdough Starter
- 11 g (1¾ teaspoons) salt
- sesame seeds for coating

1. Day 1: mix. Measure both flours and and set aside. Combine the water, starter, flours, and salt in a medium mixing bowl. With clean hands, mix until it comes together in a shaggy mass, then mix it in the bowl for 3 to 5 minutes more, alternately breaking the dough up and folding it back onto itself. At this point, the dough will still look shaggy and feel sticky and weak. Get as much dough from your hands back into the bowl as possible, scraping down your hands and the bowl. Cover the bowl with a tea towel and let rest at room temperature (65° to 75°F) for 2 hours, giving the dough a four-fold every 30 minutes. During the first hour, the folds can be aggressive, but fold more gently during the second hour. After the 2 hours, transfer the dough to a lightly oiled container, cover with a lid, and move to the refrigerator to rest overnight.
2. Day 2: preshape. Pull the dough from the fridge, then cover and rest at room temperature for 30 minutes.
3. Drizzle a little water on your countertop and spread it around, so the surface is wet but not puddled. Turn the dough out onto the damp countertop and divide it into two 500-gram pieces. Preshape each piece by giving it a four-fold, then turn it over, so it is seam-side down. The loaves will look like square-ish pouches. Cover with a tea towel and leave them to rest at room temperature for 45 minutes.
4. Shape. Place a large baking stone and hotel pan on the highest rack in your oven they will fit on. Preheat the oven to 475°F. Have ready a spray bottle of water and a linen couche. Dust the couche with flour.
5. Pour the sesame seeds into a large shallow dish or a quarter sheet pan. Lightly flour the countertop, then one at a time, flip each loaf over, pat it down a bit, and roll it under your palms into a fat cylinder about 4 by 10 inches that is pointed at the ends. To seed each loaf, spray it with water and slip your hand beneath it, pick it up, and roll the wet top side in the sesame seeds. Then place each loaf seeded-side down on the floured couche, gently peeling your hand from the loaf. Make little folds in the couche between the rows to support the loaves. Fold the excess couche over the loaves (or cover with a tea towel) and set aside to rest at room temperature for 1 hour.
6. Bake. The loaves should be about 1½ times their original size. Cut a sheet of parchment paper that will fit over the back side of a half sheet pan to use as a peel. Have two towels or hot pads, a spray bottle of water, and a razor within reach.
7. Flip the loaves over onto the parchment paper, so they are seed-side up. Score with two cuts, similar to a baguette, with each cut a little over half the length of the loaf and parallel slightly in the center. Quickly but carefully open your oven, pull the rack that you are baking on partway out, and move the hot hotel pan to the stovetop. Slide the loaves and parchment paper onto the stone and cover with the hotel pan, spraying water into the pan before setting it onto the stone to trap steam.
8. Bake for 15 minutes. Then remove the hot hotel pan and rotate the loaves for even browning. Bake, uncovered, until the seeds are browned but not charred, like the skin of a russet potato, and the raised edges along the score marks are dark brown to black, another 5 to 10 minutes. Remove the loaves to racks to cool.
9. The loaves will keep in a paper bag, bread box, or cupboard at room temperature for about 4 days.

Pane Di Genzano

Pane di Genzano is a specific bread type. Genzano's specialty is this bread. It's the ultimate country-style sourdough and classic table bread. Rye adds floral aroma, acidity, and bite, and wheat flour adds structure. This is a geographically protected (IGP) bread in Italy, so we're just using Genzano as a textbook example of a beloved country bread.

Prep time: 30 minutes | Cook time: 20 minutes | Serves 2 batards, about 8 by 10 inches

- 666 g (5⅓ cups) bolted hard wheat flour
- 74 g (¾ cup) whole rye flour
- 592 g (2½ cups) water
- 150 g (¾ cup) ripe rye Sourdough Starter
- 4 g (1⅔ teaspoons) barley malt flour or powder
- 14 g (2⅓ teaspoons) salt
- wheat bran for dusting

1. Day 1: mix. Measure the wheat flour and rye flour and set aside. Combine the water, starter, reserved flours, malt flour or powder, and salt in the bowl of a stand mixer. Mix with the dough hook on low speed for 10 minutes. Transfer the dough to a lightly oiled container, cover with a tea towel, and allow to rest at room temperature (65° to 75°F) for 2 hours, giving the dough a four-fold every 30 minutes.
2. Preshape. Drizzle a little water on your countertop and spread it around, so the surface is wet but not puddled. Turn the dough out onto the countertop and cut it into two 750-gram pieces. For each loaf, fold the four edges in toward the center of the dough, then turn it over, so it is seam-side down. Cover with a tea towel and allow to rest on the countertop for 20 minutes.
3. Shape. Generously flour the bottom and sides of two medium oval bannetons or towel-lined bowls (you'll get round loaves if using the latter). Dampen your countertop again and flip each loaf over on the countertop. Fold the left and right sides in on an angle toward the center, forming a cone shape. Now roll up from the narrow bottom of the cone, forming a football shape. Set the loaves seam-side down on the countertop. Dust the tops with flour, then slip your hand beneath each loaf and gently invert it into the banneton, so it is seam-side up. Place the filled bannetons in plastic grocery bags or loosely cover with plastic wrap or beeswax wrap and leave at room temperature for 1 hour. Then move the covered loaves to the refrigerator to rest overnight.
4. Day 2: bake. Place a large baking stone and hotel pan on the highest rack in your oven they will fit on. Preheat the oven to 475°F. Remove the bannetons from the fridge and let rest at room temperature for 1 hour. Have two towels or hot pads, a spray bottle of water, and a razor within reach.
5. Dust a peel or flat board with wheat bran, then flip the loaves out onto the board, lining them up so you can easily slip them from the board to the stone. I like to score this loaf once from end to end down the center. But this bread won't have an incredible amount of oven spring, so it's a good candidate for a more elaborate scoring pattern without worrying about the loaf blowing out. If you like, get fancy and make lots of little score marks.
6. Quickly but carefully open your oven, pull the rack that you are baking on partway out, and move the hot hotel pan to the stovetop. Lay the back side of your peel or board toward the back of the stone, then tilt, shake, and slide the loaves onto the stone, quickly removing the peel. Cover the loaves with the hot hotel pan, spraying water into the pan before setting it onto the stone to trap steam.
7. Bake for 20 minutes. Then remove the hot hotel pan and rotate the loaves for even browning. Bake, uncovered, until the crust is very dark, another 15 to 20 minutes. To the untrained eye, the crust may look burnt when properly done. You want a bit of charring here and there. Don't worry; it will be delicious. Remove the loaves to a rack to cool.
8. This bread will last a good 5 to 7 days in a paper bag, bread box, or cupboard at room temperature.

Spelt Sourdough Boule

If you've read this book, you know I love spelt flour. This bread is spelt-heavy. Due to the high spelt flour content, this dough will be looser than most. The dough is folded more to build strength, and it's shaped again to make it cohesive and taut. This extra effort yields a balance of sweet and sharp flavors, an open crumb, and a chewy crust.

Prep time: 20 minutes | Cook time: 20 minutes | Serves 2 boules, about 8-inch diameter

- 427 g (3½ cups) whole-grain spelt flour
- 284 g (2¼ cups) bolted hard wheat flour
- 569 g (2⅓ cups) water
- 107 g (½ cup) ripe spelt Sourdough Starter
- 14 g (2⅓ teaspoons) salt
- wheat or spelt bran for dusting

1. Day 1: mix. Measure both flours and set aside. Combine the water, starter, and flours in the bowl of a stand mixer. Mix with the dough hook on low speed for 8 minutes. Early in this mix, the dough should be very slack and stick to the sides of the bowl. It should take some time for it to gather enough strength to grab the hook and clear the sides of the bowl. If it builds strength too quickly in the first 8 minutes of mixing, you can add up to 10% of the flour weight in water (up to about 75 grams of water). Add this additional water incrementally, in thirds (25 grams at a time), and continue mixing after each addition.
2. After mixing for 8 minutes, cover the dough with a tea towel and allow to rest for about 20 minutes. Add the salt and resume mixing on low speed for another 8 minutes. Cover the dough with a tea towel and leave to rest at room temperature (65° to 75°F) until the dough shows some signs of fermentation (such as bubbles under the surface), 2 to 3 hours, depending on the ambient temperature. About halfway through that time, give the dough a four-fold.
3. Preshape. Once the dough shows signs of fermentation, drizzle some water on your countertop and spread it around, so the surface is wet but not puddled. Turn the dough out onto the counter and divide it into two 700-gram pieces. Give each piece a little shape: fold the four edges in toward the center of the dough, then roll it over, so it is seam-side down. Cover and allow to rest on the countertop for 20 minutes.
4. Shape. Generously flour the bottom and sides of two medium round bannetons or towel-lined bowls. Set up a bowl of flour for dusting the loaves. Dampen your countertop again and shape each loaf into a boule: roll the dough in a circle on your countertop, pressing down and cupping your hands around the dough to increase the surface tension all around it as you shape it into a nice taut ball. As you roll, the seam will seal and smooth out on the bottom. Dust the tops of the loaves with flour, then slip your hand beneath each loaf and invert it into the banneton, so the floured side is down, peeling your hand away from the loaf. Place the filled bannetons in plastic grocery bags or loosely cover with plastic wrap or beeswax wrap, then move the covered bannetons to the refrigerator to rest overnight.
5. Day 2: bake. Place a large baking stone and hotel pan on the highest rack they will fit on. Preheat the oven to 500°F. Have two towels or hot pads, a spray bottle of water, and a razor within reach.
6. Dust the loaves with bran (the loaves will be inverted, so the bran will end up on the bottom). Moving quickly but carefully, open the oven and pull the rack that you are baking on partway out and move the hot hotel pan to the stovetop or side of the oven. Invert the loaves one at a time onto the stone and score each loaf with four slashes to make a square on top. Cover the loaves with the hot hotel pan, spraying water into the pan before setting it onto the stone to trap steam. Close the oven and lower the temperature to 475°F. Bake for 20 minutes. Then, remove the hot hotel pan and rotate the loaves for even browning. Bake, uncovered, until the loaves are evenly browned and the raised edge along the score mark has scorched lightly, 15 to 20 minutes more. Remove to racks to cool.
7. These boules can be kept in a paper bag, bread box, or cupboard at room temperature for 5 to 6 days.

100% Sonora Slab

First fresh-milled flour bread I made was 100% whole-grain Sonora sourdough. This loaf honors a lost recipe. Short fermentation highlights the flour's nutty flavor.

Prep time: 20 minutes | Cook time: 50 minutes | Serves 2 free-form loaves, about 8 by 10 inches

- 505 g (4¼ cups) whole-grain Sonora flour
- 177 g (1 cup) ripe Sonora Sourdough Starter
- 505 g (2⅛ cups) water
- 13 g (2⅛ teaspoons) salt

1. Mix. Measure the flour and set aside. About 1 hour before your starter is ready, mix the flour and water by hand in a medium bowl for about 3 minutes. Cover and leave to hydrate at room temperature (65° to 75°F) until the starter is ripe. When ready, add the starter and salt and mix again by hand for about 3 minutes, alternately breaking the dough up and folding it back onto itself. At this point, the dough will still look shaggy and feel sticky and weak. Get as much dough from your hands back into the bowl as possible, scraping down your hands and the bowl. Cover the bowl with a tea towel and leave to rise at room temperature for 3 hours, giving the dough a four-fold every 30 minutes.
2. Shape. After 3 hours, the dough should be showing clear signs of fermentation, such as bubbles under the surface. Lay out a couche or large tea towel on a sheet pan and generously dust it with flour. Heavily flour a section of the countertop and turn the dough out. Fold the top edge of the dough down a third of the way, then fold the bottom edge up a third, like folding a letter into a rectangle. Pat it out gently to a rectangle about 12 by 8 inches, then use a bench knife to divide the dough in half, making two rectangles, each about 6 by 8 inches. Coat the rectangles all over with flour. Gently lift each loaf onto the couche, leaving about 3 inches between the loaves. Lift the fabric in between the loaves to support their shape against one another, then fold the ends of the fabric loosely over the loaves. Leave to ferment until the loaves are puffy and significantly risen, about 1 hour and 45 minutes.
3. Bake. Place a large baking stone and hotel pan on the highest rack in your oven they will fit on. Preheat the oven to 450°F. Cut a sheet of parchment paper that will fit over the back side of a half sheet pan to use as a peel. Have two towels or hot pads and a spray bottle of water within reach, too.
4. Gently roll a loaf onto your hand, then transfer it to the parchment paper. If the dough is really loose, just roll it from the couche. The top can be the bottom or the bottom the top. Repeat with the second loaf, lining up both loaves evenly on the parchment.
5. Quickly but carefully open your oven, pull the rack that you are baking on partway out, and move the hot hotel pan to the stovetop. Slide the parchment paper and loaves onto the stone and cover with the hot hotel pan, spraying water into the pan before setting it onto the stone to trap steam. Close the oven and bake for 20 minutes. Then remove the hot hotel pan and bake, uncovered, for 10 minutes. Rotate the loaves, then bake until they are evenly browned, another 5 to 10 minutes. Remove to racks to cool.
6. This bread can be kept in a paper bag, bread box, or cupboard at room temperature for 5 to 6 days.

Buckwheat Buttermilk Bread

In 2018, local Philadelphia buckwheat made this bread possible. Flavors worked. Buttermilk's tang lifted buckwheat's low tannic notes. This dough feels great because buttermilk acid tightens the gluten. We serve this bread with entrees, but it's good any time of day. The dough requires buckwheat groats.

Prep time: 50 minutes | Cook time: 50 minutes | Serves 2 boules, about 10-inch diameter

SOAKER
- 82 g (½ cup) whole buckwheat groats
- 49 g (3⅓ tablespoons) water

DOUGH
- 726 g (5¾ cups) bolted hard wheat flour
- 363 g (1½ cups) buttermilk
- 254 g (1⅛ cups) water
- 109 g (½ cup) ripe whole-wheat sourdough starter
- 17 g (2¾ teaspoons) salt
- 131 g (¾ cup) soaker (from above)
- raw sunflower seeds for topping
- wheat bran for dusting

1. Day 1: make soaker. In the evening, toast the buckwheat groats in a dry sauté pan over medium heat until fragrant, just a few minutes, shaking the pan for even browning. Transfer to a small container and let cool. Add the water and let soak overnight.
2. Day 2: mix. Measure the flour and set aside. Combine the buttermilk, water, and flour in a bowl (a stand mixer bowl is ideal), stirring just until incorporated. Cover with a tea towel and let rest at room temperature (65° to 75°F) for 2 hours.
3. Combine the buttermilk mixture, starter, and salt in the bowl of a stand mixer and mix with the dough hook on low speed for 4 minutes. Switch to medium speed and mix for 3 minutes. The dough will be somewhat loose, but it will come together when you fold it later. Add the soaker and mix just until incorporated, about a minute. Transfer the dough to an oiled bowl and allow it to rest at room temperature for 2½ hours, with a four-fold every 30 minutes.
4. Preshape. Drizzle a little water on your countertop and spread it around so the surface is wet but not puddled. Turn the dough out onto the countertop and divide it into two 800-gram pieces. Give each piece some shape by stretching up and folding all four edges in toward the center. Roll the dough onto its seam, cover with a tea towel, and let rest seam-side down on the countertop for 20 minutes.
5. Shape. Set up a wide shallow bowl of raw sunflower seeds to coat the tops of the loaves. Flour two large round bannetons or large towel-lined bowls. Dampen your countertop again, then shape each piece of dough into a ball by rolling the dough in a circle on the countertop, cupping your hands around the dough, and applying pressure all around it to increase the surface tension. This dough is loose but make the ball as taut as possible. To seed each loaf, spray it with water and slip your hand beneath the loaf, pick it up, and invert it into the seeds to coat the top, then transfer it to the floured banneton with the seeds down, peeling your hand from the dough. Repeat with the other loaf.
6. Place the filled bannetons in plastic grocery bags or loosely cover with plastic wrap or beeswax wrap, then move the covered loaves to the refrigerator to rest overnight.
7. Day 3: bake. Place a large baking stone and hotel pan on the highest rack in the oven they will fit on. Preheat the oven to 450°F. Have two towels or hot pads, a spray bottle of water, and a razor within reach.
8. Dust the loaves with the wheat bran. Quickly but carefully open your oven, pull the rack that you are baking on partway out, and move the hot hotel pan to the stovetop. Gently invert the loaves onto the hot stone and quickly score each one (I like four slashes to make a square). Cover the loaves with the hot hotel pan, spraying water into the pan before setting it onto the stone to trap steam. These are larger loaves, and they will really fill the space. If you are worried about their touching each other or bumping the hotel pan, they can also be baked one at a time. The upside of really filling the hotel pan is more humidity for better oven spring and crust formation.
9. Bake for 20 minutes, then remove the hot hotel pan and rotate the loaves for even browning. Bake, uncovered, until the crust is as dark as you can get it without the seeds burning, 15 to 20 minutes more. The crust itself should be medium brown. Remove the loaves to a rack to cool.
10. This bread will keep in a paper bag, bread box, or cupboard at room temperature for 5 to 6 days.

Omni Bread

My favorite Ursa Bakery bread. Whole grains, seeds, crust, tang. Hence the name Omni. This moist, nutty, wholesome bread is perfect for baking and eating all week. It keeps well and can be used for sandwiches, toast, soups, stews, and more.

Prep time: 30 minutes | Cook time: 20 minutes | Serves 2 roundish oval loaves, about 12-inch diameter

SOAKER
- 24 g (3 tablespoons) pumpkin seeds and/or flax seeds
- 24 g (3 tablespoons) sunflower seeds and/or poppy or sesame seeds
- 20 g (1¾ tablespoons) polenta
- 73 g (5 tablespoons) water

DOUGH
- 605 g (4¾ cups) bolted hard wheat flour
- 67 g (9 tablespoons) whole-grain spelt flour
- 538 g (2¼ cups) water
- 134 g (¾ cup) ripe rye sourdough starter
- 15 g (2½ teaspoons) salt
- 141 g (⅞ cup) soaker (from above)
- 1 cup pumpkin seeds (and/or flax seeds) for topping
- 1 cup sunflower seeds (and/or poppy or sesame seeds) for topping
- wheat bran for dusting

1. Day 1: make soaker. In a medium skillet, toast all the seeds and the polenta over medium heat, until they smell nutty and fragrant, 2 to 3 minutes, shaking the pan to prevent burning. Pour the water into the pan while it's still hot and leave at room temperature (65° to 75°F) for about 3 hours.
2. Mix. Measure both flours and set aside. Combine the water, starter, and flours in a large mixing bowl. With clean hands, mix until it comes together in a shaggy mass, then mix it in the bowl for a few minutes more, alternately breaking the dough up and folding it back onto itself. The dough will be sticky and ragged, and that's okay. Get as much dough from your hands back into the bowl as possible, scraping down your hands and the bowl. Cover with a tea towel and let rest at room temperature for 30 minutes. Add the salt and hand-mix again for 3 minutes. At this point, the dough should start to have some strength. Cover and let rest again for 30 minutes. Smear the soaker over the dough and give the dough a few folds to distribute the seeds, but don't worry about their being perfectly distributed. Cover and let rest for about 2 hours, giving the dough a four-fold during that time.
3. Preshape. Drizzle a little water on your countertop and spread it around so the surface is wet but not puddled. Turn the dough out onto the counter and divide it into two 750-gram pieces. Give each piece some shape by gently pulling four sides of the dough up and outward and then folding in toward the center. Cover and let rest for 10 minutes.
4. Shape. Dampen your countertop again, then flip the loaves over onto the damp area. Shape the loaves into batards: fold in the left and right sides, then gently stretch and fold the bottom in toward the center and continue rolling the loaf toward the top, keeping pressure on the dough with your palms to create a taut oblong shape.
5. Lightly flour two medium oval bannetons or towel-lined bowls (obviously, you'll get a round loaf if using the latter). Pour all the seeds for the topping into a large shallow dish just larger than the loaves (or use a quarter sheet pan). To seed each loaf, slip your hand beneath it, pick it up, and roll the wet side in the seed mixture, coating it well. Then place each loaf seed-side down in the banneton, gently peeling your hand from the loaf. Place the bannetons in a covered container or loose plastic bag and move to the refrigerator to rest overnight.
6. Day 2: bake. Place a large baking stone and hotel pan on the highest rack in the oven they will fit on. Preheat the oven to 500°F. Have two towels or hot pads, a spray bottle of water, and a razor within reach.
7. Dust the loaves with wheat bran. Quickly but carefully open your oven, pull the rack that you are baking on partway out, and move the hot hotel pan to the stovetop. Invert the loaves one at a time onto the stone and score each loaf with a diamond pattern about ½ to ¾ inch deep. Cover the loaves with the hotel pan, spraying water into the pan before setting it onto the stone to trap steam. Lower the oven temperature to 475°F and bake for 20 minutes.
8. Remove the hot hotel pan and rotate the loaves for even browning. Bake, uncovered, until the loaves are evenly browned and the raised edges along the score marks have scorched lightly, another 10 to 15 minutes. Remove to racks to cool. This bread will keep for 5 to 6 days at room temperature in a paper bag, bread box, or cupboard.

Ciabatta Grano Arso With Einkorn

I burn whole einkorn berries to make grano arso (burnt grain), a nod to the old Italian practice of torching wheat fields after harvest to kill weeds and fertilize the soil for the next year. Grano arso adds flavor depth. This isn't white sandwich bread, and it doesn't have a large open crumb like ciabatta. Serve with winter stews and braises or on hearty sandwiches.

Prep time: 20 minutes | Cook time: 30 minutes | Serves 2 free-form loaves, about 8 by 10 inches

STARTER
- 108 g (¾ cup + 1¾ tablespoons) bolted hard wheat flour
- 22 g (1¾ tablespoons) ripe rye sourdough starter
- 70 g (4¾ tablespoons) water

SOAKER
- 37 g (¼ cup) whole einkorn berries
- 32 g (2⅛ tablespoons) water
- DOUGH
- 309 g (2½ cups) bolted hard wheat flour
- 309 g (2½ cups) whole-grain einkorn flour
- 501 g (2⅛ cups) water
- 155 g (¾ cup) starter (from above)
- 69 g (⅔ cup) soaker (from above)
- 17 g (2¾ teaspoons) salt

1. Day 1: build starter. In the evening, measure the flour and set aside. Combine the starter, water, and flour in a small bowl. Cover and leave at cool room temperature (50° to 65°F) to rise overnight.
2. Day 2: make soaker. In the morning, toast the einkorn berries in a dry pan over high heat until burnt, shaking the pan for even burning. Yes, you want the grains totally burnt. Spread them on a sheet pan to cool. When cooled, crack the burnt grain in a flour mill set very coarsely or with a few pulses of a coffee or spice grinder. Pour the burnt flour into a small bowl, and mix in the water. Set aside for 1 hour.
3. Mix dough. Measure both flours and set aside. Combine the water and starter in a large mixing bowl. Then add the flours. With clean hands, mix until the dough comes together in a shaggy mass, then mix it in the bowl for a few minutes more, alternately breaking the dough up and folding it back onto itself. At this point, the dough will still look shaggy and feel sticky and weak. Get as much dough from your hands back into the bowl as possible, scraping down your hands and the bowl. Cover the bowl with a tea towel and leave to rise at room temperature (65° to 75°F) for 1 hour.
4. After an hour, add the soaker and salt to the dough. Mix them in thoroughly with several rounds of folding the dough and then breaking it up by hand. Cover and leave to rise for 1 hour.
5. Give the dough a gentle four-fold. By now, you should be seeing some signs of fermentation activity such as small bubbles at the surface of the dough. The dough should also be smooth and quite extensible. Cover and leave to rise again for about 1 hour. By then, the dough should show signs of moderate fermentation, such as a small increase in volume and some bubbles under the surface. To check, you could slash the edge of the dough with a sharp knife or razor to peek inside and look for bubbles.
6. Shape. Place a large baking stone and hotel pan on the highest rack in the oven they will fit on. Preheat the oven to 500°F. Have a couche or tea towel, flour for dusting, and a bench knife ready.
7. Liberally dust your countertop with flour. Turn the dough out, using a bowl scraper to get all of it. Fold in the left and right sides toward the center of the dough, so it is a rough rectangle on the counter. Then pat out the rectangle, so it's about 12 by 8 inches. Dust again liberally with flour and use a bench knife to divide the rectangle in half, making two rectangles, each about 6 by 8 inches. Toss a little more flour on the cut surfaces. The goal here is to evenly coat the entire outside of each ciabatta with flour. Unlike most breads, surface tension is not a crucial consideration here. Dust the couche with flour. Then, handling gently so you don't de-gas the dough, lift each ciabatta up by slipping your hands beneath the dough on either side as if you were scooping water into your hands and set the ciabatta onto the couche. (To get a pretty tiger-stripe pattern on the tops of the loaves, you've got to create wrinkles on the bottom. The scoop-and-lift maneuver should crumple the bottom of the loaf sufficiently so that it has the wrinkles when flipped to bake; all that extra flour will prevent the wrinkles from sealing and will create a slackness that will be filled up during the bake, creating the tiger stripes.) Support the sides of the ciabatta by folding ridges in the couche. Cover and let rest for 15 minutes.
8. Bake. Cut a sheet of parchment paper that will fit over the back side of a half sheet pan to use as a peel. Have two towels or hot pads and a spray bottle of water within reach, too.
9. Pull the ends of the couche to spread it out and smooth out the support folds. You are going to invert and transfer the ciabatta, but the dough is very delicate. To do this properly, have your parchment-paper-and-sheet-pan setup nearby. Then lift up one side of the couche to roll the first ciabatta right-side up, put one hand beside the ciabatta, palm up (or use a narrow paddle), and roll the loaf into your hand. Quickly roll it off your hand onto one-half of the parchment paper on the sheet pan.
10. Quickly but carefully open your oven, pull the rack that you are baking on partway out, and move the hot hotel pan to the stovetop. Slide the parchment paper and ciabatta onto the stone and cover with the hot hotel pan, spraying water into the pan before setting it onto the stone to trap steam. Close the oven and bake for 12 minutes. Then remove the hot hotel pan and rotate the loaves for even browning. Bake, uncovered, for about another 12 minutes. These ciabatta are very floury, but the crust peeking through should have a tortoiseshell mottling from tan to dark brown. Remove the loaves to racks to cool.
11. The ciabatta can be kept in a paper bag, bread box, or cupboard at room temperature for 4 to 5 days.

Sourdough Baguette

Traditional baguettes are yeast breads created during the Industrial Revolution, which sped up and advanced life. Many bakers now use natural leavening. I used Ian Lowe's recipe for this dish. I blindly followed someone else's instructions and felt very uncomfortable. It worked great. The bread's crust, crumb, texture, and flavor improve in the oven. Sourdough crusts are chewier and have a tangier flavor than yeast baguettes.

Prep time: 20 minutes | Cook time: 50 minutes | Serves 4 baguettes, 16 to 18 inches long

- 655 g (5¼ cups) bolted hard wheat flour
- 462 g (2 cups) water
- 67 g (⅓ cup) ripe bolted wheat Sourdough Starter
- 3 g (1¼ teaspoons) barley malt flour or powder
- 13 g (2⅛ teaspoons) salt

1. Day 1: mix. In the evening, measure the wheat flour and set aside. Combine the water, starter, reserved flour, malt flour or powder, and salt in the bowl of a stand mixer. Mix with the dough hook on low speed for 5 minutes. Make sure that no flour has clumped at the bottom of the bowl. If it has, manually scrape these clumps into the main dough mass, then mix for an additional 2 minutes. Transfer the dough to a lightly oiled container with a lid and leave to rest at warm room temperature (75° to 85°F) for 1 hour. During that time, give the dough a four-fold every 15 minutes. Then move the covered container to the fridge and retard overnight.
2. Day 2: preshape. Pull the container from the fridge and allow to rest at room temperature (65° to 75°F) for 1 hour. Turn the dough out onto a lightly floured countertop and divide it into four 300-gram pieces. Give each piece some shape by loosely folding all four edges in toward the center, then rolling the dough over so it is seam-side down. Let rest for 15 minutes.
3. Shape. Set up a lightly floured couche or tea towel. Turn each loaf seam-side up and gently pat it down. Then roll it into a fat cylinder, stretching it out just a bit. Now, starting with one hand in the center of the cylinder, press lightly and begin rolling the baguette back and forth. Add your second hand and, pressing evenly, roll while stretching the baguette out. It will probably take a few passes to get the baguette to the right length of 16 to 18 inches. On the final pass from the center outward, press the tips out to a taper. Place each baguette seam-side up on the couche, pulling up a little ridge of fabric in between each baguette. Once all four baguettes are nestled in, fold the excess fabric over (or cover with a tea towel) to keep them from drying out. Leave to rest at room temperature for 45 minutes.
4. Bake. Place a large baking stone and hotel pan on the highest rack in the oven they will fit on. Preheat the oven to 500°F. Cut a sheet of parchment paper that will fit over the back side of a half sheet pan to use as a peel (or line a large cutting board with parchment). Have a spray bottle of water, two towels or hot pads, and a razor within reach.
5. Gently lift and transfer two baguettes to the parchment paper, flipping them over so they are seam-side down. Adjust them so they are straight and evenly spaced from each other. To score, tilt the razor blade and hold it at an angle so that your cut will produce a flap instead of an open wound. Slash each baguette three to five times quickly in a few almost perfectly centered lines from end to end.
6. Now quickly but carefully open your oven, pull the rack that you are baking on partway out, and move the hot hotel pan to the stovetop or side of the oven. Slide the parchment paper onto the stone. Still working quickly, but without burning yourself or smooshing the baguettes, cover the baguettes with the hotel pan, spraying water into the pan before setting it onto the stone to trap steam. Close the oven and bake for 8 minutes. Then remove the hotel pan and rotate the loaves from side to side and front to back to ensure even color. Close the oven and bake until the predominant color all over the baguettes is a light terra-cotta, an additional 10 minutes or so. Remove the baguettes to a rack to cool. Repeat scoring and baking the remaining baguettes.
7. Try to eat the baguettes within 36 hours. You could also freeze them or use them to make Panzanella or Ribollita.

Blueberry-Lemon Sourdough Country Bread

Our family picks berries every summer. Sierra foothill blueberry picking is hot, sticky, and satisfying. This bread has lemon and blueberries.

Prep time: 35 minutes | Cook time: 45 minutes | Serves 1 loaf

FOR THE STARTER
- 15 grams sourdough starter (1 tablespoon) or ⅛ teaspoon instant yeast
- 60 grams water (¼ cup plus 3 tablespoons)
- 60 grams all-purpose flour (⅔ cup)

FOR THE DOUGH
- 325 grams water, divided (1⅓ cups plus 2 teaspoons)
- 80 grams active starter (½ cup)
- 100 grams whole-wheat flour (¾ cup)
- 300 grams bread flour (2 cups plus 2 tablespoons)
- 8 grams sea salt (1½ teaspoons)
- Zest of 1 lemon (¼ to ½ teaspoon)
- 80 grams fresh blueberries (⅓ to ½ cup)
- Rice flour or semolina, for dusting proofing bowl

1. **Refresh the starter:** About 6 to 10 hours before mixing your dough, place the sourdough starter in a clean container. Add the water and flour, stir well, and cover. Leave out at room temperature until it doubles in volume and becomes bubbly. (See tips for substituting instant yeast.)
2. **Weigh the ingredients:** Making sure to tare after each addition, combine 315 grams of water, 80 grams of active starter, the whole-wheat flour, and the bread flour in a large mixing bowl.
3. **Mix:** Using a spoon, mix all the ingredients together by hand or in a stand mixer until there are no dry spots of flour left.
4. **Autolyse:** Cover the bowl and let the dough rest for 20 minutes.
5. **Add the salt:** After the resting time is finished, place the bowl of dough on the scale and tare. Add the salt, then slowly pour the remaining 10 grams of water over the salt to dissolve. Massage the salt and water into the dough, rotating it and folding it to make sure it is fully mixed in. Continue folding for 3 to 5 minutes.
6. **Rest:** Cover the bowl and allow the dough to rest for 30 minutes.
7. **Stretch and fold:** Add the lemon zest and blueberries to the center of the dough. Take the dough in hand and, one-quarter at a time, pull the dough upward, then fold it back into the middle. Repeat with the other three quarters until the blueberries and lemon zest are well distributed throughout the dough.
8. **Bulk ferment:** Allow the dough to ferment at room temperature for 3 to 6 hours, until doubled in volume.
9. **Pre-shape and bench rest:** Transfer the dough to an unfloured surface. Quickly push the straight edge of a dough scraper under one-half of the dough, then fold it over itself. Push the scraper under one side of the dough and rotate in a circular motion 3 to 5 times until it's a round shape. Leave the dough to rest for 20 minutes.
10. **Prepare the proofing bowl:** Dust your proofing bowl generously with rice flour, making sure to coat the sides well.
11. **Final shape:** Flour the top of your dough. Push the straight edge of the dough scraper under the dough. Guiding with your opposite hand, flip the dough onto its floured side. Pick up the left and right edges of the dough, gently stretch outward, then fold the edges into the middle. Pinch the edges together to seal the seam. Take the end of the dough below the seam and roll it onto itself in a spiral until it seals at the opposite end. The floured side should be facing up once again. Without flipping the dough over, use the scraper to rotate the dough in a circle until it tightens into a tight ball. Quickly push the scraper under the dough and lift with your opposite hand, then flip the dough into the proofing bowl. The floured side should be down, and the sticky side should be up. Cover.
12. **Proof:** Proof for 1 to 2 hours at room temperature. To test when the proofing is completed, wet your finger and gently press the dough. If it rises back up, leaving a slight indentation, it is ready to bake.
13. **Preheat:** After 30 to 60 minutes of proofing, preheat your oven to 500°F with the Dutch oven inside on the center rack. Substitute with a metal pan filled halfway with water on the lowest rack of the oven if you are planning to bake your bread on a baking sheet.
14. **Bake:** Center an extra-long sheet of parchment paper over the proofing bowl. Holding the paper over the bowl by grasping the edges of the bowl, flip it to turn the dough out onto the parchment paper. Use a bread lame to score the top of your dough about ¼ inch deep. Carefully pick up the edges of the parchment and transfer the dough into the preheated Dutch oven (or onto the baking sheet). Cover with the lid and place it back in the oven. Spray the walls of the oven with water and shut the door. Reduce the oven temperature to 460°F and bake for 20 minutes. After 20 minutes, carefully remove the bread from the Dutch oven and place it directly on the oven rack. (Remove the steam pan if using manual steam.) Reduce the heat to 450°F and bake for an additional 20 minutes to create a golden-brown crust.
15. **Cool:** Allow the bread to cool for 1 hour on a cooling rack before slicing.

Chapter 4
All-Purpose Breads

Master No-Knead Rustic Boule

This no-knead loaf welcomes you to bread baking. While it needs to rest overnight, making and baking it won't take long.

Prep time: 25 minutes | Cook time: 45 minutes | Serves 1 loaf

- 500g (3¾ cups) all-purpose flour, plus more for dusting
- 12g (2 teaspoons) salt
- 4g (about 1 teaspoon) yeast
- 365g (1½ cups) water, 75° to 80°F
- Rice flour, for dusting
- Oil or butter, for greasing

1. **Combine:** In a large mixing bowl, use a whisk to combine the flour and salt. If using instant yeast, mix that in as well. If using active dry yeast, mix it into the water; let it dissolve and sit for a few minutes.
2. **Mix:** Add the water or water-yeast mixture to the dry ingredients. Mix everything together using a wooden spatula or Danish dough whisk until you have a loose, shaggy mixture. Continue to mix, either with a tool or with a lightly wetted hand, until you no longer see any dry bits of flour. Cover the bowl with plastic wrap or a damp towel and let the dough rest for 15 minutes.
3. **Stretch and Fold:** Lightly wet your hand with water. Starting on one side, stretch the dough up and fold it down into the center. Repeat this motion four to six more times, making your way around the dough until you have a smooth ball.
4. **Proof:** Place the dough seam-side down in the bowl, cover it, and let it rise for 45 minutes. After this initial rise, move the entire bowl, covered, into the refrigerator and let the dough rest there overnight.
5. **Season:** After placing the dough in the refrigerator, season the banneton if you plan on using it in the morning. Spray it with water, then generously dust it with rice flour or all-purpose flour. Let it sit like this overnight so that it begins to form a crust.
6. **Deflate and Shape:** In the morning, wet your hand and begin to pull the dough from around the edges of the bowl into the center; this will naturally deflate it. Turn it out onto a lightly floured work surface. Shape the dough into a tight ball by folding all the sides in. Flip the dough over so that the folded parts are down. Using a flexible dough scraper (or your hands), tuck the dough under itself, rotating the dough as you go, to build some surface tension and create a tight, rounded shape. Flour the top of the dough and then flip it over into the banneton so that the smooth top is now facing down. You can tighten up the bottom pieces if you'd like, then dust with additional flour.
7. **Second Proof:** If using a medium mixing bowl, spray it with oil or line it with butter. Then, generously coat it with either rice flour or all-purpose flour to prevent the dough from sticking. If using a banneton, generously coat it with either rice flour or all-purpose flour. Place the dough seam-side up, smooth-side down, into the seasoned banneton or prepared bowl. You can tighten the ball up by pinching the bottom seam together more tightly. Dust with flour and then cover the bowl again, letting it rise at room temperature for about 1 hour.
8. **Preheat and Score:** Place the Dutch oven or oven-safe pot into the oven. Turn the oven to 475°F and let it preheat with the Dutch oven or pot inside. Test the dough to see if it passes the "poke test". If it's ready to go, place a piece of parchment paper on top of the bowl, then flip it upside down so that the dough's seam is down on the parchment paper and the smooth side is facing up. Score the dough by cutting a shallow "X" on top, approximately ¼ inch deep.
9. **Bake:** Holding the edges of the parchment paper, carefully lift the dough and lower it into the hot Dutch oven or pot. Cover the pot and bake for 25 minutes. Remove the lid and continue baking for an additional 10 minutes. To test if the bread is done, knock on the bottom of the loaf; if it makes a clear knocking sound, it's fully baked. If it's very muffled or still feels soft, continue baking for an additional 5 minutes.
10. **Cool:** Transfer the bread to a wire rack and let it cool for at least 30 minutes. The inner core of the bread will finish cooking during this time. Then slice into it and enjoy!

Fougasse

Fougasse is shaped focaccia. Similar to focaccia, but with less water to make shaping easier. If you only want one fougasse, halve this recipe.

Prep time: 35 minutes | Cook time: 25 minutes | Serves 2 fougasse

- 500g (3¾ cups) all-purpose flour
- 12g (2 teaspoons) salt
- 4g (about 1 teaspoon) yeast
- 400g (slightly less than 1¾ cups) water, 75° to 80°F
- ¼ cup olive oil, divided
- dried herbs, for topping (optional)

1. **Create the Dough:** Follow steps 1 through 4 of the recipe for Master No-Knead Rustic Boule, using the ingredients listed in this recipe.
2. **Transfer and Shape:** Line the sheet pans with parchment paper, then drizzle ⅛ cup of olive oil over each. With wet hands, divide the dough in two and transfer one half to each pan. Gently press the doughs into a leaf shape or oval.
3. **Second Proof:** Let the doughs sit on the counter, covered, for 60 to 90 minutes. They should become quite puffy.
4. **Preheat and Shape:** Preheat the oven to 425°F and spread the remaining ⅛ cup of olive oil over the tops of both loaves. Using scissors, cut three 2- to 3-inch slashes directly down the center of the dough, cutting all the way through, each separated by 1 inch. Use your fingers to gently spread out the holes you've made just a bit; if they aren't very "open," they'll seal back up while baking. Take the scissors once again and cut three diagonal slashes on each side of the center line to make it look like a leaf. Once again, spread the holes out gently. If you'd like, top the fougasse with dried herbs.
5. **Bake:** Bake the fougasse for about 25 minutes, rotating the pan halfway through, or until golden brown.
6. **Cool:** Allow the fougasse to cool on a rack for about 20 minutes, then enjoy!

Bountiful Bagels

I love bagels on weekends. Boiling is essential for bagels' chewy texture and golden color. If this is your first time making bagels, plan ahead.

Prep time: 45 minutes | Cook time: 35 minutes | Serves 8 bagels

- 500g (3¾ cups) all-purpose flour
- 12g (2 teaspoons) salt
- 4g (about 1 teaspoon) yeast
- 320g (1⅓ cups plus 1 tablespoon) water, 75° to 80°F
- 6g (1 teaspoon) honey
- ¼ cup maple syrup
- 1 egg, beaten with 1 tablespoon water

1. **Create the Dough:** Follow steps 1 through 4 of the recipe for Master No-Knead Rustic Boule, using the ingredients listed in this recipe. Add the honey to the water during step 1.
2. **Transfer and Pre-Shape:** In the morning, line a sheet pan with parchment paper and flour a work surface. Divide the dough into 8 equal pieces. Shape each into a tight ball, dust with flour, and place them seam-side down onto the baking sheet.
3. **Second Proof:** Let the dough balls sit evenly spaced out, covered, for 60 to 90 minutes.
4. **Final Shape and Boil:** Boil about 8 cups of water and the maple syrup in a large stockpot. Shape the bagels by sticking one or both thumbs through the top of each round to create a hole in the center. Stretch it out gently so that the hole remains open. Boil the shaped bagels, 30 seconds per side, in the water-syrup mixture. Drip the water off each bagel and place them back down onto the baking sheets.
5. **Preheat and Add Toppings:** Preheat the oven to 425°F and brush the tops of the bagels with the egg wash. Top them by sprinkling on your favorite seasonings or by dipping them egg-side down into a plate full of toppings.
6. **Bake:** Bake the bagels for 30 minutes, rotating the pan halfway through.
7. **Cool:** Allow the bagels to cool on a rack for about 15 minutes. Slice and enjoy!

Pizza Dough

This pizza dough requires little active time because it rests in the fridge. After shaping dough, refrigerate it for 12 hours.

Prep time: 35 minutes | Cook time: 15 minutes | Serves 2 medium pizzas

- 500g (3¾ cups) all-purpose flour
- 12g (2 teaspoons) salt
- 4g (about 1 teaspoon) yeast
- 330g (a little less than 1½ cups) water, 75° to 80°F
- ¼ cup olive oil
- Semolina flour, for dusting

1. **Create the Dough:** Follow steps 1 through 3 of the recipe for Master No-Knead Rustic Boule, using the ingredients listed in this recipe.
2. **Proof:** Place the dough seam-side down in the bowl, cover it, and let it rise for 8 hours on the counter overnight.
3. **Transfer and Pre-Shape:** In the morning, line 2 pint-size containers with olive oil and flour a work surface. Divide the dough in half and shape each half into a tight ball. Dust with flour and place them seam-side down into their containers. Cover the containers tightly and place them in the refrigerator for 12 to 48 hours.
4. **Second Proof:** Let the dough come to room temperature inside the containers for 1 to 2 hours prior to stretching and baking.
5. **Final Shape:** Preheat the oven to 525°F with a baking stone or steel inside, if available. Line either a pizza peel, a large, thin wooden cutting board, or two baking sheets with a combination of all-purpose flour and semolina flour. Dust your hands with flour and begin to shape each pizza by picking up the dough and stretching it by hand, letting its own weight do some of the work. Work each ball into a round that is 12 to 14 inches across. If using baking sheets, the pizza will end up more in an oval shape to fit.
6. **Top and Bake:** Top the pizzas as desired and bake for 10 to 15 minutes.
7. **Cool:** Allow the pizzas to cool slightly on a rack before slicing. Enjoy!

Sesame-Coated Bâtard

This sesame-coated loaf resembles Italian deli bread. You can use a round banneton and stretch the boule into a log before baking.

Prep time: 35 minutes | Cook time: 45 minutes | Serves 1 loaf

- 500g (3¾ cups) all-purpose flour, plus more for dusting
- 12g (2 teaspoons) salt
- 4g (about 1 teaspoon) yeast
- 365g (1½ cups) water, 75° to 80°F
- ¼ cup sesame seeds
- Rice flour, for dusting

1. **Create the Dough:** Follow steps 1 through 6 of the recipe for Master No-Knead Rustic Boule, using the ingredients listed in this recipe. Coat the top of the shaped dough with the sesame seeds.
2. **Second Proof:** Generously coat the banneton or bowl with either rice flour or all-purpose flour. Place the dough coated-side down into the banneton or bowl. Dust with flour and then cover the bowl again, letting it rise at room temperature for 1 hour.
3. **Preheat and Score:** Preheat the oven to 475°F with the Dutch oven or pot inside. Test the dough to see if it passes the "poke test". If it's ready to go, place a piece of parchment paper on top of the bowl, then flip the bowl upside down. Score the seeded side of the dough by cutting a shallow "X" on top.
4. **Bake:** Holding the edges of the parchment paper, carefully lift the dough and lower it into the hot Dutch oven or pot. Cover and bake for 25 minutes. Remove the lid and continue baking for an additional 10 minutes. To test if the bread is done, knock on the bottom of the loaf; if it makes a clear knocking sound, it's fully baked. If it's very muffled or still feels soft, continue baking for an additional 5 minutes.
5. **Cool:** Transfer the bread to a wire rack and let it cool for at least 30 minutes. Then, slice into it and enjoy!

Sub Rolls

These bulky rolls are delicious. Use them as is or slice them for baguette-like party snacks. This dough can be shaped into dinner rolls.

Prep time: 35 minutes | Cook time: 25 minutes | Serves 4 personal-size rolls

- 500g (3¾ cups) all-purpose flour, plus more for dusting
- 12g (2 teaspoons) salt
- 4g (about 1 teaspoon) yeast
- 365g (1½ cups) water, 75° to 80°F
- Rice flour, for dusting

1. Create the Dough: Follow steps 1 through 4 of the recipe for Master No-Knead Rustic Boule, using the ingredients listed in this recipe.
2. Deflate and Shape: In the morning, wet your hand and begin to pull the dough from around the edges of the bowl into the center. Turn it out onto a lightly floured work surface. Cut the dough into four equal pieces, about 215g each. Shape each into a tight log shape.
3. Second Proof: Lay a kitchen linen flat on a work surface and generously spread a mixture of all-purpose flour and rice flour all over it to prevent sticking. Place each sub roll on the linen and pull the fabric up between them so that they're divided and held in shape by the linen. Dust the tops of the rolls with flour and cover with plastic wrap. Let the rolls rise for 1 hour.
4. Preheat and Score: Preheat the oven to 475°F. Test the dough to see if it passes the "poke test". If it's ready to go, place a piece of parchment paper on a baking sheet, then transfer the rolls, using a bench scraper if needed and leaving about 1 inch between them on the sheet. Score the tops with three shallow slashes on each and then spritz them with water.
5. Bake: Bake for 15 minutes, then reduce the oven temperature to 425°F and bake for another 10 minutes. The rolls may expand to touch each other as they bake, which is okay.
6. Cool: Transfer the bread to a wire rack and let it cool for at least 30 minutes. Then, slice and enjoy!

Pita Pockets

Easy pita pockets. First time I made them, I was surprised they puffed up to make a pocket. Once rolled, let them rest.

Prep time: 35 minutes | Cook time: 15 minutes | Serves 12 small pitas

- 500g (3¾ cups) all-purpose flour, plus more for dusting
- 12g (2 teaspoons) salt
- 7g (1¾ teaspoons or 1 packet) yeast
- 320g (1⅓ cups plus 1 tablespoon) water, 75° to 80°F
- 2 tablespoons olive oil

1. Create the Dough: Follow steps 1 through 3 of the recipe for Master No-Knead Rustic Boule, using the ingredients listed in this recipe. Add the olive oil during step 2 (Mix).
2. Proof: Place the dough seam-side down in the bowl, cover it, and let it rise for about 1 hour, or until doubled in size.
3. Deflate and Pre-Shape: Wet your hand and begin to pull the dough from around the edges of the bowl into the center. Turn it out onto a lightly floured work surface. Cut the dough into 12 equal pieces and shape each piece into a small ball.
4. Second Proof and Final Shape: Cover the dough balls and let them rest for 10 minutes. Preheat the oven to 500°F with two baking sheets inside. After the dough has rested for 10 minutes, flour a work surface. Using a rolling pin, roll the pitas out until they are about 5 inches across. Let them rest for 10 minutes.
5. Bake: To bake the pitas, toss two at a time into the oven and bake for 45 to 60 seconds per side. Try to move quickly so that the oven maintains its temperature. Repeat this process until all pitas are cooked.
6. Cool: Transfer the pita pockets to a clean kitchen towel and wrap them up. Keep wrapped in the towel until ready to eat.

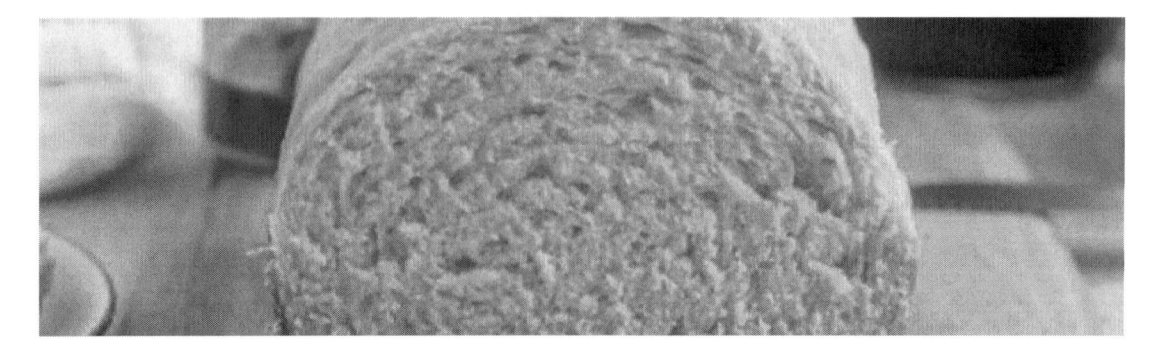

Foolproof Focaccia

If a boule or batard fails, try focaccia. It's the most forgiving bread, requires no shaping, and is fun to play with (and eat).

Prep time: 35 minutes | Cook time: 35 minutes| Serves 1 loaf

- 500g (3¾ cups) all-purpose flour
- 12g (2 teaspoons) salt
- 4g (about 1 teaspoon) yeast
- 400g (slightly less than 1¾ cups) water, 75° to 80°F
- ¼ cup olive oil, divided
- ½ tablespoon flaky sea salt

1. **Create the Dough:** Follow steps 1 through 4 of the recipe for Master No-Knead Rustic Boule, using the ingredients listed in this recipe. This dough will feel a bit more wet—that's okay!
2. **Transfer and Pre-Shape:** In the morning, line the pan with parchment paper, then drizzle ⅛ cup of olive oil over it. With wet hands, transfer the dough to the pan. Spread it to mostly fill the pan.
3. **Second Proof:** Let the dough sit on the counter, covered, for 60 to 90 minutes. It should become quite puffy.
4. **Preheat and Add Toppings:** Preheat the oven to 425°F and top the dough with the remaining ⅛ cup of olive oil and the flaky sea salt. With some olive oil on your first, middle, and fourth fingers, press gently into the dough all over to create focaccia's signature "dimples." Don't go too overboard, or you'll deflate the focaccia.
5. **Bake:** Bake the focaccia for 30 minutes, rotating the pan halfway through. Once the entire top is golden brown, it is ready.
6. **Cool:** Allow the focaccia to cool in the baking pan for 10 minutes, then transfer it to a wire rack and let it cool for 20 more minutes. Slice into it and enjoy!

Olive Oil Sandwich Loaf

Soft sandwich bread. Olive oil adds a lovely, not overpowering flavor. It's great for sandwiches, toast, and French toast. Using stale bread, make croutons.

Prep time: 35 minutes | Cook time: 65 minutes| Serves 1 loaf

- 500g (3¾ cups) all-purpose flour
- 12g (2 teaspoons) salt
- 7g (1¾ teaspoons or 1 packet) yeast
- 260g (1¼ cups) water, 75° to 80°F
- 95g (about ½ cup) olive oil, plus more for brushing

1. **Create the Dough:** Follow steps 1 through 3 of the recipe for Master No-Knead Rustic Boule, using the ingredients listed in this recipe. Add the olive oil during step 2 (Mix).
2. **Proof:** Place the dough seam-side down in the bowl, cover it, and let it rise for 1 hour, or until doubled in size.
3. **Transfer and Shape:** Line the loaf pan with parchment paper and drizzle in some olive oil to coat it. With wet or oiled hands, deflate the dough by folding the sides in and pressing it down and then shape it into a log. Place the log, smooth-side up, into the loaf pan. Brush the top with olive oil.
4. **Second Proof:** Let the dough sit on the counter, covered, for another 45 minutes. It should begin to rise and slowly reach the top of the pan.
5. **Bake:** Preheat the oven to 400°F, then bake the loaf for 45 minutes. Turn the oven temperature down to 375°F and bake for another 15 minutes.
6. **Cool:** Remove the loaf from the pan using the parchment paper and transfer it to a wire rack. Let it cool for 1 hour, then slice and enjoy!

Herbed Muffin Pan Peasant Rolls

The muffin pan makes these rolls shapeless. Because they're shapeless, they have more water, so don't be alarmed if the dough feels wet.

Prep time: 35 minutes | Cook time: 35 minutes| Serves 12 rolls

- 500g (3¾ cups) all-purpose flour
- 12g (2 teaspoons) salt
- 7g (1¾ teaspoons or 1 packet) yeast
- 430g (1¾ cups) water, 75° to 80°F
- 8g (about 2 tablespoons) dried herbs (I like a mix of basil, oregano, and thyme)
- 2 tablespoons butter or canola oil spray, divided

1. **Create the Dough:** Follow steps 1 and 2 of the recipe for Master No-Knead Rustic Boule, using the ingredients listed in this recipe. Add the herbs during step 1 (Combine). Be aware that this is a very wet dough.
2. : Cover the bowl with plastic wrap and let the dough rise for 60 to 90 minutes.
3. **Transfer and Shape:** Line the muffin pan cups with butter or spray them with canola oil. Wet your hand and gently deflate the dough by doing a round of stretch and folds around the bowl. Again, it will be very wet. Pull off pieces of the dough and fill each muffin cup until the dough reaches about the top of the cup.
4. **Second Proof:** Glaze the top of the rolls with additional butter or canola oil, then cover with plastic wrap. Let the rolls rest for an additional 20 minutes.
5. **Preheat and Bake:** Preheat the oven to 425°F. Bake the muffin pan rolls for 15 minutes, then reduce the oven temperature to 375°F and bake for an additional 5 to 10 minutes.
6. **Cool:** Allow the rolls to cool in the pan for 5 minutes, then transfer them to a cooling rack. Enjoy!

Rosemary Bread Sticks

"Grissini" are crunchy Italian bread sticks. They can be used as crackers or as a midweek snack. This recipe has no yeast or leavening, but the dough needs 30 minutes in the fridge.

Prep time: 55 minutes | Cook time: 35 minutes| Serves 50 to 70 bread sticks

- 500g (3¾ cups) all-purpose flour, plus more for dusting
- 12g (2 teaspoons) salt
- 8g (2 tablespoons) rosemary
- 200g (slightly less than 1 cup) water, 75° to 80°F
- 45g (6 tablespoons) olive oil

1. **Combine:** In a large mixing bowl, use a whisk to combine the flour, salt, and rosemary. In a separate bowl, use the whisk to combine the water and olive oil.
2. **Mix:** Add the water-oil mixture to the dry ingredients. Mix everything together using a wooden spatula or your hands until there are no dry bits of flour. You may need to squeeze the dough with your hands until you have a smooth ball.
3. **Rest:** Wrap the dough tightly in plastic wrap and let it rest in the refrigerator for at least 30 minutes or up to 3 hours.
4. **Shape:** Turn the dough out onto a lightly floured surface. Work it into a rough square or rectangle and then roll it out until it's approximately ¼ inch thick. Slice the dough into thin strands, then cut them all in half. Taking one at a time, roll them back and forth using your hands until they are a little thinner than the diameter of a pencil. You'll get anywhere from 50 to 70, depending on thickness and how short you cut them.
5. **Transfer and Bake:** Preheat the oven to 400°F. Line two or more baking sheets with parchment paper and transfer all the bread sticks to them, making sure they do not touch.
6. **Bake:** Bake for 20 to 30 minutes, keeping the pans on the middle and top racks. Rotate the pans and turn the bread sticks over midway through the bake. The ones closer to the heat source might cook faster so keep an eye on them. They're ready when slightly golden brown (not dark brown).
7. **Cool:** Let the bread sticks cool on the baking sheets. They should snap when you break them in half.

Easiest English Muffins

This easy stovetop English muffin recipe makes perfect egg sandwiches or weekend brunch treats smothered in butter and jam. They can be made in a few hours with a shorter rise.

Prep time: 35 minutes | Cook time: 25 minutes| Serves 12 muffins

- 500g (3¾ cups) all-purpose flour
- 12g (2 teaspoons) salt
- 7g (1¾ teaspoons or 1 packet) yeast
- 325g (1⅓ cups plus ½ tablespoon) water, 75° to 80°F
- 2g (½ teaspoon) baking powder
- Cornmeal or semolina flour, for dusting

1. **Create the Dough:** Follow steps 1 through 3 of the recipe for Master No-Knead Rustic Boule, using the ingredients listed in this recipe. Add the baking powder to the flour and salt during step 1 (Combine).
2. **Proof:** Place the dough seam-side down in the bowl, cover it, and let it rise for about 1 hour, or until doubled in size. While the dough is rising, line two baking sheets with parchment paper and dust with cornmeal or semolina.
3. **Deflate and Shape:** When the dough is ready, divide it into 12 equal portions, about 70g each. Using a little flour, shape them into balls by pinching the edges of the dough together at the bottom. Place the dough balls seam-side down 1 to 2 inches apart on the prepared baking sheets. Dust the tops with more cornmeal or semolina, then cover them and let them rise again for about 45 minutes.
4. **Preheat:** Preheat a large cast-iron or ungreased skillet over medium-low heat.
5. **Cook:** In an ungreased skillet over low heat, cook the muffins in batches of 6 at a time for 5 or so minutes per side. Resist the temptation to turn the heat up! When you flip them, press down on them gently to flatten them. Check the bottoms of the muffins to make sure they aren't burning. The sides should be softer but will start to firm up as they cook.
6. **Transfer and Cool:** When each muffin is finished cooking, transfer it to a wire rack to cool. Let the muffins rest for about 30 minutes, then slice and enjoy!

Chapter 5
Enriched Breads

Brioche

This recipe makes a soft, sweet brioche. This brioche recipe can be mixed by hand, unlike most. This sweet bread makes delicious French toast on weekends. Many of my customers buy brioche on Saturday for Sunday breakfast. Homemade is a treat.

Prep time: 25 minutes | Cook time: 35 minutes | Serves 2 loaves

FOR THE DOUGH
- 156 grams whole milk
- 256 grams whole eggs
- 72 grams sugar
- 6 grams yeast
- 180 grams very soft butter
- 600 grams all-purpose flour
- 12 grams salt
- Butter, oil, or cooking spray, for greasing the pans
- For the egg wash
- 1 egg
- 2 tablespoons water

1. Scale: Weigh all of the ingredients before you begin. In this case, the milk and eggs can be cold from the refrigerator, but the butter needs to be very soft (not melted) so that it can be incorporated into the dough by hand.
2. Combine: Combine the milk, eggs, sugar, yeast, and butter in a large bowl using a whisk or a fork.
3. Mix: Add the flour and salt on top of the wet ingredients and mix by hand, feeling that the ingredients are well combined, until a smooth, even, wet dough is produced. Don't worry if it seems very relaxed. The soft butter will firm up with the colder ingredients in the dough.
4. Rest: Cover the dough with a floured kitchen towel, and let it rest for 20 to 30 minutes while the flour absorbs the liquid ingredients.
5. Knead: Flour your work surface and turn the dough out onto it. Knead the dough by pushing forward into the dough with the heels of your hands and then folding the elongated dough back toward you. Give it a quarter turn, push the dough away, and fold it back again. Keep with it until you can feel that the dough has tightened up and has gotten smoother, 5 to 10 minutes.
6. Rise: Place the dough in a large bowl and cover with a floured kitchen towel or plastic wrap and let rise for 1 hour 30 minutes to 2 hours.
7. Divide and shape: Using a metal dough scraper, divide the dough into 2 pieces and shape each into a simple loaf shape: Fold the far side (12 o'clock) down to the middle, sealing the dough against itself. Fold the bottom up to meet the seam and seal it. This is a letter fold. Turn the dough so the seam is vertical, and do the letter fold again, sealing the dough to itself. You should have a nice little rounded square shape. Place your loaves into 2 greased loaf pans.
8. Proof: Let the loaves proof for 1 hour 30 minutes to 2 hours, until the dough "mushrooms" above the edges of each pan and feels light and airy.
9. Preheat: While the dough is proofing, preheat the oven to 375°F.
10. Bake: Make an egg wash by whisking the egg with the water. Brush it over the tops of the loaves with a pastry brush. Bake the loaves for 35 to 40 minutes. The finished loaves should be golden brown and will sound hollow when you thump them with your fingers.
11. Cool: Let cool in the pans for about 10 minutes, then transfer the loaves from the pans to a cooling rack for 20 more minutes before slicing.

Chocolate Babka

Babka is chocolate-filled bread. The dough is rolled with chocolate like the cinnamon swirl loaf, then halved, twisted, and braided to create a swirling, marbled masterpiece. As Seinfeld famously said, "Nothing beats a babka!"

Prep time: 25 minutes | Cook time: 35 minutes | Serves 2 loaves

FOR THE DOUGH
- 145 grams whole milk
- 205 grams whole eggs
- 60 grams sugar
- 5 grams yeast
- 150 grams very soft butter
- 500 grams all-purpose flour
- 10 grams salt
- Butter, oil, or cooking spray, for greasing the pans
- For the filling
- 85 grams cocoa powder
- 198 grams sugar
- 227 grams cream
- 113 grams salted butter
- 1 tablespoon vanilla

1. create the dough: Follow the Master Recipe for Enriched Bread through step 6 of Brioche recipe, using the ingredient amounts listed.
2. chill: After the first rise, cover the bowl with plastic wrap and refrigerate the dough for 2 hours. Chilling the dough allows it to be rolled out, shaped, and cut without sticking and making a big mess.
3. make the filling: While the dough is chilling, make the chocolate filling. I use my recipe for hot fudge, which may not be very authentic, but it has the most fantastic texture and works well with the dough. In a saucepan over medium heat, whisk together the cocoa powder, sugar, and cream until well combined and simmering. Add the butter and vanilla and stir until the butter melts. Turn off the heat and continue whisking until the mixture becomes shiny. Chill for at least 30 minutes in the refrigerator, until the filling is thick and spreadable.
4. divide and preshape: Divide the dough into 2 equal pieces. Using a rolling pin, roll out each piece of dough into a rectangle as thin as you can get it, approximately 9 by 16 inches, with the shorter side horizontal and closest to you. The thinner the dough, the more contrast you will get with lots of swirls of chocolate. Using a rubber spatula, spread 1 dough rectangle with half of the fudge filling, covering the surface but leaving a small strip of dough uncovered on the long side farthest from you; you will use this to seal the edge of the dough. Gently roll up the dough, pushing the edge of the dough away from you and rolling it up like a yoga mat. Seal the seam by pressing the dough together. Repeat with the other piece of dough, using the rest of the fudge filling, and transfer both babka ropes to a baking sheet. Put them in the freezer for 15 minutes to firm them up, which will make them easier to cut.
5. shape: Grease 2 loaf pans or line them with parchment. Take out the chilled ropes and use a sharp knife to cut each in half lengthwise. Take 2 halves and twist them around each other as much as possible (this creates the swirling marbling effect inside the dough) and place the twist into one of the loaf pans, folding and twisting to fit. Repeat with the other 2 halves and place into the other loaf pan.
6. proof: Let proof for 1 hour 30 minutes to 2 hours, until the dough is just reaching the top of the pan.
7. preheat: While the dough is proofing, preheat the oven to 375°F.
8. bake: Bake for 35 to 40 minutes. The finished loaves should be golden brown and will sound hollow when you thump them with your fingers.
9. cool: Let cool in the pans for about 10 minutes, then transfer the loaves from the pans to a cooling rack for 20 more minutes before slicing.

Challah

Challah is a Jewish holiday bread. It's a pretty, shiny braided loaf. My kids love this bread's unique look. It's fun to work with the firm-yet-supple dough.

Prep time: 25 minutes | Cook time: 45 minutes | Serves 1 large braided loaf

FOR THE DOUGH
- 145 grams whole milk
- 205 grams whole eggs
- 80 grams honey
- 5 grams yeast
- 30 grams vegetable oil
- 500 grams all-purpose flour
- 10 grams salt
- For the egg wash
- 1 egg
- 2 tablespoons water

1. **create the dough:** Follow the Master Recipe for Enriched Bread through step 6 of Brioche recipe, using the ingredient amounts listed.
2. **divide and shape:** Line a baking sheet with parchment paper. Divide the dough into 3 equal parts and let rest for 20 minutes. Take each piece and roll it between your hands and the work surface into ropes about 12 inches long (just like making snakes out of Play-Doh back in the day). There are many ornate options for braiding challah, but let's start with a simple 3-strand braid. Arrange the strands next to each other vertically. Press the 3 strands together at the top. Pick up the strand on the right and cross it over the center strand; this strand is now in the center. Then, take the left strand and cross it over the center, arriving as the new center strand. Keep crossing each side over the center until the dough gets too short to do it. Press the strands together at the bottom, and transfer to the prepared baking sheet.
3. **proof:** Make the egg wash by mixing together the egg and water. Brush the dough lightly with the egg wash using a pastry brush, reserving any left over for brushing before you bake. Cover lightly with plastic wrap. Proof for 1 hour 30 minutes to 2 hours, until very puffed and light and airy.
4. **preheat:** While the dough is proofing, preheat the oven to 350°F.
5. **bake:** Brush the dough with the remaining egg wash. Bake for 35 to 45 minutes. The finished loaf should be golden brown and will sound hollow when you thump it with your fingers.
6. **cool:** Let cool on a wire rack for at least 30 minutes to let the interior crumb set and make it easier to slice.

Springtime Challah Snails

This is another kid-friendly recipe. Soft, forgiving dough is kid-friendly. These snails are a great class project to pair with a nature-focused lesson or story time while the dough rises. Sprinkled seeds bring these rolls full circle.

Prep time: 25 minutes | Cook time: 25 minutes | Serves 6 to 8 snail rolls

FOR THE DOUGH
- 145 grams whole milk
- 205 grams whole eggs
- 80 grams honey
- 5 grams yeast
- 30 grams vegetable oil
- 500 grams all-purpose flour
- 10 grams salt
- For the egg wash
- 1 egg
- 2 tablespoons water
- For the topping (optional)
- Flaxseed, sunflower seeds, or poppy seeds

1. **create the dough:** Follow the Master Recipe for Enriched Bread through step 6 of Brioche recipe, using the ingredient amounts listed.
2. **divide and preshape:** Line a baking sheet with parchment paper. Divide the dough into 6 or 8 equal pieces. Take each piece and roll it between your hands and the work surface into ropes about 8 inches long (just like making snakes out of Play-Doh back in the day). Coil each one into a snail shape, leaving the end free. Use scissors to and snip the little end into two little snail antennae. Place the snails on the prepared baking sheet.
3. **proof:** Make the egg wash by mixing together the egg and water. Brush each snail lightly with the egg wash, reserving any left over. Let the snails proof for 1 hour to 1 hour 30 minutes, until they are light and puffy. Brush them again with the reserved egg wash and sprinkle seeds over the top, if desired.
4. **preheat:** While the dough is proofing, preheat the oven to 350°F.
5. **bake:** Bake for 25 to 35 minutes, until the snails are shiny and golden brown. Check often to see if they are done; smaller snails will cook more quickly than larger ones.
6. **cool:** Let the snails cool on a wire rack for 30 minutes before serving.

Cinnamon Wreath Bread

My family loves this all year, and it gets rave reviews whenever I share it. This bread wreath is perfect for New Year's because it symbolizes cycling through the months and starting over in January. Each New Year should begin sweetly, right? May sharing and eating this bread bring you hope and laughter as you welcome the new year.

Prep time: 47 to 52 minutes | Cook time: 30 to 35 minutes | Serves 8-12

FOR THE SWEET LEVAIN
- 30 grams active sourdough starter
- 15 grams sugar
- 50 grams water
- 100 grams all-purpose or bread flour
- For the dough
- 200 grams warm milk
- 42 grams butter, at room temperature or melted
- 180 grams of the activated sweet levain
- 380 grams bread flour
- 7 grams sea salt
- 1 large egg yolk
- For the filling
- 7 tablespoons unsalted butter, at room temperature
- ¼ cup plus 1 tablespoon brown sugar
- 1 tablespoon cinnamon

1. Make the dough: Follow the Sweet Levain Rolls Master Recipe through step 7, using the ingredients listed.
2. Prepare the filling: In a mixing bowl, beat the butter, sugar, and cinnamon together to create a smooth, creamy mixture.
3. Prepare the skillet: Line a large cast iron skillet or a baking sheet with parchment paper.
4. Shape: Transfer the dough to a floured work surface. Using a floured rolling pin, roll the dough into a 12-by-18-inch rectangle. With a spatula, spread the filling over the dough, leaving a ½-inch margin around the edges. Starting at one of the long sides of the dough, roll up the dough tightly into a long cylinder and press to seal the seam. Starting 2 inches from one end of the dough, cut the cylinder in half lengthwise, making sure the top is still connected. Starting where the dough is connected, braid the two open halves together so that the inside layers are exposed. Take the end of the braided dough and tuck it over the end that is connected and under where the braid began to create a round wreath shape. Carefully lift the wreath and place it onto the center of the parchment paper in the skillet or baking sheet.
5. Shaping Cinnamon Wreath Bread
6. Proof: Cover the dough with a kitchen towel and proof for 3 to 5 hours at room temperature, until the impression made by a finger lightly pressed into the dough slowly rises back.
7. Preheat: Preheat the oven to 375°F.
8. Bake: Bake for 30 to 35 minutes until it is golden brown on the edges.
9. Cool: Transfer the skillet or baking sheet to a cooling rack and let cool for 10 to 15 minutes to allow the melted brown sugar and butter on the base to harden and create a sweet and crunchy bottom crust. Transfer to a plate and serve.

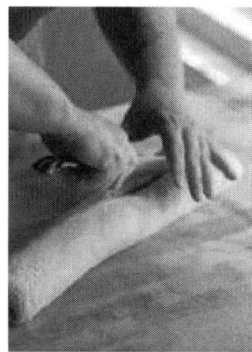

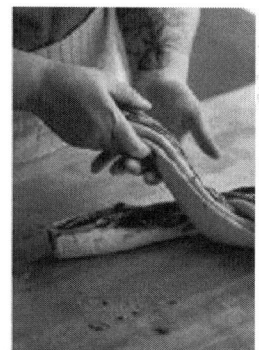

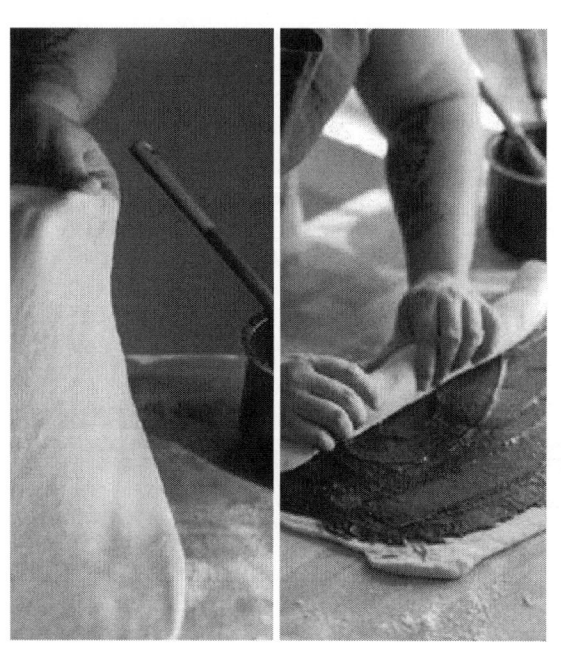

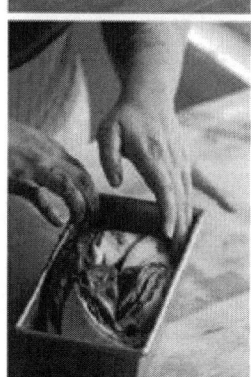

Sorghum Whole Wheat Bread (Vegan)

This no-knead recipe only requires punching down the dough before baking in a Dutch oven.

Prep time: 20 minutes, plus 3 hours 30 minutes rising time, plus 1 hour cooling time | Cook time: 45 minutes | Serves 1 slice (12 servings), yields 1 round loaf

- 1⅛ tsp (3.5 g) active dry yeast (½ packet)
- 2 cups plus 2 tbsp (240 g plus 15.2 g) whole wheat flour, divided
- 1½ cups (345 g) lukewarm water plus extra if needed
- 1 tsp (6 g) salt
- 1½ cups (182 g) sorghum flour

1. Put the yeast into a small mixing bowl and add 1½ cups of lukewarm water. Stir to dissolve and set aside for about 5 minutes until the yeast is foamy.
2. Place the sorghum flour, 2 cups of whole wheat flour, and salt into a very large plastic bowl with a lid.
3. Stir the yeast mixture into the dry ingredients with a wooden spoon. If the liquid is not enough to moisten the dough evenly, add extra water a little at a time.
4. Cover the bowl with the lid and place in a draft-free and warm part of the kitchen for about 2 hours until the dough has doubled in size.
5. Dust a cutting board or a workspace with 1 tbsp of whole wheat flour. Turn the dough out onto the floured board and punch the dough down, kneading it for only a few minutes.
6. Shape the dough into a round loaf by hand and then sprinkle the rest of the whole wheat flour over a clean, lint-free kitchen cloth. Place this cloth inside a deep bowl and then put the shaped dough ball into this bowl. Fold the ends of the kitchen cloth over the dough and allow the dough to rise for about 1½ hours until it has doubled in size again.
7. Switch on the oven about 45 minutes into the second rising of the dough and preheat to 450 degrees F (230 degrees C).
8. Place the lidded Dutch oven into the oven 25 minutes after switching on the oven.
9. Use oven mitts to remove the Dutch oven from the stove oven and set on a wooden cutting board and remove the lid.
10. Lift the risen dough out of the bowl by the ends of the kitchen cloth. Flour your hands before you remove the dough from the kitchen cloth, then carefully place the dough into the Dutch oven and put the lid on.
11. Place the Dutch oven back into the stove and bake for 30 minutes. Then remove the lid from the Dutch oven and continue baking uncovered for another 10 minutes until the bread is golden brown.
12. Remove the Dutch oven using oven mitts and tap the bottom of the loaf to do the doneness test. When the sound is hollow place the bread on a cooling rack.
13. Leave the bread to cool down for at least 1 hour before serving.

Zucchini Spice Quick Bread

My picky son loves this zucchini bread. We enjoy this bread with coffee for breakfast. This bread's moist texture and sweet, spicy flavor come from zucchini.

Prep time: 25 minutes | Cook time: 55 minutes | Serves 2 large loaves

- 2 zucchini
- 3 large eggs
- 100 grams brown sugar (½ cup)
- 100 grams white cane sugar, plus more for topping (½ cup)
- 4 grams vanilla extract (1 teaspoon)
- 6 grams salt (1 teaspoon)
- 210 grams whole-wheat flour (1½ cups)
- 210 grams all-purpose flour (1½ cups)
- 4 grams baking powder (1 teaspoon)
- 5 grams baking soda (1 teaspoon)
- 6 grams ground cinnamon (2 teaspoons)
- 2 grams ground ginger (½ teaspoon)
- 2 grams ground nutmeg (½ teaspoon)
- 1 gram ground cloves (¼ teaspoon)
- 113 grams unsalted butter, melted (½ cup)

1. Preheat: Preheat the oven to 350°F.
2. Grate the zucchini: Grate the zucchini into coarse pieces using a cheese grater. Place the zucchini in a fine mesh strainer propped over a bowl to allow excess water to drain.
3. Mix the wet ingredients: Place a large mixing bowl on the scale. Tare the bowl, then add the eggs, brown sugar, cane sugar, vanilla, and salt. Beat the ingredients together. Set aside.
4. Mix the dry ingredients: Tare a separate bowl, then add the whole-wheat flour, all-purpose flour, baking powder, baking soda, cinnamon, ginger, nutmeg, and cloves. Pour the dry mixture into the wet mixture. Stir to combine.
5. Add the zucchini and butter: Add the grated and drained zucchini to the batter. (There should be about 400 grams.) Add the melted butter and stir until combined.
6. Prepare the loaf pans: Cut two square pieces of parchment, at least 12-by-12 inches. Turn a loaf pan over and center the two parchment squares over the bottom of the pan. Use scissors to make four cuts from the edge of the paper to each corner. Turn the pan back over and use the cut slits to fold the edges of the parchment paper in to fit snugly into the corners of the pan. One piece of parchment paper goes into each loaf pan.
7. Fill the loaf pans: Use a spatula to pour the dough equally between the loaf pans. For an extra crispiness on top, sprinkle 1 to 2 tablespoons of sugar on top of the loaves.
8. Bake: Place the pans in the oven and bake for 50 to 55 minutes. The bread should be golden brown on top, and a knife inserted into the center should come out clean.
9. Cool: Allow the loaves to cool for about 20 minutes before slicing.

Star Bread

Star Bread looks complicated, but shaping is easy. It's a great holiday bread for Advent, St. Lucia's Day, and Christmas. I've included a spice-filled winter version and a berry-filled summer version. The fruit jam-filled star bread has beautiful colors and textures, while the pistachio spice filling has a complex, sweet flavor. The filling's butter makes the bread flakier. Decide which method of making bread you prefer.

Prep time: 55 minutes | Cook time: 35 minutes | Serves 1 loaf

FOR THE SWEET LEVAIN

- 30 grams active sourdough starter
- 15 grams sugar
- 50 grams water
- 100 grams all-purpose or bread flour
- For the dough
- 200 grams warm milk
- 42 grams unsalted butter, at room temperature or melted
- 180 grams of the activated sweet levain
- 380 grams bread flour
- 7 grams sea salt
- 1 large egg
- For the fruit jam filling
- ⅔ cup strawberry jam or another berry jam
- Zest of 1 lemon
- 1 large egg white
- For the pistachio spice filling
- ½ cup plus 2 tablespoons unsalted butter, at room temperature
- 1½ tablespoons sugar
- ½ cup pistachios, finely chopped
- 1 teaspoon cinnamon
- ¼ teaspoon ground cardamom
- For the icing (optional)
- ½ cup sifted confectioners' sugar
- 2½ teaspoons milk
- 1 teaspoon vanilla extract
- ⅓ cup pistachios, coarsely chopped

1. Make the dough: Follow the Sweet Levain Rolls Master Recipe through step 7, using the ingredients listed.
2. Prepare the jam filling: If making the jam filling, purée the jam until it's spreadable, if needed. In a medium bowl, mix together the jam and lemon zest. In a small bowl, whisk the egg white until frothy.
3. Prepare the pistachio spice filling: If making the pistachio spice filling, in a medium bowl mix together the butter, sugar, pistachios, cinnamon, and cardamom until it is smooth and creamy.
4. Divide: Transfer the dough from the bowl to a clean, floured work surface. Divide the dough into 4 equal pieces, either visually or by weighing the dough on the scale, and roll them into balls.
5. Prepare the baking sheet: Line a baking sheet with parchment paper.
6. Roll and fill: Place 1 piece of the dough onto a floured work surface. Using a floured rolling pin, roll out the dough to a 12-inch circle (it's okay if the circle is not perfect). Place the rolled-out dough onto the parchment paper. If you are using the jam filling, brush the dough with the egg wash, leaving a 1-inch margin around the edges. (The pistachio filling does not need the egg wash.) Spread one-third of your chosen filling over the dough, leaving a 1-inch margin around the edges. Lightly flour the work surface. Take a second piece of the dough and roll it out to a 12-inch circle. Place the dough over the first piece of dough and press the edges to seal it to the uncovered edge of the dough below it. Spread the next one-third of filling over the dough, following the instructions above. Repeat with the third piece of dough and the remaining filling. You should have 3 layers of dough spread with filling stacked on top of each other. Roll out the last piece of dough to the same size and place it on top of the three layers, and seal the edges together.
7. Filling and layering dough
8. Shape: Using a 2- to 3-inch diameter circular biscuit cutter, place it in the center of the top circle. Do not cut or press it down—this is a guide to make the cuts around the edge of the dough. Using a sharp knife, make 4 equally spaced cuts radiating out from the edge of the biscuit cutter. Cut each quarter in half and then each section in half again to end up with 16 equal cuts fanning out around the circle. Using your hands, pick up two sections of dough next to each other, twist them 2 times away from each other, and press the ends of the dough together to form a point. Pick up the next two sections and repeat. Continue picking up and twisting pairs of sections until they all have been twisted and the dough has formed an 8-point star. Remove the biscuit cutter.
9. Shaping star bread
10. Proof: Cover with a kitchen towel and proof for 3 to 5 hours at room temperature until the layers are puffy.
11. Preheat: 30 minutes before the proofing is done, place a baking stone on the center rack of the oven (if using). Preheat the oven to 375°F.
12. Bake: Carefully slide the shaped star bread onto the baking stone along with the parchment paper. If you're not using a baking stone, put baking sheet with the shaped star bread and parchment paper into the oven. Bake for 30 to 35 minutes until golden brown and the filling is bubbling.
13. Cool: Transfer to a cooking rack and let cool for 20 to 30 minutes.
14. Make the icing: If you'd like to drizzle the fruit jam-filled star bread with vanilla icing, in a small bowl, whisk together the confectioners' sugar, milk, and vanilla until smooth. Drizzle the icing over the bread and sprinkle with chopped pistachios.
15. Serve: Transfer the bread to a serving platter. If serving the pistachio spice-filled bread, serve as is or dust the top with confectioners' sugar. Cut into wedges.

Berry Scones

Flaky, buttery scones with summer berries are my favorite. They're great for brunch, bridal showers, and baby showers. Flaky scones require cold butter and minimal mixing.

Prep time: 25 minutes | Cook time: 25 minutes | Serves 12 scones

FOR THE DOUGH
- 150 grams berries, such as blueberries, blackberries, or combination, divided (1 cup)
- 400 grams all-purpose flour (2½ cups)
- 200 grams white cane sugar, plus more for topping (1 cup)
- 15 grams baking powder (1 tablespoon)
- 4 grams salt (½ teaspoon)
- Zest of 1 lemon
- 226 grams unsalted butter, cold (1 cup)
- 200 grams whole milk, chilled (¾ cup)

FOR THE GLAZE
- 65 grams powdered sugar (about ½ cup)
- 1 to 3 teaspoons freshly squeezed lemon juice

1. Prepare the pie dish and the frozen berries: Line a pie dish with parchment paper and fill with 10 to 20 berries. Place the pie dish in the freezer.
2. Prepare the baking sheets: Line two baking sheets with parchment paper and set aside.
3. Weigh the ingredients: Making sure to tare your bowl on the scale after each addition, combine the flour, sugar, baking powder, salt, and lemon zest. Stir.
4. Add the butter: Cut the cold butter in half, then cut each half into eight pieces and add to the dry mixture. With two forks or a pastry cutter, cut the butter into the flour mixture so that the smaller pieces distribute through the dough until crumbly and sandy. Some big pieces are okay, but aim for pieces no bigger than a pea.
5. Mix: Add the chilled milk and stir to combine, making sure not to overmix. Gently fold in the remaining berries until just incorporated.
6. Shape: Lightly flour the parchment papers. Place one-half of the dough on each sheet. Gently pat each half of the dough into a large circle that is about 1 inch thick. Take out the nearly frozen berries and press them into the top.
7. Chill: Cover the dough and place in the refrigerator to chill for 10 to 20 minutes, or freeze.
8. Preheat: Preheat the oven to 400°F.
9. Divide: Cut each circle of dough into 6 wedges (like a pizza). Carefully spread the scones out on the baking sheets, making sure they are at least 2 inches apart.
10. Bake: Place the baking sheets in the oven and bake for 18 to 20 minutes, until the scones are golden brown on the edges and a toothpick inserted in the thickest part of each scone comes out clean.
11. Cool: Allow the scones to cool at room temperature for about 20 minutes.
12. Glaze and serve: Whisk together the powdered sugar and lemon juice until it reaches a good consistency for drizzling. Drizzle the glaze over the cooled scones and serve.

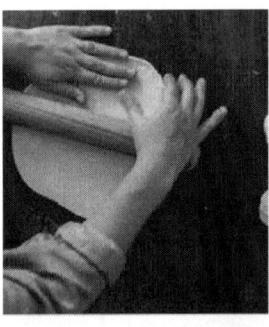

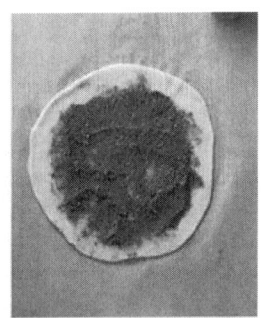

Potato Burger Buns

Soft, easy-to-make burger buns. These make great burger buns for summer barbecues.

Prep time: 55 minutes | Cook time: 25 minutes | Serves 8 large hamburger buns

FOR THE DOUGH

- 300 grams potato, peeled, cooked, and mashed (about 1 cup after mashing, from 2 medium to large potatoes)
- 120 grams milk (¼ cup plus 3 tablespoons)
- 100 grams warm water, divided (¼ cup plus 3 tablespoons)
- 68 grams unsalted butter, at room temperature (¼ cup)
- 15 grams brown sugar (1 tablespoon)
- 6 grams instant yeast (2 teaspoons)
- 450 grams bread flour (3 cups)
- 50 grams whole-wheat flour (⅓ cup)
- 10 grams salt (1½ teaspoons)
- 2 large eggs

FOR THE EGG WASH

- 1 large egg
- ½ teaspoon water
- Pinch salt
- 1 tablespoon poppy seeds or sesame seeds (optional)

1. Cook the potatoes: Peel and quarter the potatoes. Bring a large pot of water to a boil. Add the potatoes and reduce the heat to medium or medium-low to simmer. Cover and cook for 20 to 25 minutes, until the potatoes are fork-tender. Once the potatoes are finished cooking, immediately strain them using a colander, then run them under cool water to stop further cooking.
2. Mash the potatoes: Put the cooked potatoes in a mixing bowl and mash until smooth. If using an electric mixer, mash the potatoes using the paddle mixing tool until there are almost no lumps—don't overwhip the potatoes or they will become too starchy. Set aside.
3. Warm the milk: Heat the milk until it reaches a temperature of 115°F to 120°F.
4. Weigh the ingredients: Tare a separate large mixing bowl, then combine 300 grams of mashed potatoes, 100 grams of warm milk, 90 grams of water, and the butter. Add the sugar and instant yeast; allow the sugar to dissolve. Finally, add the bread flour and whole-wheat flour.
5. Mix: Mix the ingredients together until a shaggy dough forms, then add the salt, the remaining 10 grams of water, and the eggs. Mix to combine.
6. Fold: Stretch and fold the dough by hand for 10 to 15 minutes or 5 to 10 minutes using a dough hook in a stand mixer, until the dough no longer sticks to the sides of the bowl and pulls away easily.
7. Bulk ferment: Cover the dough and allow it to ferment for 1½ to 2 hours, until doubled in volume.
8. Prepare the baking sheets: Place two large pieces of parchment paper on two flat baking sheets.
9. Divide: Turn the dough out onto a floured work surface. Divide the dough into 8 equal pieces (about 163 grams each).
10. Shape: This dough is very soft and can be difficult to shape. Use a floured surface and a dough scraper to fold the bottom of the dough over the top. Then rotate, using the dough scraper to maneuver the dough in a circular motion, tightening it into a smooth, taut ball. Gently pick up the bun and place it on one of the prepared baking sheets. Repeat with the rest of the dough. There should be four buns on each baking sheet.
11. Proof: Cover the shaped buns with plastic wrap or a cloth and proof for 30 to 60 minutes, until the rolls are puffy and at least 1½ times larger.
12. Preheat: Preheat the oven to 375°F.
13. Make the egg wash: Beat together the egg, water, and salt in a small bowl or cup. Use a pastry brush to brush the egg wash all over the tops of the buns. Sprinkle on ¼ to ½ teaspoon of poppy seeds.
14. Bake: Place the baking sheets with proofed rolls into the preheated oven, spray the walls of the oven with water, and close the door to trap the steam. Bake for 20 to 24 minutes, until the rolls are golden brown on top.
15. Cool: Let the rolls cool for at least 30 minutes before serving.

Cheese-Filled Challah

Shavuot celebrates tradition and the land of milk and honey. Some families enjoy dairy-baked challah, which is avoided at other holidays. Soft challah with rosemary flavor and melted cheese.

Prep time: 45 minutes | Cook time: 35 minutes | Serves 2 loaves

FOR THE STARTER
- 30 grams sourdough starter (2 tablespoons) or ⅛ teaspoon instant yeast
- 15 grams white cane sugar (1 tablespoon)
- 50 grams water (3½ tablespoons)
- 100 grams all-purpose flour (⅔ cup)

FOR THE DOUGH
- 100 grams warm water, divided (about ½ cup)
- 3 grams instant yeast (1 teaspoon)
- 150 grams starter (about ¾ cup)
- 50 grams white cane sugar or honey (¼ cup)
- 500 grams bread flour (3½ cups)
- 70 grams oil, such as olive oil or avocado oil (⅓ cup)
- 3 large eggs
- 10 grams salt (1½ teaspoons)
- 6 grams fresh rosemary, minced (1 to 2 tablespoons)

FOR THE FILLING
- 200 grams mozzarella cheese, grated (2½ cups, loosely filled)
- 40 grams Parmesan cheese, freshly grated (⅔ cup, loosely filled)

FOR THE EGG WASH
- 1 large egg
- ⅛ teaspoon water
- 20 to 30 grams mozzarella cheese, grated, for topping (about ¼ cup)

1. **Make the starter:** About 8 to 12 hours before mixing your dough, combine the starter or yeast, sugar, water, and flour in a clean container. Cover and leave at room temperature. It will increase in volume and become bubbly.
2. **Weigh the ingredients:** Making sure to tare after each addition, combine 90 grams of warm water, the instant yeast, 150 grams of starter, and the sugar. Allow the sugar to dissolve, then add the bread flour.
3. **Mix:** Mix the ingredients until a shaggy dough forms, then add the oil, the eggs, the salt, the remaining 10 grams of water, and the rosemary. Mix to combine.
4. **Knead:** Turn the dough out onto a work surface and knead by hand for 10 to 15 minutes or 3 to 8 minutes with a dough hook in a stand mixer, until the dough is smooth, is no longer sticky, and releases easily from the bowl or work surface.
5. **Bulk ferment:** Cover the dough and ferment for 1½ to 2 hours, until doubled in volume.
6. **Divide the dough:** Divide the dough into four equal pieces for two medium-size loaves.
7. **Shape:** Line a baking sheet with parchment paper. Lightly flour a work surface and roll out a piece of dough into a 9-by-7-inch rectangle. Sprinkle on one-quarter of the grated mozzarella and Parmesan cheeses, leaving at least 1-inch clear around the edges. Take the long edge of the rectangle and fold it up over the cheese. Pinch the edges together to seal around the cheese to make one length of dough. Repeat the filling and folding with another piece of dough. Take the two filled lengths of dough and intertwine them. Pinch the ends together to seal. Place on one side of the parchment-lined baking sheet. Repeat with the rest of the dough and cheese.
8. **Proof:** Cover and proof for 45 to 60 minutes, until the bread is about 1½ times larger. Touching the dough with a fingertip should leave an indentation.
9. **Preheat:** Preheat the oven to 350°F. Place a steam pan filled with water on the lowest rack.
10. **Make the egg wash:** Beat together the egg with the water and brush the mixture onto the challah. Then sprinkle the mozzarella on top.
11. **Bake:** Place the loaves in the oven and quickly spray the oven walls with water. Bake for 25 minutes. Remove the steam pan and continue baking for 10 to 15 minutes longer, until the loaves are a shiny golden brown.
12. **Cool:** Transfer to a cooling rack and cool for 1 hour before serving.

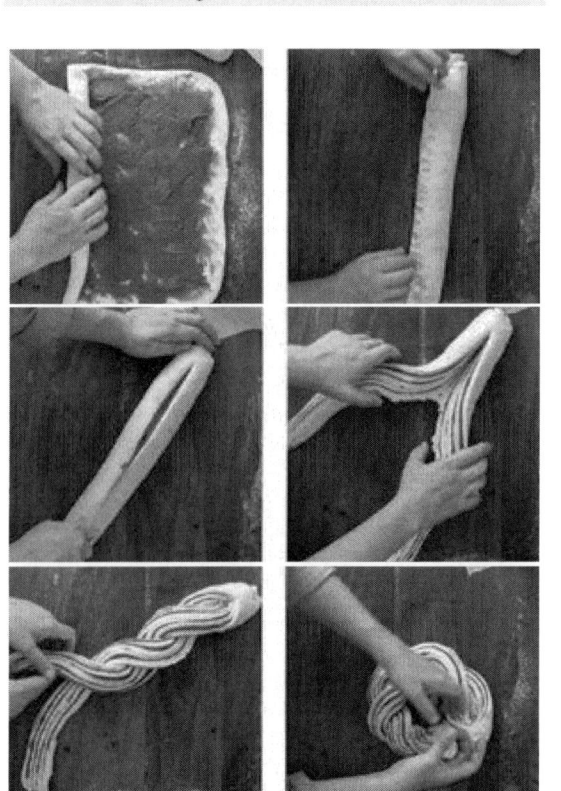

Rosemary-Tomato Focaccia

This bread is a delicious way to use summer tomatoes and herbs. Best with olive oil and balsamic vinegar.

Prep time: 35 minutes | Cook time: 25 minutes | Serves 1 large loaf

FOR THE STARTER
- 15 grams sourdough starter (1 tablespoon) or ⅛ teaspoon instant yeast
- 60 grams water (¼ cup plus 3 tablespoons)
- 60 grams all-purpose flour (⅔ cup)

FOR THE DOUGH
- 370 grams warm water, divided (1½ cups plus 1 tablespoon)
- 15 grams white cane sugar or honey (1 tablespoon)
- 2 grams instant yeast (½ teaspoon)
- 100 grams starter (½ cup)
- 450 grams all-purpose flour (3 cups plus 3½ tablespoons)
- 50 grams whole-wheat flour (⅓ cup)
- 10 grams salt (1½ teaspoons)
- 40 grams olive oil, plus more for the pan (3½ tablespoons)
- 6 grams fresh rosemary, minced (1 to 2 tablespoons)

FOR THE TOP
- 20 to 30 grams olive oil or avocado oil (2 to 3 tablespoons)
- 200 to 250 grams grape tomatoes, halved (½ to 1 cup)
- 10 to 15 grams coarse sea salt, for topping (1 to 2 teaspoons)

1. Make the starter: About 6 to 10 hours before mixing your dough, mix together the starter or yeast, water, and flour in a bowl. Cover and leave at room temperature until doubled in volume and bubbly.
2. Weigh the ingredients: Making sure to tare your bowl after each addition, combine 360 grams of warm water, the sugar, instant yeast, and 100 grams of starter. Let the sugar dissolve, then add the all-purpose flour and whole-wheat flour.
3. Mix: Stir the ingredients together until a shaggy dough forms, then add the salt, oil, and rosemary. Pour the remaining 10 grams of water over the salt to dissolve it. Mix to combine.
4. Fold: Gather a portion of the dough, stretch it up, and fold it over the bulk. Rotate the bowl 90 degrees and repeat for 5 to 10 minutes or use a dough hook in a stand mixer for 4 to 8 minutes, until the dough is smooth, is no longer sticky, and releases easily from the bowl.
5. Bulk ferment: Place the dough in a clean bowl, cover, and ferment for 1½ to 2 hours, until doubled in volume.
6. Shape: Spread about 1 tablespoon of oil on a piece of parchment paper with your fingertips. Place the dough on the oiled parchment. Gently spread the dough with oiled fingertips into a 10-inch wide circle with uniform thickness. If the dough resists shaping, allow it to relax for 10 minutes. Top the bread with the oil, using your fingertips to make dimples in the dough. Evenly spread the tomatoes across the top of the bread, cut-side up, and gently press them down into the dough.
7. Proof: Proof for 30 to 60 minutes at room temperature.
8. Preheat: After 30 minutes of proofing, preheat the oven to 475°F with a steam pan filled with water on a lower rack and a baking stone on the center rack (or you can bake your loaf on a baking sheet).
9. Bake: Before the focaccia goes into the oven, sprinkle the top with the coarse salt. Use a bread peel or baking sheet to transfer the focaccia and parchment to the preheated baking stone. Close the oven and reduce the temperature to 450°F. Bake for 25 to 30 minutes, removing the steam pan after 10 minutes.
10. Cool: Allow the loaf to cool for 30 to 60 minutes on a cooling rack before serving.

Chapter 6
Keto Breads

Low Carb Bun For One

Try this easy 2-minute bun recipe. If you like overbaked buns, bake for 20 minutes.

Prep time: 15 minutes | Cook time: 35 minutes| Serves 1

- 1 tbsp coconut oil
- 1 egg
- 1 tbsp coconut milk
- 1 tbsp almond flour
- 1 tbsp coconut flour
- 1/8 tsp baking soda
- sesame seeds- to sprinkle over

1. Blend together the coconut oil, egg, coconut milk, almond flour, coconut flour and the baking soda.
2. Mix everything well and then pour the batter in to a greased cake pan.
3. Preheat your oven at 350 degrees Fahrenheit
4. Put the cake pan in preheated oven for about 18 to 20 minutes.
5. If you want to prepare the bun in microwave, you can make it in 2 minutes or even less.
6. Sprinkle over the sesame seeds on top.
7. Cool and then serve.

Low Carb Vanilla Bread

This simple low carb bread is a basic keto diet recipe. This breakfast food is delicious.

Prep time: 15 minutes | Cook time: 35 minutes| Serves 5

- 5 eggs
- 4tbsp coconut flour
- 4tbsp granulated sweetener
- 1tsp baking powder
- 2tsp vanilla extract
- 3tbsp full fat milk
- 125 grams melted butter

1. Separate the egg whites and the egg yolks and beat the egg whites until they form in to stiff peaks.
2. In another bowl, beat the egg yolks, coconut flour, granulated sweetener and the baking powder.
3. Now slowly and gradually pour in the melted butter carefully and mix it to make sure that you have a very smooth consistency of your batter.
4. Now add in the full fat milk and the vanilla extract.
5. With the help of a rubber spatula, now very gently fold in the egg whites in the mixture.
6. Try to keep as much as air and fluffiness that you can for better results.
7. Preheat your oven at 350 degrees Fahrenheit and put the pan to bake in preheated oven for 30 minutes or until it is golden brown.
8. Cool and then serve!

Keto Blueberry Lemon Bread

Keto dieters crave dessert. Here's a keto dessert recipe that's low in carbs and easy to make. Two joys on one plate!

Prep time: 35 minutes | Cook time: 55 minutes| Serves 16

- 3 cups almond flour
- 2 tbsp egg white protein powder
- 1tsp cream of tartar
- ½ tsp baking soda
- ¼tsp celtic sea salt
- 6 eggs
- 1 tbsp lemon zest
- ½ tbsp vanilla extract
- ½ tsp vanilla stevia
- 1 cup blueberries

1. In a food processor, blend together the almond flour, egg white protein powder, cream of tartar, baking soda and the salt.
2. Now add in the eggs, lemon zest, vanilla extract and the vanilla stevia.
3. Now fold in the blue berries.
4. Mix the batter well and then pour the batter in to a prepared greased pan.
5. Preheat your oven at 350 degrees Fahrenheit.
6. Put the pan to bake in preheated oven for 45 to 50 minutes or until baked to perfection.
7. Cool and then serve!

Grain Free Cashew Sourdough Bread

Easy culturing instructions for low-carb bread. The health benefits of this dish alone make it worth trying.

Prep time: 25 minutes | Cook time: 35 minutes | Serves 12

- 10 cashews
- 4 ounces water
- probiotic capsules- equal to 30-40 billion strains
- 2 eggs, separated
- 1 tbsp water
- ½ tsp baking soda
- ¼ tsp salt
- 1 tbsp egg yolk plus water

1. Blend the cashews with filtered water
2. Put the mixture in to a bowl, add in the probiotic capsules and then mix them well.
3. Cover the bowl and put in the oven which should not be more than 110 degrees for 12 hours at least.
4. The longer you let it sit the more sour it will become
5. When it is ready, preheat the oven on 325 degrees.
6. Put the cashew mixture in to a bowl.
7. Separate both the egg yolks and the egg whites and add the egg yolks in the cashew mixture with the water.
8. Now add the baking soda and salt in the cashew mixture.
9. Beat the egg whites until soft peaks form and then fold them in the egg yolks and cashew mixture.
10. Pour the mixture in to a prepared loaf tin.
11. Mix the egg yolk and the water and use the pastry brush for the egg wash.
12. Bake at 325 degrees for 50 minutes.
13. Serve when cool.

Easy Low Carb Baked Bread

The following is an excellent recipe for low-carb bread that is not only simple to prepare but also beneficial to one's health.

Prep time: 15 minutes | Cook time: 25 minutes | Serves 12

- 2 ½ cups almond flour
- 2 tsp baking powder
- ¼ tsp baking soda
- ¼ tsp salt
- ¼ cup softened butter
- 2 tbsp egg white protein powder
- 3 eggs
- 4 tsp anise extract

1. Preheat your oven at 350 degrees Fahrenheit.
2. Mix almond flour, baking powder, baking soda and salt in a bowl
3. In a separate bowl, beat the butter.
4. Now add in the eggs, anise extract and beat them with butter
5. Now mix in the flour and the egg white protein powder and form the dough.
6. Cut the dough lengthwise and place the slices on to a prepared baking sheet.
7. Put the slices to bake in preheated oven for about 10 minutes or until both sides turn brown.
8. Cool and serve!

Keto Pumpkin Bread

These tasty keto pancakes are great for weight watchers or those who want to maintain a healthy weight.

Prep time: 15 minutes | Cook time: 35 minutes | Serves 6

- 2 ounces freshly ground flax seeds
- 2 ounces ground hazelnuts
- 28 grams egg white protein
- 1 tsp baking powder
- 1 tbsp chai masala mix
- 1 tsp vanilla extract
- 1 cup coconut cream
- 3 eggs
- ½ cup pumpkin puree
- 4-5 stevia drops
- 1 tbsp swerve
- coconut oil for greasing

1. Firstly, you need mix all the dry ingredients, the ground flax seeds, ground hazelnuts, egg white protein, baking powder, chai masala mix and the vanilla extract in a bowl.
2. Now add in the coconut cream, eggs, pumpkin puree, stevia drops and the swerve. Make sure that all the dry and wet ingredients are properly mixed.
3. Brush a loaf pan with the coconut oil and pour in the prepared batter.
4. Put the loaf tin in preheated oven at 350 degrees Fahrenheit for 25 to 30 minutes or until the bread is set.
5. Sprinkle over the chai masala mix before serving.

Keto Baked French Toast Bread

Here's a recipe for low-carb French toast that's perfect for healthy morning breakfasts. This bread has nutritious ingredients.

Prep time: 15 minutes | Cook time: 55 minutes | Serves 18

PROTEIN BREAD:
- 12 separated eggs
- 1 cup whey protein
- 4 oz cream cheese

FRENCH TOAST:
- 2 eggs
- ½ cup unsweetened almond milk
- 1tsp vanilla extract
- 1tsp cinnamon

SYRUP:
- ½ cup butter
- ½ cup swerve
- ½ cup unsweetened almond milk

DIRECTIONS FOR BAKING THE BREAD:

1. First, for baking the bread, preheat your oven at 325 degrees Fahrenheit.
2. Separate the eggs and beat the egg whites until they become very stiff. Now very gently fold in the protein powder in to the egg whites.
3. Now it your choice whether you mix the reserved egg yolks or the cream cheese in to the egg white mixture.
4. Now grease a bread pan and place the dough in to the bread pan and put it to bake in preheated oven for 40 to 45 minutes or until it turns golden brown.
5. Let the bread cool completely before cutting it in to slices.

DIRECTIONS FOR THE FRENCH TOAST:

6. Heat coconut oil in to a skillet on a medium high heat.
7. In a bowl, beat the eggs, unsweetened almond milk, vanilla extract and the cinnamon.
8. Dip the prepared bread slices in to the mixture and then in the skillet to fry.
9. Cook until your French toast turns golden brown from both the sides. Repeat this process with the remaining bread slices.

DIRECTIONS FOR THE SAUCE:

10. Heat butter in a sauce pan so that it can melt. Wait for the butter to turn golden brown.
11. When the butter turns golden brown, add in the swerve and keep on mixing it.
12. Immediately after you put in the swerve, add in the unsweetened almond milk and keep stirring until your sauce reaches the consistency that you desire. Pour the sauce in to a mason jar and let it cool completely before using it.

Keto Pumpkin Bread Loaf

Make sure to give this keto pumpkin bread a try because it is the ideal choice for a diet that is low in calories.

Prep time: 25 minutes | Cook time: 25 minutes | Serves 10

3 EGG WHITES
1 cup unsweetened apple sauce
1/4 cup cream
1 tsp vanilla extract
1 cup no calorie sweetener
1 cup almond flour
1 tsp baking soda
1 tbsp pumpkin pie spice
1 tsp cinnamon
½ cup pineapple chunks
½ cup dried cranberries
½ cup chopped almonds

1. Preheat oven to 350 degrees.
2. In a bowl beat the egg whites until they turn stiff.
3. Now add the apple sauce, cream, sweetener, almond flour, baking soda, pumpkin pie spice and the cinnamon.
4. Mix all the ingredients in the egg white bowl properly.
5. Now fold the pineapple, cranberries and the chopped almonds in teh mixture.
6. Pour the batter in a greased baking to bake until a toothpick inserted in it comes out clean.

Keto Bun And Roll Recipe

Being on keto doesn't mean you can't have soft buns for dinner or lunch. This keto bun recipe makes a healthy side.

Prep time: 25 minutes | Cook time: 45 minutes| Serves 6

- 1 cup almond flour
- 3 egg whites
- 300 ml hot water
- 5 tbsp psyllium husk
- 2 tbsp apple cider vinegar
- 2 tsp baking powder
- 1 tsp salt
- sesame seeds

1. Preheat your oven at 375 degrees Fahrenheit.
2. In a bowl, add almond flour, egg whites, hot water, psyllium husk, apple cider vinegar, salt and baking powder.
3. Knead the dough properly and then divide it in 6 parts.
4. Make six balls from the dough and flat then either by hands or rolling pin gently to avoid crooked shape or cracks.
5. Glaze with egg yolk and sprinkle sesame seeds over it.
6. Put it to bake in preheated oven for 30 to 40 minutes.
7. Cool and serve!

Best Keto Bread

This recipe for keto bread is the greatest you'll find due to its simplicity and low carb content.

Prep time: 15 minutes | Cook time: 45 minutes| Serves 20 slices

- 1 ½ cups almond flour
- 6 eggs
- 4 tbsp melted butter
- 3 tsp baking powder
- ¼ tsp cream of tartar
- a pinch salt
- 6 drops liquid stevia

1. Preheat your oven at 375 degrees Fahrenheit.
2. Separate the yolks from the eggs.
3. Beat the egg whites with the cream of tartar until soft peaks are formed.
4. In a food processor, mix the almond flour, egg yolks, melted butter, baking powder, salt and the liquid stevia.
5. Now add in the egg whites mixture in the processed batter
6. Do not over mix the batter.
7. Pour the batter in to a greased loaf pan and then put it to bake in a preheated oven for 30 minutes.
8. Cut the slices once the bread cools down. .

Keto Mummy Dogs

Keto diet allows rapid food, especially for kids. So, fat kids forced to go on keto by mom can still eat hot dogs. Ask your mum to bake you a low-carb cake.

Prep time: 15 minutes | Cook time: 35 minutes| Serves 4

- ½ cup almond flour
- 4 tbsp coconut flour
- ½ tsp salt
- 1 tsp baking powder
- 2 2/ 3 oz butter
- 1 ½ cups shredded cheese
- 2 egg
- 1 lb sausages

1. Preheat your oven at 350 degrees Fahrenheit.
2. Assemble almond flour, coconut flour, salt and the baking powder in a bowl.
3. Take a pan and melt the butter and the cheese.
4. Once the butter and cheese gets melted, remove the pan from heat and add an egg.
5. Beat it well and then add in the flour mixture to form a dough.
6. Flatten the dough in a rectangular form.
7. Cut it in to long strips.
8. Now wrap the dough strips around the sausage and then brush the dough with egg wash.
9. Place the hot dog on a baking sheet and then put to bake in preheated oven for 15 to 20 minutes or until it is golden brown.
10. Cool and then serve!

Chapter 7
French Breads

Fougasse

This crusty bread can be topped with herbs, olives, cheese, or olive oil and eaten warm. Its shape is also a great canvas for creativity. Simple cuts can produce leaflike designs, ladders, and complicated rounds.

Prep time: 45 minutes | Cook time: 25 minutes | Serves 4 loaves

- 1¾ cups (400 grams) water, at room temperature, divided
- 2 teaspoons (6 grams) instant yeast, divided
- 5 cups minus 1½ tablespoons (590 grams) bread flour (or T55 flour), divided, plus more for shaping
- 2 tablespoons (25 grams) olive oil, plus more for drizzling
- 1 tablespoon (9 grams) kosher salt, plus more for sprinkling

1. Make a pâte fermentée: In a bowl, stir together ½ cup (100 grams) of water with a pinch of yeast. Add 1¼ cups (150 grams) of flour and 1 teaspoon (3 grams) of salt. Stir until a shaggy dough comes together. Turn the dough onto your bench and knead until well combined, 1 to 2 minutes. The mixture will be sticky. Return the dough to the bowl, cover with a towel, and set aside for 2 to 4 hours at room temperature or refrigerate overnight. It should double in size.
2. Make the dough: Add the remaining 1¼ cups (300 grams) of water and remaining yeast to the pâte fermentée, using your fingers to break up the dough into the liquid. Add the remaining 3⅔ cups (440 grams) of flour, the oil, and the remaining 2 teaspoons (6 grams) of salt and mix until a shaggy dough forms, about 1 minute.
3. Turn out the dough onto a clean bench and knead for 8 to 10 minutes (or transfer to a stand mixer and knead for 6 to 8 minutes at low speed) until smooth, stretchy, and supple. If you're kneading by hand, resist the urge to add more flour; the dough will naturally become less sticky as you work it.
4. Stretch the dough to check for proper gluten development. If it rips too quickly and feels rough, continue to knead until smooth and supple.
5. If kneading by hand, return the dough to the bowl. Cover with a towel and set aside for 1 hour or until doubled in size. (This timing will vary, depending on your kitchen temperature.)
6. Shape and bake: Lightly flour your bench and use a plastic bench scraper to release the dough from the bowl. Use a metal bench scraper to portion the dough into 4 equal sections (about 250 grams each). Cover with a towel and rest for 5 to 10 minutes. Line two baking sheets with parchment paper.
7. Dust the balls with flour and flatten each to a rough oval a little over ¼ inch thick, using first your fingertips (photo A) and then a rolling pin, if desired (photo B).
8. Use a paring knife held at a 45-degree angle to cut decorative lines into the dough. Make sure you cut all the way through the dough, and space the cuts at least ½ inch apart (photos C and D).
9. Gently transfer two loaves to each prepared baking sheet, spacing them a few inches apart. Stretch them gently to make sure the cuts remain open while baking (the holes will shrink and narrow as the bread expands in the oven).
10. Cover the loaves with towels and set aside to proof for 30 to 45 minutes or until marshmallow-y in texture. If you poke the dough, it should spring back slightly, leaving an indent. After 15 minutes of proofing, preheat the oven to 475°F.
11. When the loaves are ready to bake, put the baking sheets in the oven. Spritz the loaves with water 4 or 5 times, and close the door. Spray again after 3 minutes of baking, and again after another 3 minutes, working quickly to not lose oven heat. Bake for 18 to 20 minutes total, until the loaves are a deep golden brown, rotating the position of the trays halfway through baking for even browning. Remove the trays from the oven and set aside to cool slightly.
12. Drizzle with olive oil and sprinkle with salt before serving.

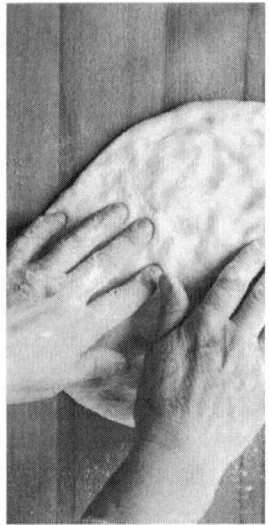

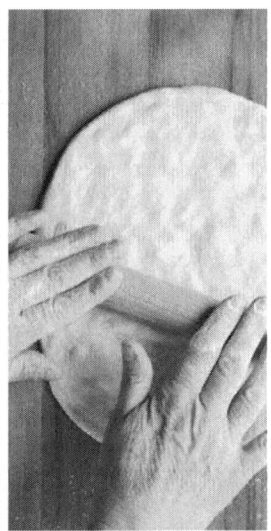

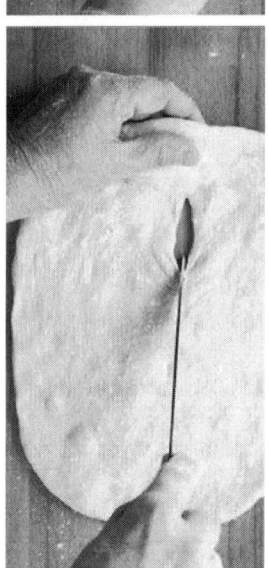

Pain Complet

Pain complet is 100% whole wheat. It's great for sandwiches or breakfast with jam, butter, honey, or marmalade. We made a bâtard. You can use other whole-grain blends or bread flour for a more open crumb.

Prep time: 35 minutes | Cook time: 25 minutes | Serves 1 loaf

- ¾ cup (175 grams) water, at room temperature, divided
- 2 tablespoons (42 grams) honey
- 1½ teaspoons (4 grams) instant yeast, divided
- 2¼ cups (250 grams) whole wheat flour (or T150 flour), divided, plus more for shaping
- 1½ teaspoons (5 grams) kosher salt

1. Make a poolish: In a medium bowl, stir together ½ cup (100 grams) of water, the honey, and a pinch of yeast, then a scant 1 cup (100 grams) of flour. Stir until a thick paste forms. Cover with a towel and set aside for 2 to 4 hours at room temperature or refrigerate overnight. It should double in size.
2. Make the dough: Add the remaining ¼ cup (75 grams) of water and remaining yeast to the preferment, using your fingers to break up the dough into the liquid. Add the remaining 1¼ cups (150 grams) of flour and the salt, and mix until a shaggy dough forms, about 1 minute. Turn the dough out onto a clean bench and knead for 8 to 10 minutes (or transfer to a stand mixer and knead for 6 to 8 minutes at low speed) until smooth, stretchy, and supple. If you're kneading by hand, resist the urge to add more flour; the dough will naturally become less sticky as you work it. If kneading by hand, return the dough to the bowl. Cover with a towel and set it aside for 1 hour or until doubled in size. (This timing will vary, depending on your kitchen temperature.)
3. Shape and bake: Lightly flour your bench and use a plastic bench scraper to release the dough from the bowl.
4. Using your fingertips, pull the edges of the dough inward, working around the dough clockwise until all edges are folded into the center. Pinch lightly to adhere (see step-by-step photos in the boule de pain recipe, for method). You should see the folds of dough meeting in the center, creating a seam. (Take care to not knead the dough or deflate it too aggressively.) Flip the dough over. Cup both hands around the base and, using the grip of the table, pull the round toward you, rotating as you go, to tighten the seam. Cover with a towel and rest for 5 to 10 minutes.
5. Use your fingertips to gently press the round to a rough oval (photo A). Fold the top third of the dough toward you and press lightly along the seam to adhere. Roll the dough over itself toward you again, to create a log (photo B), using the heel of your hand or your fingertips to seal the seam. Make sure your bench is lightly floured. You don't want too much pressure on the dough, but nor do you want the dough to slide instead of roll. If the dough slides, brush away excess flour and wet your hands lightly.
6. Gently flip the dough so the seam is on the bottom, and use your hands to rock the ends of the loaf back and forth to create a football shape (bâtard). Then work your hands from the center of the loaf out toward the edges to elongate it slightly to about 8 inches long (photo C). Transfer to a baking sheet lined with parchment paper.
7. Cover the dough with a towel and set aside for about 1 hour, until it has a marshmallow-y texture. If you poke the dough, it should spring back slightly, leaving an indent. After 30 minutes of proofing, preheat the oven to 450°F.
8. When the loaf is ready to bake, hold a lame at a 30-degree angle and decoratively score, using quick, light movements to create parallel diagonal lines down the length of the loaf. It will look almost like a scored sausage (saucisson) about to be cooked!
9. Put the baking sheet in the oven, spritz the loaf with water 4 or 5 times, and close the door. Spray again after 3 minutes of baking, and again after another 3 minutes, working quickly to not lose oven heat. Bake for 20 to 25 minutes total, until the loaf is a deep golden brown and the internal temperature registers about 200°F.
10. Transfer the loaf to a cooling rack for 15 to 20 minutes before slicing.

Le Cramique

These thick, sweet buns are baked with brioche-like dough and procedure. Le cramique (kramiek in Flemish) began in Belgium in the 13th century and became cramiche in France (loaf).

Prep time: 35 minutes | Cook time: 25 minutes | Serves 14 buns

- ¾ cup (175 grams) whole milk
- 2 teaspoons (6 grams) instant yeast
- 3 (150 grams) large eggs, divided
- 4⅛ cups (500 grams) bread flour (or T55 flour), plus more for shaping
- 3 tablespoons (40 grams) granulated sugar
- 1 tablespoon (9 grams) kosher salt
- 9 tablespoons (125 grams) unsalted butter, at room temperature (65 to 70°F)
- ⅔ cup (100 grams) dark raisins, soaked in ⅔ cup (150 grams) warm water for at least 1 hour or overnight
- ¼ cup (50 grams) pearl sugar (optional)

1. Make the dough: In a medium bowl, lightly stir together the milk, yeast, and 2 (100 grams) eggs. Add the flour, sugar, and salt, and stir until a shaggy dough comes together. Turn the dough onto a clean bench and knead for 6 to 8 minutes (or transfer to a stand mixer and knead for 4 to 5 minutes at low speed) until smooth. Return the dough to the bowl and mix in the butter a bit at a time, either by hand or with the dough hook, and continue to knead until the butter is well incorporated. You may need to scrape down the bowl with a spatula occasionally while kneading.
2. Cover with a towel and set aside for 1 to 1½ hours at room temperature. The dough should double in size. (This timing will vary, depending on your kitchen temperature.)
3. Transfer the bowl to the refrigerator for at least 2 hours and up to overnight. The colder the dough, the easier and less sticky it will be to work with.
4. Line two baking sheets with parchment paper. Once the dough is cold, lightly flour your bench and press the dough out to a ½-inch-thick rectangle. Strain the raisins and transfer to a paper towel to dry for 2 minutes, then spread them evenly over the dough, pressing lightly to adhere. Fold the dough in half to enclose the raisins.
5. Evenly divide the dough into 14 pieces with a metal bench scraper, ideally by using a scale. Sprinkle the top of each piece lightly with flour.
6. Shape and bake: On a clean bench, gently flatten a piece of dough, then use your fingertips to pull the corners of the dough into the center and pinch to shape into a rough round. Flip the round over. Cup the dough within your hand and, using the grip of your bench, rotate to tighten the seam. Dust the top with flour if necessary to prevent it from sticking to your hand. Work quickly to avoid the fat warming too fast. Repeat with the remaining rounds.
7. Transfer the buns to the prepared baking sheets seam-side down, spacing them at least 3 inches apart. Cover with a towel and set aside for 1 to 1½ hours, until marshmallow-y in texture. If you poke the dough, it should spring back slightly, leaving an indent. After 45 minutes of proofing, preheat the oven to 400°F.
8. Whisk the remaining 1 egg (50 grams) with a splash of water and use a pastry brush to gently brush this glaze over each bun. Use kitchen shears to snip the top of each round to create an X. Fill each X with a sprinkle of pearl sugar (if using).
9. Bake the buns for 20 to 24 minutes, until they are golden brown. Serve warm.

French Baguette

This baguette is easy and quick to make. You can make a baguette for very little money using common kitchen tools and supplies.

Prep time: 20 minutes plus 1 hour 45 minutes for rising time | Cook time: 15 minutes | Serves 1 large loaf or 6 mini loaves

- 3 ¼ cups (394 g) all-purpose flour, plus extra if needed
- 1 tsp (4 g) white sugar
- 2 tsp (6 g) active dry yeast
- 2 tsp (27.3 g) vegetable oil
- 1 ½ tsp (9 g) salt
- 1 ½ cups (345 g) water hot

1. Place the hot water and sugar into a 2-cup measure and stir to dissolve. Add the yeast and give the mixture a gentle stir. Allow the yeast to stand for about 5 minutes until it is foamy.
2. Place the salt and flour into a large mixing bowl and combine. Make a well in the center of the mixture and add the yeast mixture into the well. Use a wooden spoon and stir, starting in the middle until you have a sticky dough.
3. Knead the dough for about 10 minutes in the mixing bowl, adding small amounts of flour if needed until the dough is no longer sticky. The dough is ready when it is elastic.
4. Oil a deep mixing bowl and place the dough inside. Turn the dough over to make sure all surfaces are coated. Cover with plastic wrap or a damp kitchen cloth and set aside to rise for 1 hour.
5. Fill a large roasting pan with water and place it on the bottom rack in the oven. Line a baking sheet with parchment paper or a silicone baking mat and set aside. Preheat the oven to 425 degrees F (220 degrees C).
6. Punch the dough down in the mixing bowl and then place it on a floured work surface. You can shape the dough into one large oblong or oval loaf or divide it into six equal pieces for individual mini baguettes. Place the loaf or mini loaves onto the prepared baking sheet.
7. Score the bread by making four diagonal slashes across (mini loaves should have one diagonal slash). Cover with a dry kitchen cloth and allow to rise for 40 minutes until it has doubled in size.
8. Remove the kitchen cloth and place the baking sheet on the center rack in the oven and bake for between 15 to 20 minutes—time will depend on the size of loaf or loaves—until golden brown.
9. Place on a wire cooling rack to cool down for 10 minutes before slicing.

Fouée

Fouée is like pita bread. This French bread round is baked in a wood-fired oven, split open, and stuffed with pig rillettes and white beans. If you roll the dough too thick or skip the final proof, it won't puff. Too thin, it's a cracker.

Prep time: 45 minutes | Cook time: 15 minutes | Serves 8 bread rounds

- 1½ cups (350 grams) water, at room temperature
- 2 teaspoons (6 grams) instant yeast
- 5 cups minus 1½ tablespoons (590 grams) all-purpose flour (or T55 flour), plus more for shaping
- 1 tablespoon (9 grams) kosher salt
- Oil, for greasing baking sheet (optional)

1. Make the dough: In a bowl, combine the water and yeast, then stir in the flour and salt. Knead by hand for 6 to 8 minutes (or 4 to 6 minutes in a stand mixer at low speed) until well combined and smooth. If working in a mixer, you may need to finish the dough by hand, as it's a bit heavy. Cover with a towel or plastic wrap, and set aside for 1 hour or until doubled in size. This will vary depending on your kitchen temperature.
2. Shape and bake: Lightly flour your bench and use a plastic bench scraper to release the dough from the bowl. Use a metal bench scraper to portion into 8 equal pieces, about 115 grams each.
3. Using your fingertips, pull the edges of one piece of dough inward, working around the dough clockwise until all edges are folded into the center. Pinch lightly to adhere.
4. Flip each round over. Cup both hands around the base, and using the grip of the table, pull the round toward you, rotating as you go, to tighten the seam. Repeat with the remaining rounds. Cover with a towel and rest for 5 to 10 minutes.
5. Transfer 4 rounds to a small plate, cover with a towel or plastic wrap, and transfer to the refrigerator. Cover the remaining rounds and rest for 5 to 10 minutes.
6. Preheat the oven to 475°F. Put a baking stone or oiled heavy baking sheet on the center rack of the oven.
7. Dust your bench with flour and roll the 4 unrefrigerated dough rounds to ¼-inch-thick circles. Be precise about the thickness: Dough that is too thick will not puff, and those that are too thin will become crackers. If the dough is shrinking back while you're rolling, cover it, rest for an additional 10 minutes, then try again.
8. Proof, uncovered, for 15 to 20 minutes or until lightly puffed. In the meantime, roll out the 4 refrigerated rounds.
9. Quickly and gently place the first 4 pieces on the baking stone or baking sheet, spacing them at least 2 inches apart. Bake for 8 to 10 minutes, until puffed and lightly golden brown in spots.
10. Remove from the oven, set on a cooling rack, and bake the remaining pieces when they're lightly puffed and have rested for 15 to 20 minutes.
11. Cool for 5 to 10 minutes before splitting and filling.

Croissants

Cold butter forms flaky layers in chilled dough. Warm butter and dough will make a biscuit instead of a croissant. Under-proofed croissants are gummy. Rolling dough and butter must be perfect, therefore use a ruler.

Prep time: 1 hour 30 minutes | Cook time: 35 minutes | Serves 10

- ¾ cup plus 1 tablespoon (180 grams) whole milk
- 2 teaspoons (6 grams) instant yeast
- 2⅔ cups (312 grams) all-purpose flour (or T55 flour), plus extra for shaping
- 1 tablespoon plus 1½ teaspoons (20 grams) granulated sugar
- 2 teaspoons (6 grams) kosher salt
- 1 cup (225 grams) unsalted butter, at room temperature (65 to 70°F), divided
- 1 (50 grams) large egg

1. Make the dough: In a medium bowl, stir together the milk and yeast, then add the flour, sugar, salt, and butter and stir until a shaggy dough forms. Turn the dough out onto a clean bench and knead for 8 to 10 minutes (or transfer to a stand mixer and knead for 6 to 8 minutes at low speed) until smooth, stretchy, and supple.
2. If kneading by hand, return the dough to the bowl. Cover with a towel and set aside for 1 hour or until doubled in size. (This timing will vary, depending on your kitchen temperature.)
3. Turn the dough out onto a clean bench and press lightly to an 8-inch square. Wrap with plastic wrap and refrigerate for 1 hour. This is known as the dough block (détrempe). The dough block and butter block should have a similar temperature and consistency, so chilling is essential.
4. After 30 minutes of chilling the dough block, place the remaining ¾ cup (170 grams) of butter on a piece of parchment paper. Top with an additional sheet of parchment paper and use a rolling pin and plastic bench scraper to shape the butter into a 6-by-8-inch rectangle. Slide the packet of parchment paper onto a baking sheet and transfer to the refrigerator for 15 to 20 minutes, until firm but pliable. You should be able to bend the packet without it snapping into shards.
5. Set the butter block aside on your bench while you shape the dough. This will ensure that it's the correct temperature (not too cold) before incorporation. Dust your bench and the top of the dough with flour and roll the dough block into a 9-by-13-inch rectangle. Brush off excess flour. Unwrap the butter and flip it onto the center of the dough, so its edges almost meet the sides of the dough block (photo A). Fold the top and bottom portions of dough over the butter block, meeting in the center. Thoroughly pinch the center and end seams closed (photo B). Temperature is crucial, so work quickly.
6. Dust your bench with flour and rotate the dough so the center seam is pointing toward you. Roll the dough out, using a back-and-forth motion, to create a 7-by-21-inch rectangle, working carefully so no butter escapes from the dough (photo C). If butter peeks through, pinch the dough around it to cover and dust with flour. Brush off excess flour before folding.
7. Fold the top third of the dough toward the center, then fold the bottom third of the dough over the center to create a letter fold (photo D). Brush off excess flour.
8. Wrap the dough in plastic wrap and chill for 30 minutes.
9. Repeat step 6, starting with the folded edge of the dough on your left side, rolling the dough into a 7-by-21-inch rectangle, and creating a letter fold (photo E). Wrap the dough again and chill for 45 minutes.
10. Repeat this step once more, then wrap the dough and chill for at least 1 hour or overnight.
11. Shape and bake: Line a baking sheet with parchment paper.
12. Dust your bench with flour and roll the dough into a ¼-inch-thick rectangle, about 9 by 20 inches (similar to photo C). Use a paring knife to mark 4-inch sections along the length of the long side. Use a chef's knife to cut the rectangle at the 4-inch marks, creating five 4-by-9-inch sections (photo F). Halve each of these sections diagonally to create a total of 10 triangles (photo G).
13. Stretch the bottom of each triangle lightly to elongate it a bit. Starting on the long side, roll the triangles to create a croissant shape (photos H and I). When you've almost reached the end of the roll, pull the tip a bit to elongate it and wrap it around the croissant, pinching lightly to seal. Place each croissant on the prepared baking sheet with the tips on the bottom to keep them from opening while proofing and baking. Space them a few inches apart.
14. Cover the tray with plastic wrap and set aside to proof at room temperature for 1½ to 2½ hours. (This timing will vary, depending on your kitchen temperature, but the ideal temperature is 75°F to 80°F.) Proof until it reaches a marshmallow-y consistency and an increase in volume. If you poke the dough, it should spring back slightly, leaving an indent.
15. After 1 hour of proofing, preheat the oven to 400°F.
16. In a small bowl, whisk the egg with a splash of water and use a pastry brush to brush the glaze over the croissants. Brush them once more, for extra shine.
17. Bake for 30 to 35 minutes until the croissants are a deep golden brown. Serve warm.

Buckwheat French Bread

This robust buckwheat bread is great for French bread pizza. Gluten-free buckwheat flour is combined with spelt and bread flour for structure and rise.

Prep time: 35 minutes | Cook time: 25 minutes | Serves 2 15-inch loaves

- 100g (½ cup) active starter
- 420g (1¾ cups) water
- 28g (2 tablespoons) olive oil
- 90g (¾ cup) buckwheat flour
- 107g (1 cup) spelt flour
- 420g (3½ cups) bread flour
- 1 teaspoon salt

1. Make the Dough. In a large bowl, whisk together the starter, water, and oil. Add all three flours and the salt and mix to combine. Finish by hand, mixing until a rough dough forms. Cover the bowl and let the dough rest for 1½ to 2 hours.
2. Stretch and Fold. Begin by pulling up on one edge of the dough as high as you can stretch it without tearing and fold it in the middle of the dough. Give the bowl a quarter-turn and stretch and fold again. Repeat another two times, until you have made one complete rotation of the bowl. Repeat this step three more times, spacing them about 30 minutes apart.
3. Bulk Ferment. Remove the dough. Lightly grease the bowl, return the dough to the bowl, and flip it once to coat the other side. Cover the bowl with a damp towel and let rise for about 8 hours, until doubled in size.
4. Shape. Line a large baking sheet with parchment paper. Turn the dough out onto a lightly floured surface and divide in half. Working with one portion at a time, pat the dough into a thick 9-by-13-inch rectangle. Starting at one long side, roll the dough up tightly and pinch the seam to seal. Arrange the loaf seam-side down on the lined baking sheet. Repeat to make a second loaf.
5. Proof. Cover with greased plastic wrap or a kitchen towel and let rise for about 2 hours, or until noticeably puffy and nearly doubled in size. Near the end of the rise, position a rack in the center of the oven and preheat the oven to 375°F.
6. Score the Bread. Uncover the dough. With a very sharp knife or baker's lame, cut 4 or 5 slashes at an angle on the top of each loaf.
7. Bake. Bake for 25 to 30 minutes, until the crust is browned and the bread has reached an internal temperature of 190°F.
8. Cool. Remove from the oven and let cool for at least 2 hours before slicing.

La Charbonée De Boulanger

I finally found James MacGuire, who helped translate Calvel's work. Calvel described the dish as pork shoulder cubes cooked like boeuf bourguignon. My variation of the dish.

Prep time: 35 minutes | Cook time: 65 minutes | Serves 4 to 6

- About 2 pounds pork shoulder roast, cut into 2-inch cubes
- Salt and pepper
- ½ large yellow onion, sliced
- 2 carrots, sliced
- 4 sprigs thyme
- 2 sprigs savory
- 3 bay leaves
- 1 bottle red wine, preferably a Chinon or other Loire Valley red
- 3 tablespoons vegetable oil with a high smoke point, such as grapeseed oil
- 3 tablespoons all-purpose flour
- 15 pearl onions, peeled and left whole
- 15 small button mushrooms
- 1 to 2 cups chicken stock
- 5 cloves garlic, skin-on, lightly smashed
- Small potatoes, peeled and boiled if desired for serving.

1. Season the pork generously with salt and pepper. Place half of the yellow onion and half the carrots, 1 sprig thyme, 1 sprig savory, and 2 bay leaves in a baking dish or bowl, cover with the pork cubes, and add just enough wine to cover the meat, pouring it over the top and reserving at least ½ cup. Cover and refrigerate overnight.
2. Strain the solids from the marinade, reserving all the liquid. Reserve the pork and discard the vegetables and herbs. Dry the pork thoroughly with paper towels.
3. Preheat the oven to 450°F, or if you have been baking bread, leave the baking stone in and lower the oven to 200°F once the bread is out.
4. In a Dutch oven or other heavy, ovenproof pan with a lid, heat the oil over high heat, then brown the pork in batches so as not to overcrowd the pan. Brown the pork well on all sides, then remove and reserve; brown the rest of the meat. Turn the heat to medium and brown the remaining yellow onion, remaining carrots, flour, pearl onions, and mushrooms. Return the meat to the pan and deglaze with the reserved marinade and the reserved ½ cup of the wine.
5. Add enough chicken stock so that the liquid almost covers the meat. Add the garlic and remaining thyme, savory, and bay leaf. Cover the pot and bake for 1 hour. Turn the oven to 250°F and bake for 1 more hour. Serve with the potatoes or bread, if desired.

Croque Monsieur

A croque monsieur and pilsner are other favorites. Croque madame sandwich: add a fried egg. Serve with toast to sop up cheese and sauce.

Two-day-old bread works best for this; the slices can sit out overnight to dry out. If you're short on time, dry the bread slices in a low oven (200oF).

Prep time: 15 minutes | Cook time: 35 minutes| Serves 2 sandwiches

BÉCHAMEL
- 1 tablespoon unsalted butter
- 1 tablespoon plus 1 teaspoon all-purpose flour
- ¾ cup whole milk
- Pinch of freshly grated nutmeg
- Salt and ground white pepper
- SANDWICHES
- 4 slices Pain de Mie
- 2 slices boiled ham
- 2 slices Emmenthaler cheese, plus ¾ cup grated
- 4 tablespoons unsalted butter, melted

1. To make the béchamel, melt the butter in a heavy saucepan over medium heat. Add the flour, stirring constantly with a wooden spoon, and cook for a minute or two. Whisk in ¼ cup of the milk until smooth with no lumps, then whisk in the remaining ½ cup milk. Continue to cook, whisking constantly, until thick enough to coat a spoon, 2 to 3 minutes. Add the nutmeg and season to taste with salt and pepper. Keep warm.
2. Adjust the oven rack 4 inches from the broiler and heat the broiler.
3. To make the sandwiches, spread one side of each bread slice generously with the béchamel. Top 2 of the bread slices with a piece of ham, followed by a piece of cheese. Place a second slice of bread on top of the cheese, sauce side down. Brush both sides of the sandwich with melted butter and cook in a cast-iron skillet over medium heat until browned and crispy on one side, 4 to 5 minutes. You can also weight down the sandwich with a second pan on top. Flip the sandwiches and cook the other side until browned and crispy, another 4 to 5 minutes. Remove from the heat.
4. Leaving the sandwiches in the pan, sprinkle the grated cheese on top. Broil the sandwiches until the cheese is melted and browned on top, 3 to 5 minutes. Serve at once.

Oysters with Mignonette

For brinier Atlantic oysters, serve this classic French mignonette sauce with Pain de Seigle, salted butter, and a mineral-rich white wine like Muscadet or Sancerre. Make mignonette a day ahead so flavors may blend.

Prep time: 25 minutes | Cook time: 30 minutes| Serves several dozen oysters or a full tower of fruits desmer

- 1 teaspoon peppercorns
- Pinch of coarse sea salt
- ¾ cup good-quality red wine vinegar
- 1 shallot, diced (about 2 tablespoons)
- 2 to 3 dozen fresh oysters
- Crushed ice or rock salt for serving

1. Using a mortar and pestle, coarsely crush the peppercorns with the salt; don't overdo it, or the pepper will disappear into the vinegar.
2. Transfer to a bowl and add the vinegar and shallot and stir to combine. Refrigerate for at least 1 day. The mignonette keeps for up to 1 month in the refrigerator and continues to be more refined over several days, so make it in advance if you can.
3. Shuck the oysters and serve them on a platter embedded in crushed ice or rock salt, along with the mignonette sauce.

Chapter 8
Pan Loaves

Sandwich Bread

Lunchtime crowd-pleaser sandwich bread. Milk, butter, and honey fill this soft bread. We've baked this bread with oat milk, olive oil, and agave syrup. Substitute as desired. Add 15 grams (1 tablespoon) water to granulated sugar in place of honey.

Prep time: 25 minutes | Cook time: 55 minutes | Serves 1 loaf

- 320 grams scalded milk
- 30 grams unsalted butter
- 30 grams honey (1½ tablespoons)
- 12 grams salt (2 teaspoons)
- 520 grams all-purpose or bread flour
- 150 grams sourdough starter
- Cooking oil, for greasing
- 1 tablespoon milk, to brush on the dough before baking

1. Scald the milk by warming it to 180°F in a microwave or on the stove. Because of evaporation, you may want to start with 330 grams of milk.
2. Add the butter, honey, and salt to the hot milk to dissolve them, then chill the mixture in the refrigerator down to about 90°F. This should take about 15 minutes.
3. Combine the flour, sourdough starter, and milk mixture in a medium bowl and mix thoroughly. Transfer the dough to a floured countertop and knead it by hand for 2 to 3 minutes.
4. Cover the dough and let it bulk ferment for 6 to 12 hours at room temperature, or until it has just about doubled in size.
5. Flour your countertop, scrape the dough out onto it, and shape the dough into a tube.
6. While the dough rests on its seam, lightly oil your loaf pan, then place the dough in the pan, seam-side down.
7. Cover and proof the dough for 2 to 4 hours. You can also retard the dough in the refrigerator overnight or longer. The dough is ready to bake when it has doubled in size or its highest part crests over the lip of a 9-by-5-by-2¾-inch loaf pan.
8. Place one of your oven racks in the second-from-the-bottom position. Preheat your oven to 350°F for about 15 minutes.
9. Brush the milk on the top of the loaf and put the pan in the oven.
10. Bake for 45 to 50 minutes, or until the interior of the loaf is over 190°F.
11. When the bread has finished baking, immediately remove it from the pan. Cool it on a rack on its side to discourage settling of the crumb for at least 1 hour before slicing.
12. Once completely cooled, store the bread in a plastic bag or beeswax wrap to keep it soft.

Light Wheat Bread

This pan loaf introduces whole grain flour to sandwich bread. You can use whole wheat flour (hard red spring wheat) and other wheat kinds. Gluten strength and hydration will vary by wheat type, but differences should be tolerable because half the flour is all-purpose or bread flour. If the dough is too dry, add additional milk; if it's too moist, stretch and fold it.

Prep time: 25 minutes | Cook time: 50 minutes | Serves 1 loaf

- 330 grams scalded milk
- 30 grams unsalted butter
- 30 grams honey (1½ tablespoons)
- 12 grams salt (2 teaspoons)
- 260 grams all-purpose or bread flour
- 260 grams whole grain flour
- 150 grams sourdough starter
- Cooking oil, for greasing
- 1 tablespoon milk, to brush on the dough before baking

1. Scald the milk by warming it to 180°F in the microwave or on the stove. Because of evaporation, you may want to start with 340 grams of milk.
2. Add the butter, honey, and salt to the hot milk to dissolve them, then chill the mixture in the refrigerator down to about 90°F. This should take about 15 minutes.
3. Combine the flours, sourdough starter, and milk mixture in a medium bowl and mix thoroughly. Transfer the dough to a floured countertop and knead by hand for 2 to 3 minutes.
4. Cover the dough and let it bulk ferment for 6 to 12 hours at room temperature, or until it has just about doubled in size.
5. Flour your countertop, scrape the dough out onto it, and shape the dough into a tube.
6. While the dough rests on its seam, lightly oil your loaf pan, then place the dough in the pan, seam-side down.
7. Cover and proof the dough for 2 to 4 hours. You can also retard the dough in the refrigerator overnight or longer. The dough is ready to bake when it has doubled in size or its highest part crests over the lip of a 9-by-5-by-2¾-inch loaf pan.
8. Place one of your oven racks in the second-from-the-bottom position. Preheat your oven to 350°F for about 15 minutes.
9. Brush the milk on the top of the loaf and put the pan in the oven.
10. Bake for 45 to 50 minutes, or until the interior of the loaf is over 190°F.
11. When the bread has finished baking, immediately remove it from the pan. Cool it on a rack on its side to discourage settling of the crumb for at least 1 hour before slicing.
12. Once completely cooled, store the bread in a plastic bag or beeswax wrap to keep it soft.

Whole Wheat Pan Loaf

This pan loaf is 100% whole grain wheat. It's great for sandwiches, avocado toast, and soups. This recipe calls for sprouted wheat flour. Sprouted grains absorb additional nutrients. Sprouted wheat is sweeter and ferments faster. You can use whole grain flour beginning, but all-purpose is great too.

Prep time: 25 minutes | Cook time: 45 minutes | Serves 1 loaf

- 390 grams scalded milk
- 30 grams unsalted butter
- 30 grams honey (1½ tablespoons)
- 12 grams salt (2 teaspoons)
- 520 grams whole grain flour
- 150 grams sourdough starter
- Cooking oil, for greasing
- 1 tablespoon milk, to brush on the dough before baking

1. Approximately 4 to 8 hours before you want to start mixing your dough, build a whole grain sourdough starter by taking ½ teaspoon of your existing starter and mixing it with 35 grams of whole grain flour and 35 grams of water. (After the starter's expansion has peaked, feed it again if you need more starter or want the starter to have even less of the original all-purpose flour.) Note that the starter will ferment a little faster than refined flour starter, and it'll have fewer surface bubbles due to a weaker gluten network.
2. Scald the milk by warming it to 180°F in the microwave or on the stove. Because of evaporation, you may want to start with 400 grams of milk.
3. Add the butter, honey, and salt to the hot milk to dissolve them, then chill the mixture in the refrigerator down to about 90°F. This should take about 15 minutes.
4. Combine the flour, starter, and milk mixture in a medium bowl and mix thoroughly. If you find this dough too wet to knead by hand, let it rest for 15 to 30 minutes and give it a round of stretching and folding (see step 2 in the Cinnamon Raisin Light Wheat Pan Bread recipe).
5. Cover the dough and let it bulk ferment for 6 to 12 hours at room temperature, or until it has just about doubled in size.
6. Flour your countertop, scrape the dough out onto it, and shape the dough into a tube.
7. While the dough rests on its seam, lightly oil your loaf pan, then place the dough in the pan seam-side down.
8. Cover and proof the dough for 2 to 4 hours. The dough is ready to bake when it has doubled in size or its highest part crests over the lip of a 9-by-5-by-2¾-inch loaf pan.
9. Place one of your oven racks in the second-from-the-bottom position. Preheat your oven to 350°F for about 15 minutes.
10. Brush the milk on the top of the loaf and put the pan in the oven.
11. Bake for 45 to 50 minutes, or until the interior of the loaf is over 190°F.
12. When the bread has finished baking, immediately remove it from the pan. Cool it on a rack on its side for at least an hour before slicing.
13. Once completely cooled, store the bread in a plastic bag or beeswax wrap to keep it soft.

Cinnamon Raisin Light Wheat Pan Bread

Cinnamon raisin bread has beautiful colors and luscious raisins. Make a sweet-savory sandwich with this toasted, buttered bread. Cinnamon slows fermentation, so we use water instead of milk and whole grain flour.

Prep time: 25 minutes | Cook time: 55 minutes | Serves 1 loaf

- 350 grams all-purpose or bread flour
- 170 grams whole grain flour
- 340 grams water
- 150 grams sourdough starter
- 30 grams honey (1½ tablespoons)
- 12 grams salt (2 teaspoons)
- 6 grams cinnamon (2 teaspoons)
- 120 grams raisins
- Cooking oil, for greasing

1. Thoroughly mix the flours, water, starter, honey, salt, and cinnamon in a medium bowl. Add the raisins and continue mixing until they're evenly distributed. (Separating the mixing into two steps prevents dry flour from getting trapped in the crevices of the dried fruit.)
2. Cover and let the dough rest for 15 minutes, then give it a round of stretching and folding: With damp fingertips, stretch and fold the dough, lifting the edge of one side of the dough and folding it over to the other side. Go around the bowl two or three times, stretching and folding each side, and stop when the dough feels tighter.
3. Let the dough bulk ferment for 6 to 10 hours at room temperature, or until it has just about doubled in size.
4. Flour your countertop, scrape the dough out onto it, and shape the dough into a tube.
5. Cover and proof the dough for 2 to 4 hours. You can also retard the dough in the refrigerator overnight or longer. The dough is ready to bake when it has doubled in size or its highest part crests over the lip of a 9-by-5-by-2¾-inch loaf pan.
6. Place one of your oven racks in the second-from-the-bottom position. Preheat your oven to 350°F for about 15 minutes.
7. If the top of your dough isn't damp already, brush or spray water on it. You may want to score this dough to control the oven spring.
8. Bake for 50 minutes, or until the interior of the loaf is over 190°F.
9. When the bread has finished baking, immediately remove it from the pan. Cool it on a rack on its side (to discourage settling of the crumb) for at least 1 hour before slicing.
10. Once completely cooled, store the bread in a plastic bag or beeswax wrap to keep it soft.

Multiseed Light Wheat Pan Bread

This multiseed light wheat sourdough is great for grilled cheese and toast. Sunflower, chia, and hemp seeds give this a nutty, crunchy, and buttery flavor.

Prep time: 25 minutes | Cook time: 50 minutes | Serves 1 loaf

- 60 grams sunflower seeds, divided
- 25 grams chia seeds (2 tablespoons)
- 20 grams hemp seeds (3 tablespoons)
- 400 grams water, divided
- 260 grams bread flour or all-purpose flour
- 260 grams whole grain flour
- 150 grams sourdough starter
- 30 grams olive oil (2 tablespoons)
- 12 grams salt (2 teaspoons)
- Cooking oil, for greasing

1. Reserve 30 grams of sunflower seeds for bread crust.
2. Combine the remaining 30 grams of sunflower seeds with the chia seeds and hemp seeds in a small bowl with 100 grams of water. Cover and let the mixture sit for about 1 hour.
3. In a medium bowl, combine the flours, the remaining 300 grams of water, the sourdough starter, oil, and salt and mix thoroughly. Add the seed mixture along with any water left in the bowl. Continue mixing until the seeds are distributed through the dough.
4. Cover and let the dough rest for 15 to 30 minutes. Then with damp fingertips, stretch and fold the dough, lifting the edge of one side of the dough and folding it over to the other side. Go around the bowl two or three times, stretching and folding each side, and stop when the dough feels tighter.
5. Bulk ferment the dough for 6 to 10 hours at room temperature, or until it has just about doubled in size.
6. Flour your countertop, scrape the dough out onto it, and shape the dough into a tube.
7. While the dough rests on its seam, lightly oil your loaf pan, then place the dough in the pan seam-side down.
8. Cover and proof the dough for 2 to 4 hours. You can also retard the dough in the refrigerator overnight or longer. The dough is ready to bake when it has doubled in size or its highest part crests over the lip of a 9-by-5-by-2¾-inch loaf pan.
9. Place one of your oven racks in the second-from-the-bottom position. Preheat your oven to 350°F for about 15 minutes.
10. Brush or spray water on the dough if the top of it isn't damp already, then sprinkle the reserved sunflower seeds on the dough. Score the dough to control the oven spring. (Dragging your lame through the seeds is a bit tricky.)
11. Bake for 50 minutes, or until the interior of the loaf is over 190°F.
12. When the bread has finished baking, immediately remove it from the pan. Cool it on a rack on its side (to discourage settling of the crumb) for at least 1 hour before slicing.
13. Once completely cooled, store the bread in a plastic bag or beeswax wrap to keep it soft.

New York Deli Rye Pan Bread

Whole grain rye flour and caraway seeds combine to create New York deli rye bread. This bread has more rye flour than store-bought rye. This bread is great for tuna sandwiches with cream cheese and buttered toast with eggs and potatoes.

Prep time: 25 minutes | Cook time: 55 minutes | Serves 1 loaf

- 350 grams all-purpose or bread flour
- 170 grams whole grain rye flour (also called dark rye)
- 320 grams water
- 150 grams sourdough starter
- 30 grams honey (1½ tablespoons)
- 24 grams olive oil (2 tablespoons)
- 10 grams caraway seeds (1½ tablespoons)
- 12 grams salt (2 teaspoons)
- Cooking oil, for greasing

1. Combine the flours, water, starter, honey, oil, caraway seeds, and salt in a medium bowl and mix thoroughly. This dough is too sticky and wet to knead by hand, but you can let it rest for 15 to 30 minutes and then give it a round of stretching and folding: With damp fingertips, lift the edge of one side of the dough and fold it over to the other side. Go around the bowl two or three times, stretching and folding each side, and stop when the dough feels tighter.
2. Cover the dough and let it bulk ferment for 6 to 10 hours at room temperature, or until it has just about doubled in size.
3. Flour your countertop, scrape the dough out onto it, and shape the dough into a tube.
4. While the dough rests on its seam, lightly oil your loaf pan, then place the dough in the pan seam-side down.
5. Cover and proof the dough for 2 to 4 hours. You can also retard the dough in the refrigerator overnight or longer. The dough is ready to bake when it has doubled in size or its highest part crests over the lip of a 9-by-5-by-2¾-inch loaf pan.
6. Place one of your oven racks in the second-from-the-bottom position. Preheat your oven to 350°F for about 15 minutes.
7. Brush or spray water on the top of the dough if it isn't damp already.
8. If you haven't let your dough expand as much as recommended in step 5, then score it to control the oven spring.
9. Bake for 50 minutes, or until the interior of the loaf is over 190°F.
10. When the bread has finished baking, immediately remove it from the pan. Cool it on a rack on its side to discourage settling of the crumb. Give this loaf at least 2 hours to cool before slicing because rye

bread needs more time to set, or solidify.
11. Once completely cooled, store the bread in a plastic bag or beeswax wrap to keep it soft.

Turmeric Fennel Pan Loaf

This yellow bread is a visual pleasure. Sweet fennel scent, anti-inflammatory turmeric and black pepper in the bread. It pairs well with meat, cheese, butter, or fresh tomatoes.

Prep time: 25 minutes | Cook time: 55 minutes | Serves 1 loaf

- 520 grams all-purpose or bread flour
- 320 grams water
- 150 grams sourdough starter
- 30 grams honey (1½ tablespoons)
- 24 grams olive oil (2 tablespoons)
- 12 grams salt (2 teaspoons)
- 6 grams ground turmeric (2 teaspoons)
- 6 grams fennel seeds (1 tablespoon)
- ¼ to ½ teaspoon ground black pepper
- Cooking oil, for greasing

1. Combine the flour, water, starter, honey, oil, salt, turmeric, fennel seeds, and pepper in a medium bowl and mix thoroughly. If you find the dough too wet to knead by hand, let it rest for 15 to 30 minutes and then give it a round of stretching and folding: With damp fingertips, lift the edge of one side of the dough and fold it over to the other side. Go around the bowl two or three times, stretching and folding each side, and stop when the dough feels tighter.
2. Cover the dough and let it bulk ferment for 6 to 10 hours at room temperature, or until it has just about doubled in size.
3. Flour your countertop, scrape the dough out onto it, and then shape the dough into a tube. This dough is on the wet side, so you may need to roll the dough a second time.
4. While the dough rests on its seam, lightly oil your loaf pan, then place the dough in the pan seam-side down.
5. Cover and proof the dough for 2 to 4 hours. You can also retard the dough in the refrigerator overnight or longer. The dough is ready to bake when it has doubled in size or its highest part crests over the lip of a 9-by-5-by-2¾-inch loaf pan.
6. Place one of your oven racks in the second-from-the-bottom position. Preheat your oven to 350°F for about 15 minutes.
7. Dust the top of the dough with flour and score down the center. This dough tends to expand during baking, and a score will prevent a rupture on the side of the loaf.
8. Bake for 50 minutes, or until the interior of the loaf is over 190°F.
9. When the bread has finished baking, immediately remove it from the pan. Cool it on a rack on its side (to discourage settling of the crumb) for at least 1 hour before slicing.
10. Once completely cooled, store the bread in a plastic bag or beeswax wrap to keep it soft.

Buckwheat Pan Bread

Buckwheat is a healthy rhubarb seed. This fresh-tasting bread is perfect for sandwiches and toast. At 20% of the flour, buckwheat flavor shines while gluten structure stays firm. If you like the flavor and are prepared to sacrifice airiness, add more buckwheat.

Prep time: 25 minutes | Cook time: 55 minutes| Serves 1 loaf

- 420 grams all-purpose or bread flour
- 100 grams buckwheat flour
- 280 grams water
- 150 grams sourdough starter
- 65 grams plain yogurt
- 12 grams salt (2 teaspoons)
- Cooking oil, for greasing

1. Combine the flours, water, sourdough starter, yogurt, and salt in a medium bowl and mix thoroughly. If you find this dough too wet to knead by hand, let it rest for 15 to 30 minutes and then give it a round of stretching and folding: With damp fingertips, lift the edge of one side of the dough and fold it over to the other side. Go around the bowl two or three times, stretching and folding each side, and stop when the dough feels tighter.
2. Cover the dough and let it bulk ferment for 6 to 10 hours at room temperature, or until it has just about doubled in size.
3. Flour your countertop, scrape the dough out onto it, and then shape the dough into a tube. This dough is on the wet side, so you may need to roll the dough a second time.
4. While the dough rests on its seam, lightly oil your loaf pan, then place the dough in the pan seam-side down.
5. Cover and proof the dough for 2 to 4 hours. You can also retard the dough in the refrigerator overnight or longer. The dough is ready to bake when it has doubled in size or its highest part crests over the lip of a 9-by-5-by-2¾-inch loaf pan.
6. Place one of your oven racks in the second-from-the-bottom position. Preheat your oven to 350°F for about 15 minutes.
7. Dust the top of the dough with flour and score down the center. This dough tends to expand during baking, and a score will prevent a rupture on the side of the loaf.
8. Bake for 50 minutes, or until the interior of the loaf is over 190°F.
9. When the bread has finished baking, immediately remove it from the pan. Cool it on a rack on its side (to discourage settling of the crumb) for at least 1 hour before slicing.
10. Once completely cooled, store the bread in a plastic bag or beeswax wrap to keep it soft.

Einkorn Pan Loaf

This all-einkorn pan loaf is excellent, with a delicate, sweet flavor and no bitterness. Einkorn is the oldest wheat that behaves differently from contemporary wheat. Faster fermentation and more air pockets, but the dough isn't flexible or fluffy.

Prep time: 25 minutes | Cook time: 65 minutes| Serves 1 loaf

- 260 grams scalded milk
- 22 grams honey (1 tablespoon)
- 12 grams salt (2 teaspoons)
- 148 grams water
- 600 grams einkorn wheat flour
- 100 grams sourdough starter
- 1 tablespoon milk, to brush on the dough before baking
- Cooking oil, for greasing

1. Approximately 4 to 8 hours before you want to start mixing your dough, build an einkorn wheat sourdough starter by taking ½ teaspoon of your existing starter and mixing it with 35 grams of einkorn flour and 35 grams of water. (After the starter's expansion has peaked, feed it again if you need more starter or want the starter to have even less of the original all-purpose flour.) Note that the starter will ferment faster than refined flour starter, and it will have fewer surface bubbles due to a weaker gluten network.
2. Scald the milk by warming it to 180°F in the microwave or on the stove. Because of evaporation, you may want to start with 270 grams of milk.
3. Dissolve the honey and salt in the hot milk, then add the water. Chill the mixture in the refrigerator down to about 90°F. This should take less than 10 minutes.
4. Combine the flour, sourdough starter, and milk mixture in a bowl and mix thoroughly.
5. Cover the dough and let it bulk ferment for 5 to 7 hours, or until it has grown by 75%.
6. Flour your countertop, scrape the dough out onto it, and shape the dough into a tube. Use your bench knife to maneuver the sticky dough.
7. Lightly oil your loaf pan, then place the dough in the pan seam-side down. Again, use your bench knife.
8. Dip a spatula into a bowl of water and smooth the surface of the dough.
9. Cover and proof the dough for 1 hour 30 minutes to 3 hours. You can also retard the dough in the refrigerator overnight or longer. The dough is ready to bake when it is about ¾ inch under the top of a 9-by-5-by-2¾-inch loaf pan.
10. Place one of your oven racks in the second-from-the-bottom position. Preheat your oven to 350°F for about 15 minutes.
11. Brush the milk on the top of the loaf and put the pan in the oven.
12. Bake for 50 minutes to 1 hour, or until the interior of the loaf is over 200°F.

13. When the bread has finished baking, immediately remove it from the pan. Cool it on a rack on its side to discourage settling of the crumb. If possible, wait 8 to 12 hours before cutting to let the crumb set.
14. Once completely cooled, store the bread in a plastic bag or beeswax wrap to keep it soft.

Flaxseed Pan Bread

Flaxseed sourdough bread is nutty and strong in omega-3 fatty acids. This bread adds nutrition to toast and sandwiches. Flaxseed meal texture affects absorbency, so add water gently. Store entire seeds in the fridge or freezer and ground them as needed, or buy flaxseed meal and freeze it.

Prep time: 25 minutes | Cook time: 50 minutes | Serves 1 loaf

- 440 grams all-purpose or bread flour
- 80 grams flaxseed meal
- 350 grams water
- 150 grams sourdough starter
- 12 grams salt (2 teaspoons)
- Cooking oil, for greasing

1. Combine the flour, flaxseed meal, water, starter, and salt in a medium bowl and mix thoroughly. If you find this dough too wet to knead by hand, let it rest for 15 to 30 minutes and then give it a round of stretching and folding. With damp fingertips, lift the edge of one side of the dough and fold it over to the other side. Go around the bowl two or three times, stretching and folding each side, and stop when the dough feels tighter.
2. Cover the dough and let it bulk ferment for 6 to 10 hours at room temperature, until it has just about doubled in size.
3. Flour your countertop, scrape the dough out onto it and shape the dough into a tube. This dough is on the wet side, so you may need to roll the dough a second time.
4. While the dough rests on its seam, lightly oil your loaf pan, then place the dough in the pan seam-side down.
5. Cover and proof the dough for 2 to 4 hours. You can also retard the dough in the refrigerator overnight or longer. The dough is ready to bake when it has doubled in size or its highest part crests over the lip of a 9-by-5-by-2¾-inch loaf pan.
6. Place one of your oven racks in the second-from-the-bottom position. Preheat your oven to 350°F for about 15 minutes.
7. Brush the top of the dough with water if it isn't damp already, and score the dough down the center, as this dough may expand during baking.
8. Bake for 50 minutes, or until the interior of the loaf is over 190°F.
9. When the bread has finished baking, immediately remove it from the pan. Cool it on a rack on its side (to discourage settling of the crumb) for at least 1 hour before slicing.
10. Once completely cooled, store the bread in a plastic bag or beeswax wrap to keep it soft.

Whole Wheat Chocolate Babka

In an episode of Seinfeld, they tried to order the last babka for a dinner party. Cinnamon adds flavor and vinegar improves rising.

Prep time: 65 minutes | Cook time: 50 minutes | Serves 2 8-inch loaves

FOR THE DOUGH

- 424g (3¾ cups) white whole wheat flour
- 99g (½ cup) granulated sugar
- 1 teaspoon salt
- 100g (½ cup) active starter
- 1 tablespoon apple cider vinegar (optional)
- 3 large eggs, at room temperature
- 1 large egg yolk, at room temperature
- 80g (⅓ cup) whole milk
- 1 teaspoon vanilla extract
- 140g (10 tablespoons) unsalted butter, at room temperature

FOR THE FILLING

- 112g (8 tablespoons) unsalted butter, at room temperature
- 63g (½ cup) powdered sugar
- 33g (⅓ cup) Dutch-process cocoa
- ½ teaspoon ground cinnamon
- 170g (1 cup) chopped bittersweet chocolate
- For the syrup
- 120g (½ cup) water
- 99g (½ cup) granulated sugar

1. Make the Dough. In the bowl of stand mixer, stir together the flour, granulated sugar, salt, and vital wheat gluten (if using). Add the starter, vinegar (if using), whole eggs, egg yolk, milk, and vanilla. Snap on the dough hook and mix on low speed until a dough comes together. Beat in the butter, 1 tablespoon at a time. Cover the bowl with a damp towel and let rest for 20 minutes.
2. Knead. On medium speed, knead with the dough hook for about 10 minutes.
3. Bulk Ferment. Place the dough in a lightly greased bowl, turning the dough so it is evenly coated. Cover with a damp towel and let the dough rise for 6 to 8 hours, until doubled in size.
4. Prepare the Pans. Grease or butter two 8½-by-4½-inch loaf pans. Line the pans with parchment paper, leaving overhang so the parchment can be used to lift the loaves out later.
5. Make the Filling. In a bowl, beat together the butter, powdered sugar, cocoa, and cinnamon until combined. Set aside.

Kamut Cinnamon-Raisin Swirl Bread

Cinnamon-raisin swirl bread is one of my favorite breakfast breads. I thought it couldn't get any better until I tried Kamut flour in sourdough. Kamut's buttery flavor goes nicely with cinnamon and brown sugar. After baking, you can brush the crust with melted butter.

Prep time: 25 minutes | Cook time: 45 minutes | Serves One 8-inch loaf

FOR THE DOUGH
- 100g (½ cup) active starter
- 240g (1 cup) whole milk
- 56g (4 tablespoons) unsalted butter, melted
- 50g (¼ cup) granulated sugar
- 2 large eggs, at room temperature
- 180g (1½ cups) bread flour
- 180g (1½ cups) Kamut flour
- 1½ teaspoons salt
- 80g (½ cup) raisins
- Egg wash: 1 large egg beaten with 1 tablespoon water

FOR THE FILLING
- 71g (⅓ cup packed) light brown sugar
- 28g (2 tablespoons) ground cinnamon
- 2 teaspoons flour

1. Make the Dough. In a large bowl, whisk together the starter, milk, melted butter, granulated sugar, and eggs. Add both flours and the salt and mix to combine. Finish by hand, until a rough dough forms. Cover the bowl with a damp towel and let the dough rest for 30 minutes.
2. Add the Raisins. Mix in the raisins by hand until evenly distributed. Cover again and let the dough rest for 1 to 1½ hours.
3. Stretch and Fold. Begin by pulling up on one edge of the dough as high as you can stretch it without tearing and fold it in the middle of the dough. Give the bowl a quarter-turn and stretch and fold again. Repeat another two times, until you have made one complete rotation of the bowl. Repeat this step three more times, spacing them 30 minutes apart.
4. Bulk Ferment. Cover the bowl with a damp towel and let the dough rise at room temperature for 6 to 8 hours, until doubled in size with a smooth and domed top.
5. Make the Filling. In a small bowl, combine the brown sugar, cinnamon, and flour. Set aside.
6. Shape. Remove the dough from the bowl and place it on a lightly floured work surface. Roll the dough into an 18-by-8-inch rectangle. Brush the dough with the egg wash. Spread the filling over the dough evenly, pressing it down slightly. Starting on a short side, roll the dough into a log and tuck the ends underneath. Let it rest for 5 to 10 minutes. Place the log seam-side down in a lightly greased 8½-by-4½-inch loaf pan.
7. Proof. Cover the dough with a clean towel or shower cap and let rise for 1½ to 2 hours, until it has risen to the top of the pan and gotten puffy. Near the end of the rise, position a rack in the center of the oven and preheat the oven to 375°F.
8. Bake. Uncover the dough and bake for 45 to 50 minutes, until the crust is golden brown and the bread has reached an internal temperature of 190°F.
9. Cool. Let the bread cool in the pan for 10 minutes, then transfer the loaf to a wire rack to cool for at least 2 hours before slicing.

New York Deli Rye

Caraway compliments the sourness of the sourdough to make delicate, moist rye sandwich bread. This bread goes well with morning scrambled eggs.

Prep time: 35 minutes | Cook time: 45 minutes | Serves One 8-inch loaf

- 100g (½ cup) active starter
- 1 tablespoon sugar
- 42g (3 tablespoons) unsalted butter, melted
- 1 large egg, at room temperature
- 480g (2 cups) whole milk
- 212g (2 cups) light rye flour
- 424g (3¾ cups) bread flour
- 1½ teaspoons salt
- 1½ tablespoons caraway seeds

1. **Make the Dough.** In a large bowl, whisk together the starter, sugar, melted butter, egg, and milk. Add both flours and the salt and mix to combine. Finish by hand, until a rough dough forms. Cover with a damp towel and let the dough rest for 30 minutes to 1 hour.
2. **Add the Caraway Seeds.** Mix in the caraway seeds by hand until evenly distributed.
3. **Stretch and Fold.** Begin by pulling up on one edge of the dough as high as you can stretch it without tearing, then fold it to the middle of the dough. Give the bowl a quarter-turn and stretch and fold again. Repeat another two times, until you have made one complete rotation of the bowl. Repeat this step three more times, spacing them 30 to 45 minutes apart.
4. **Bulk Ferment.** Cover the bowl with a damp towel and let the dough rise at room temperature for 8 to 10 hours, until doubled in size and the top of the dough is domed and smooth.
5. **Shape.** Remove the dough from the bowl and place it on a lightly floured work surface. Roll the dough into an 8-by-4-inch rectangle, then roll up the rectangle into a log and tuck the ends underneath. Let it rest for 5 to 10 minutes. Place the log seam-side down in a lightly greased 8½-by-4-inch loaf pan.
6. **Proof.** Cover the dough with a clean towel or shower cap and let rise for 1½ hours to 2 hours, until it has risen above the edge of the pan. Near the end of the rise, position a rack in the center of the oven and preheat the oven to 350°F.
7. **Bake.** Uncover the dough and bake for 40 to 45 minutes, until the crust is golden brown and the bread has reached an internal temperature of 190°F.
8. **Cool.** Let the bread cool in the pan for 10 minutes, then transfer the loaf to a wire rack to cool for at least 2 hours before slicing.

Millet Hamburger Buns

Mild, gluten-free millet flour and bread flour create delicate, chewy hamburger buns. Sesame seeds offer crunch and honey adds sweetness. Summer barbecues need sourdough buns.

Prep time: 45 minutes | Cook time: 25 minutes | Serves 8 buns

- 200g (1 cup) active starter
- 120g (½ cup) water
- 120g (½ cup) whole milk
- 42g (2 tablespoons) honey
- 28g (2 tablespoons) unsalted butter, melted
- 1 large egg, at room temperature
- 210g (1½ cups) millet flour
- 180g (1½ cups) bread flour
- 1½ teaspoons salt
- Egg wash: 1 large egg beaten with 1 tablespoon water
- Sesame seeds, for garnish

1. **Make the Dough.** In a large bowl, whisk together the starter, water, milk, honey, melted butter, and egg. Add both flours and the salt and mix to combine. Finish by hand, mixing until a rough dough forms. Cover the bowl with a damp towel and let the dough rest for 1½ to 2 hours.
2. **Stretch and Fold.** Begin by pulling up on one edge of the dough as high as you can stretch it without tearing and fold it in the middle of the dough. Give the bowl a quarter-turn and stretch and fold again. Repeat another two times, until you have made one complete rotation of the bowl. Repeat this step three more times, spaced about 30 minutes apart.
3. **Bulk Ferment.** Cover the bowl with a damp towel and let the dough rise at room temperature for 6 to 8 hours, until it is doubled in size and has a rounded, smooth top.
4. **Shape.** Remove the dough from the bowl and place it on a lightly floured work surface. Divide the dough into 8 equal portions. Shape each into a ball and place on a parchment-lined baking sheet.
5. **Proof.** Cover the dough with lightly greased plastic wrap and let the buns rise for 1½ to 2 hours, until slightly risen and puffy. Near the end of the rise, position a rack in the center of the oven and preheat the oven to 375°F.
6. **Bake.** Uncover the dough and brush each bun with the egg wash, then sprinkle on the sesame seeds. Bake for 15 to 20 minutes, until the crust is golden brown and the bread has reached an internal temperature of 190°F.
7. **Cool.** Let the buns cool on the baking sheet for 10 minutes, then transfer to a wire rack to cool completely.

Chapter 9
Sandwich Breads and Pizza

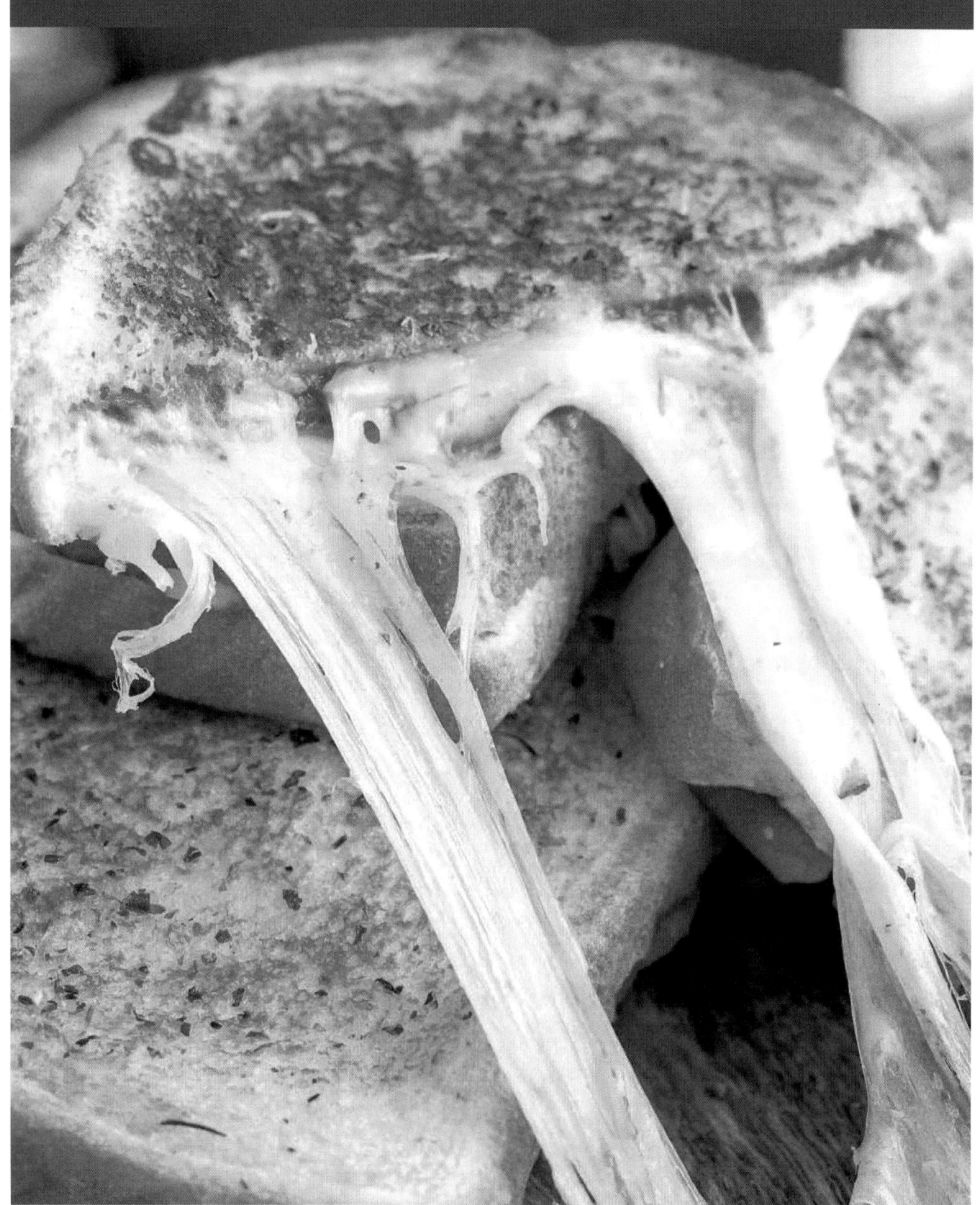

Sandwich Loaf Bread

Good gluten-free bread doesn't need to be toasted. The surface is crisp and the inside is soft and fluffy. This gluten-free bread is larger than typical store-bought varieties.

Prep time: 15 minutes | Cook time: 1 hour 10 minutes | Serves 1 (2-pound) loaf

- 550g high-protein flour
- 472g lukewarm water (65°F)
- 4 large egg whites (120g), at room temperature, lightly beaten, or 120g more lukewarm water (65°F)
- 24g sunflower seed oil

1. **Combine:** In a large bowl with a dough whisk or in the bowl of a stand mixer fitted with the paddle attachment, mix together the High-Protein Flour, water, egg whites, and sunflower seed oil on low speed until combined. Increase the speed to medium and beat for 3 minutes to add air to the dough.
2. **Shape:** Grease a loaf pan with nonstick cooking spray. Transfer the dough into the loaf pan and, using a wet offset spatula or spoon, gently smooth out the surface.
3. **Proof:** Cover loosely with plastic wrap and proof at room temperature until the dough domes over the edge of the pan, about 1½ hours.
4. **Preheat:** Place an inverted rimmed baking sheet on the middle rack of the oven and preheat to 425°F.
5. **Bake:** Bake for 15 minutes, then reduce the heat to 350°F and bake for 30 minutes more. Remove the loaf from the pan, set on the preheated baking sheet, and bake until golden and the internal temperature measures 208°F, 20 to 25 minutes more.
6. **Cool:** Let cool completely, about 1 hour, on a wire rack.

Pizza Crust

My goal was to create a low-maintenance dough that rolled out easily, puffed well, and tasted great. Success! I also wanted to freeze a prebaked crust for instant use. Baked pizza crusts can be frozen for 1 month; thaw before topping and baking.

Prep time: 15 minutes | Cook time: 60 minutes | Serves 2 (8½-inch) pizzas

- 320g all-purpose flour, plus more for dusting
- 7g (one ¼-ounce package) instant yeast
- 4g (1 teaspoon) granulated sugar
- 6g (1 teaspoon) salt
- 177g lukewarm water (65°F)
- 2 large egg whites (60g), at room temperature, lightly beaten, or 60g lukewarm water (65°F)
- 24g olive oil, plus more for brushing
- 112g (½ cup) store-bought or homemade pizza sauce, for topping, divided
- Various toppings, such as thinly sliced bell peppers, onions, mushrooms, pepperoni, cooked sausage slices, mozzarella, Parmesan cheese, olives

1. **Combine:** In a large bowl, use a dough whisk to combine the All-Purpose Flour, yeast, sugar, and salt. Add the water, egg whites, and olive oil. Using a wooden spoon, beat until the dough pulls away from the sides of the bowl.
2. **Shape:** Divide the dough into two equal pieces. Dust a piece of parchment paper lightly with All-Purpose Flour and transfer one of the dough portions onto it. Dust it with more All-Purpose Flour and, using your fingertips or a rolling pin, press the dough out to a circle about 8½ inches across and ¼ inch thick. Repeat with the second portion of dough.
3. **Proof:** Cover loosely with plastic wrap and proof at room temperature for about 30 minutes.
4. **Preheat:** Place an inverted rimmed baking sheet on the bottom rack of the oven and preheat to 450°F.
5. **Bake:** One portion of dough at a time, slide the dough with its parchment paper onto the preheated baking sheet and bake until puffy, golden, and crisp on the bottom, about 8 minutes. Repeat with the remaining dough.
6. **Make The Pizza:** Working with one pizza crust at a time, brush with olive oil. Spoon on about 56g (¼ cup) of pizza sauce, leaving a ½-inch border, then cover with your favorite toppings. Bake until the crust is golden, about 8 minutes. Repeat with the remaining crust and toppings.
7. **Cool:** Let cool slightly on a wire rack, about 5 minutes, then transfer each pizza to a cutting board and, using a pizza cutter or serrated knife, cut each round into four pieces.

The Complete Cosori Air Fryer Cookbook | 71

Sesame Sandwich Bread Squares

Once I mastered gluten-free pizza dough, ciabatta-like squares followed. I call them bread squares because I spread out 34-inch-thick dough and cut them into four squares. When making a sandwich, slice it crosswise and fill it.

Prep time: 15 minutes | Cook time: 1 hour 10 minutes | Serves 4 (4-ounce) sandwich squares

- 320g all-purpose flour, plus more for dusting
- 7g (one ¼-ounce package) instant yeast
- 4g (1 teaspoon) granulated sugar
- 6g (1 teaspoon) salt
- 177g lukewarm water (65°F)
- 2 large egg whites (60g), at room temperature, lightly beaten, or 60g lukewarm water (65°F)
- 24g olive oil, plus more for brushing
- Sesame seeds, for sprinkling

1. **Combine:** In a large bowl, use a dough whisk to combine the All-Purpose Flour, yeast, sugar, and salt. Add the water, egg whites, and olive oil. Using a wooden spoon, beat until the dough pulls away from the sides of the bowl, about 3 minutes.
2. **Shape:** Lightly dust a piece of parchment paper with All-Purpose Flour. Turn the dough onto the parchment and lightly dust the top with more All-Purpose Flour. Using your fingertips or a rolling pin, press the dough out into an 8-inch square about ¾ inch thick.
3. **Proof:** Cover loosely with plastic wrap and proof at room temperature until the dough is puffy, about 30 minutes.
4. **Preheat:** Place an inverted rimmed baking sheet on the middle rack of the oven and preheat to 450°F. Cut the dough into four equal pieces. Spray lightly with water and sprinkle with sesame seeds.
5. **Bake:** Slide the dough pieces with their parchment paper onto the preheated baking sheet and bake until puffy and crisp on the bottom, about 10 minutes.
6. **Cool:** Let cool completely, about 20 minutes, on a wire rack.

Cinnamon-Raisin Sandwich Bread

This sandwich bread is great toasted with butter or made into French toast. Curry chicken salad, ham and Cheddar, and Thanksgiving leftovers are some of my favorite sandwich ingredients.

Prep time: 15 minutes | Cook time: 4 hours | Serves 1 (2-pound) loaf

- 550g high-protein flour
- 472g lukewarm water (65°F)
- 4 large egg whites (120g), at room temperature, lightly beaten, or 120g more lukewarm water (65°F)
- 24g sunflower seed oil
- 50g packed brown sugar
- 13g ground cinnamon, divided
- 225g raisins
- 50g granulated sugar
- Melted unsalted butter, for brushing

1. **Combine:** In a large bowl with a dough whisk or in the bowl of a stand mixer fitted with the paddle attachment, mix together the High-Protein Flour, water, egg whites, sunflower seed oil, brown sugar, 8g (1 tablespoon) of cinnamon, and raisins on low speed until combined. Increase the speed to medium and beat for 3 minutes to add air to the dough.
2. **Shape:** Grease a loaf pan with nonstick cooking spray. Transfer the dough into the loaf pan and, using a wet offset spatula or spoon, gently smooth out the surface.
3. **Proof:** Cover loosely with plastic wrap and proof at room temperature until the dough domes over the edge of the pan, about 1½ hours.
4. **Preheat:** Place an inverted rimmed baking sheet on the middle rack of the oven and preheat to 425°F.
5. **Bake:** Bake for 15 minutes, then reduce the heat to 350°F and bake for 30 minutes more. Remove the loaf from the pan, set on the preheated baking sheet, and bake until golden and the internal temperature measures 208°F, 20 to 25 minutes more.
6. **Cool:** In a small bowl, stir together the granulated sugar and remaining 5g (2 teaspoons) of cinnamon. Remove the loaf from the oven and brush with butter, then quickly coat it in the cinnamon sugar. Let cool completely, about 1 hour, on a wire rack.

Honey, Nuts, And Oats Sandwich Bread

These bread's nostalgic taste combinations are a nod to my childhood cereal of choice, Honey Bunches of Oats and Honey Nut Cheerios.

Prep time: 15 minutes | Cook time: 4 hours | Serves 1 (2-pound) loaf

- 550g high-protein flour
- 413g lukewarm water (65°F)
- 4 large egg whites (120g), at room temperature, lightly beaten, or 120g more lukewarm water (65°F)
- 42g honey, plus more for brushing
- 24g sunflower seed oil
- 65g chopped pecans
- gluten-free oat bran, for coating
- gluten-free old-fashioned rolled oats, for sprinkling

1. **Combine:** In a large bowl with a dough whisk or in the bowl of a stand mixer fitted with the paddle attachment, mix together the High-Protein Flour, water, egg whites, honey, sunflower seed oil, and pecans on low speed until combined. Increase the speed to medium and beat for 3 minutes to add air to the dough.
2. **Shape:** Grease a loaf pan with nonstick cooking spray and coat the sides with oat bran. Transfer the dough into the loaf pan and, using a wet offset spatula or spoon, gently smooth out the surface.
3. **Proof:** Cover loosely with plastic wrap and proof at room temperature until the dough domes over the edge of the pan, about 1½ hours.
4. **Preheat:** Place an inverted rimmed baking sheet on the middle rack of the oven and preheat to 425°F.
5. **Bake:** Bake for 15 minutes, then reduce the heat to 350°F and bake for 30 minutes more. Remove the loaf from the pan, set on the preheated baking sheet, and bake until golden and the internal temperature measures 208°F, 20 to 25 minutes more. Remove from the oven, brush generously with honey, and sprinkle with oat bran and rolled oats.
6. **Cool:** Let cool completely, about 1 hour, on a wire rack.

Garlic Butter Focaccia Bread

To create this dish, I combined two of my all-time favorite foods: garlic bread and focaccia. To tell the truth, you could get by with just eating this focaccia bread dusted with coarse salt.

Prep time: 15 minutes | Cook time: 2 hours 20 minutes | Serves 1 (17.5-by-13.5-inch) focaccia

FOR THE DOUGH
- 550g high-protein flour
- 413g lukewarm water (65°F)
- 4 large egg whites (120g), at room temperature, lightly beaten, or 120g more lukewarm water (65°F)
- 24g olive oil, plus more for greasing

FOR THE GARLIC BUTTER
- 57g (¼ cup) unsalted butter, melted
- 2g (¾ teaspoon) garlic powder
- 3g (½ teaspoon) salt

1. **Combine:** In a large bowl with a dough whisk or in the bowl of a stand mixer fitted with the paddle attachment, mix together the High-Protein Flour, water, egg whites, and olive oil on low speed until combined. Increase the speed to medium and beat for 3 minutes to add air to the dough.
2. **Shape:** Generously grease a rimmed baking sheet with olive oil. Transfer the dough to the prepared baking sheet. Lightly grease your hands and use your fingertips to gently dimple the dough, stretching it to the edges of the baking sheet.
3. **Proof:** Cover loosely with plastic wrap and proof at room temperature until the dough is puffy, about 1½ hours.
4. **Preheat:** Place an inverted rimmed baking sheet on the middle rack of the oven and preheat to 400°F.
5. **Bake:** Place the baking sheet with the dough on the preheated baking sheet and bake until golden, 20 to 25 minutes.
6. **Make The Garlic Butter:** Meanwhile, in a small saucepan over medium-low heat, combine the butter, garlic powder, and salt, stirring occasionally, until melted. Reduce the heat to low, cover, and keep warm.
7. **Cool:** Remove the focaccia from the oven and use a pastry brush to coat it thoroughly with the garlic butter. Let cool slightly on a wire rack, about 5 minutes, then transfer to a cutting board and use a pizza cutter or serrated knife to slice into pieces.

Chicago Deep-Dish Pepperoni Pan Pizza

Deep-dish pizza, whether from Pizza Hut, Giordano's, or Lou Malnati's, is characterized by a thick, chewy dough that allows for an abundance of toppings.

Prep time: 15 minutes | Cook time: 2 hours 20 minutes | Serves 2 (9-inch) pizzas

- 550g high-protein flour, plus more for dusting
- 413g lukewarm water (65°F)
- 4 large egg whites (120g), at room temperature, lightly beaten, or 120g more lukewarm water (65°F)
- 24g olive oil, plus more for greasing
- 112g (½ cup) store-bought or homemade pizza sauce
- 169g (1½ cups) shredded mozzarella
- 24 small slices gluten-free pepperoni

1. **Combine:** In a large bowl with a dough whisk or in the bowl of a stand mixer fitted with the paddle attachment, mix together the High-Protein Flour, water, egg whites, and olive oil on low speed until combined. Increase the speed to medium and beat for 3 minutes to add air to the dough.
2. **Shape:** Generously grease two 9-inch round cake pans with olive oil. Divide the dough into two equal pieces. Dust a piece of parchment paper lightly with High-Protein Flour and transfer one of the dough portions onto it. Using a floured rolling pin, roll the dough into a 9-inch circle and place in one of the prepared pans. Repeat with the second portion of dough.
3. **Proof:** Cover the pans loosely with plastic wrap and proof at room temperature until the dough is puffy, about 1½ hours.
4. **Preheat:** Place an inverted rimmed baking sheet on the middle rack of the oven and preheat to 400°F.
5. **Bake:** Top each pizza round equally with sauce, mozzarella, and pepperoni. Bake until golden and bubbling, 20 to 25 minutes.
6. **Cool:** Let cool slightly on a wire rack, about 5 minutes, then transfer to a cutting board and use a pizza cutter or serrated knife to cut each round into four pieces.

Parmesan Pull-Apart Pizza Breadsticks

Think back to your favorite pizza delivery place. You won't have to wait long for those nostalgic pangs of chewy crunchiness to be satisfied by these imitation breadsticks.

Prep time: 15 minutes | Cook time: 2 hours 10 minutes | Serves 12 (10-inch) breadsticks

- 550g high-protein flour, plus more for dusting
- 343g lukewarm water (65°F)
- 2 large egg whites (60g), at room temperature, lightly beaten, or 60g more lukewarm water (65°F)
- 60g olive oil, plus more for greasing and brushing
- 12g salt, divided
- 9g (1 tablespoon) garlic powder, divided
- 7g (2 tablespoons) Italian seasoning blend
- Grated Parmesan cheese, for sprinkling
- Homemade or store-bought marinara sauce, warmed, for dipping

1. **Combine:** In a large bowl with a dough whisk or in the bowl of a stand mixer fitted with the paddle attachment, mix together the High-Protein Flour, water, egg whites, olive oil, 6g (1 teaspoon) of salt, and 3g (1 teaspoon) of garlic powder on low speed until combined. Increase the speed to medium and beat for 3 minutes to add air to the dough. In a small bowl, stir together the Italian seasoning blend, remaining 6g (2 teaspoons) of garlic powder, and remaining 6g (1 teaspoon) of salt to make a pizza seasoning. Set aside.
2. **Shape:** Generously grease a rimmed baking sheet with olive oil. Dust a piece of parchment paper lightly with High-Protein Flour and transfer the dough onto it. Using a floured rolling pin, roll out the dough into a 9-by-13-inch rectangle about ½ inch thick. Using a pizza cutter or sharp knife, cut into 12 equal strips and place on the prepared baking sheet about ⅛ inch apart. Use a pastry brush to coat the dough with olive oil and sprinkle generously with Parmesan cheese and the pizza seasoning.
3. **Proof:** Cover loosely with plastic wrap and proof at room temperature until the dough is puffy, about 1½ hours.
4. **Preheat:** Place an inverted rimmed baking sheet on the middle rack and preheat the oven to 400°F.
5. **Bake:** Place the baking sheet with the dough on the preheated baking sheet and bake until golden brown, about 25 minutes. Serve hot with the marinara dipping sauce.

Einkorn Sandwich Bread

Einkorn flour is the oldest kind of wheat, seeded 12,000 years ago. This ancient grain makes soft, zesty, crunchy sandwich bread. This whole-grain bread may fool you into thinking it's not.

Prep time: 35 minutes | Cook time: 45 minutes | Serves One 8-inch loaf

- 75g (⅓ cup) active starter
- 1 tablespoon honey
- 180g (¾ cup) whole milk
- 240g (1 cup) water
- 600g (6¼ cups) whole-grain einkorn flour
- 2 teaspoons salt

1. Make the Dough. In a large bowl, whisk together the starter, honey, milk, and water. Add the flour and salt and mix to combine. Finish by hand, mixing until a rough dough forms. Cover with a damp towel and let the dough rest for 2 hours.
2. Stretch and Fold. Begin by pulling up on one edge of the dough as high as you can stretch it without tearing and fold it in the middle of the dough. Give the bowl a quarter-turn and stretch and fold again. Repeat another two times, until you have made one complete rotation of the bowl. Repeat this step three more times, spacing them 30 minutes apart.
3. Bulk ferment. Cover the bowl with a damp towel and let the dough rise at room temperature for 8 to 12 hours, until it no longer looks dense and has doubled in size.
4. Shape. Remove the dough from the bowl and place it on a floured surface. Roll the dough into an 8-by-4-inch rectangle, then roll up the rectangle into a log and tuck the ends underneath. Let it rest for 5 to 10 minutes. Place the log seam-side down in a lightly greased 8½-by-4½-inch loaf pan.
5. Proof. Cover the dough with a clean towel or shower cap and let rise for 3 to 4 hours, until the dough looks puffy and has risen 1 inch above the rim of the pan. Near the end of the rise, position a rack in the center of the oven and preheat the oven to 375°F.
6. Bake. Uncover the dough and bake for 40 to 45 minutes, until the crust is light golden brown and the bread has reached an internal temperature of 190°F.
7. Cool. Transfer the bread to a wire rack to cool for at least 2 hours before slicing.

Whole Wheat Sandwich Bread

This whole wheat sourdough sandwich bread makes great sandwiches. This honey-sweetened whole wheat loaf is delicate and moist. Sourdough starter and whole-grain flour add flavor to your sandwich.

Prep time: 45 minutes | Cook time: 45 minutes | Serves One 9-inch loaf

- 100g (½ cup) active starter
- 425g (3½ cups) water
- 60g (¼ cup) orange juice
- 42g (2 tablespoons) honey
- 28g (2 tablespoons) oil
- 600g (5 cups) whole wheat flour
- 1½ teaspoons salt

1. Make the Dough. In a large bowl, whisk together the starter, water, orange juice, honey, and oil. Add the flour and salt and mix to combine. Finish by hand, mixing until a rough dough forms. Cover with a damp towel and let the dough rest for 1½ to 2 hours.
2. Stretch and Fold. Begin by pulling up on one edge of the dough as high as you can stretch it without tearing, then fold it to the middle of the dough. Give the bowl a quarter-turn and stretch and fold again. Repeat another two times, until you have made one complete rotation of the bowl. Repeat this step three more times, spacing them 30 to 45 minutes apart.
3. Bulk Ferment. Cover the bowl with a damp towel and let the dough rise at room temperature for about 8 hours, or until it no longer looks dense and has doubled in size.
4. Shape. Remove the dough from the bowl and place it on a lightly floured surface. Roll the dough into a 9-by-5-inch rectangle, then roll up the rectangle into a log and tuck the ends underneath. Let it rest for 5 to 10 minutes. Place the log seam-side down in a lightly greased 9-by-5-inch loaf pan.
5. Proof. Cover the dough with a clean towel or shower cap and let rise for 1 to 2 hours, until the dough looks puffy and has risen 1 inch above the rim of the pan. Near the end of the rise, position a rack in the center of the oven and preheat the oven to 375°F.
6. Bake. Uncover the dough and bake for 40 to 45 minutes, until the crust is light golden brown and the bread has reached an internal temperature of 190°F.
7. Cool. Transfer the bread to a wire rack to cool for at least 2 hours before slicing.

Focaccia Picnic Sandwiches

Warm or cold, serve these summer sandwiches. Melted cheese helps them stay together, making them perfect for travel, picnics, and housewarming gifts.

Prep time: 35 minutes | Cook time: 35 minutes | Serves 1 large loaf (makes about 16 small sandwiches)

FOR THE STARTER
- 15 grams sourdough starter (1 tablespoon) or ⅛ teaspoon instant yeast
- 60 grams water (¼ cup plus 3 tablespoons)
- 60 grams all-purpose flour (⅔ cup)

FOR THE DOUGH
- 370 grams warm water, divided (1½ cups plus 1 tablespoon)
- 15 grams white cane sugar or honey (1 tablespoon)
- 2 grams instant yeast (½ teaspoon)
- 100 grams starter (about ½ cup)
- 450 grams all-purpose flour (3 cups plus 3½ tablespoons)
- 50 grams whole-wheat flour (⅓ cup)
- 11 grams salt (1½ teaspoons)
- 40 grams olive oil, plus more for the pan (3½ tablespoons)

FOR THE TOP
- 20 to 30 grams olive oil or avocado oil (2 to 3 tablespoons)
- 10 to 15 grams coarse sea salt (1 to 2 teaspoons)
- FOR THE FILLING
- 30 to 60 grams pesto (2 to 4 tablespoons)
- 125 grams mozzarella cheese, grated (1½ cups, loosely filled)
- 1 tomato, thinly sliced

1. Make the starter: About 6 to 10 hours before mixing your dough, mix together the starter or yeast, water, and flour in a bowl. Cover and leave at room temperature until doubled in volume and bubbly.
2. Weigh the ingredients: Making sure to tare after each addition, combine 360 grams of warm water, the sugar, instant yeast, and starter in a large bowl. Let the sugar dissolve, then add the all-purpose flour and whole-wheat flour.
3. Mix: Stir the ingredients together until a shaggy dough forms. Add the salt and oil. Pour the remaining 10 grams of water over the salt to dissolve it. Mix to combine.
4. Fold: Stretch and fold the dough by hand for 8 to 10 minutes or 3 to 8 minutes using a dough hook in a stand mixer, until the dough no longer sticks to the sides of the bowl and pulls away easily.
5. Bulk ferment: Place the dough in a clean bowl, cover, and ferment for 1½ to 2 hours, until doubled in volume.
6. Shape: Spread about 1 tablespoon of oil (avocado or olive) on parchment paper with your fingertips. Place the dough on the oiled parchment, then gently spread it out with oiled fingertips into a 10-inch circle with uniform thickness. If the dough resists shaping, leave it to rest for 10 minutes.
7. Proof: Proof for 30 to 60 minutes at room temperature.
8. Preheat: After 30 minutes of proofing, preheat the oven to 475°F with a steam pan filled with water on a lower rack and a baking stone on the center rack.
9. Top the focaccia: Before baking, top the dough with the oil; use your fingertips to make dimples in the top of the dough. Sprinkle coarse salt on top to taste.
10. Bake: Use a bread peel or baking sheet to transfer the focaccia and parchment onto the preheated baking stone. (Bake directly on a baking sheet if not using a stone.) Close the oven door and reduce the temperature to 450°F. Bake for 25 to 30 minutes, until golden brown. Remove the steam pan after 10 minutes.
11. Cool: Allow to cool for 30 to 60 minutes.
12. Preheat: Preheat the oven to 400°F.
13. Cut the bread: Once the bread is cool enough to handle, cut into four large pieces. Turn each piece of bread onto its cut side and slice through the middle to divide the top from the bottom.
14. Assemble the sandwiches: Place the four bottom pieces of cut focaccia on a large piece of aluminum foil. Spread half of the pesto on the bottom layer of focaccia bread. Add the mozzarella and tomato slices. Spread the rest of the pesto on the underside of the top pieces, place them on top, and wrap the aluminum foil around the sandwiches to seal.
15. Heat the sandwiches: Place the wrapped sandwiches in the oven for 8 to 12 minutes.
16. Finish slicing the sandwiches and serve: Remove the sandwiches from the oven and carefully unwrap. Cut the sandwiches into quarters so that there are 16 small sandwiches total. Serve.

Marbled Rye Sandwich Bread

Marbled rye's sour flavor makes it a popular sandwich bread. This bread is perfect for a summer picnic. Rye has less gluten, thus kneading is ineffectual. Mix the dough well.

Prep time: 50 minutes | Cook time: 35 minutes | Serves 1 loaf

FOR THE STARTER

- 30 grams sourdough starter (2 tablespoons) or ⅛ teaspoon instant yeast
- 15 grams white cane sugar (1 tablespoon)
- 50 grams water (3½ tablespoons)
- 100 grams all-purpose flour (⅔ cup)

FOR THE DOUGH

- 120 grams milk (¼ cup plus 3 tablespoons)
- 205 grams warm water, divided (¾ cup plus 1¾ tablespoons)
- 150 grams starter (about ¾ cup)
- 200 grams rye flour (1⅓ cups)
- 300 grams all-purpose flour (2 cups)
- 30 grams molasses (2 tablespoons)
- 5 grams caraway seeds (2 teaspoons)
- 10 grams sea salt (1½ teaspoons)
- 10 grams cacao powder (1 tablespoon)

1. **Make the starter:** About 8 to 12 hours before mixing your dough, combine the starter or yeast, sugar, water, and flour in a clean container. Cover and leave at room temperature. It will increase in volume and become bubbly.
2. **Warm the milk:** Heat the milk until it reaches a temperature of 115°F to 120°F.
3. **Weigh the ingredients:** Making sure to tare after each addition, combine 100 grams of warm milk, 190 grams of warm water, 150 grams of starter, the rye flour, all-purpose flour, molasses, and caraway seeds in a mixing bowl.
4. **Mix:** Mix the ingredients together until a shaggy dough forms, then add the salt. Add the remaining 10 grams of water to dissolve the salt. Mix until well combined, being careful not to overmix.
5. **Divide the dough:** Divide the dough in half (about 512 grams per half). Place one half in a separate bowl and cover.
6. **Mix in the cacao powder:** Add the cacao powder and the remaining 5 grams of water to the remaining half of the dough. Mix well until all the cacao powder is incorporated into the dough to create a darker-hued dough, then cover.
7. **Bulk ferment:** Ferment both bowls of dough in a warm place for 3 to 6 hours, until doubled in volume.
8. **Prepare a loaf pan:** Line a loaf pan with parchment trimmed to fit or liberally grease the loaf pan.
9. **Shape:** Lightly flour a work surface. Divide the lighter colored dough in half. Using a rolling pin, roll one of the halves into a 10-by-12-inch rectangular shape. Divide the darker colored dough in half. Take one of the halves and roll out to the same size, then lay it on top of the rolled-out lighter dough. Repeat with the second half of each dough so that you have four layers with dark and light dough alternating. Take the short (10-inch) side of the dough and roll the dough into a cylinder. Press or pinch the seam to seal and place the dough seam-side down. Press the coiled ends down and seal them to the bottom of the loaf. Place the shaped dough in the prepared loaf pan.
10. **Proof:** Cover and proof for 1½ to 3 hours, until the dough rises to the top of the loaf pan.
11. **Preheat:** About 20 to 30 minutes before the proofing is done, put a steam pan filled with water on the bottom oven rack and preheat the oven to 500°F.
12. **Bake:** Place the loaf pan in the oven and quickly spray the oven walls with water. Reduce the oven temperature to 450°F and bake for 20 minutes. Remove the steam pan and bake for 15 to 20 minutes longer, until the loaf is a deep brown color. If the top is browning too quickly, tent aluminum foil over the top of the pan.
13. **Cool:** Place the loaf on a cooling rack and cool for at least 1 hour before slicing.

Sesame Spelt Sandwich Bread

This sandwich bread has a soft dough, substantial oven spring, and moist crumb from spelt flour. Sesame seeds give crispness before baking.

Prep time: 35 minutes | Cook time: 45 minutes | Serves One 8-inch loaf

- 50g (¼ cup) active starter
- 400g (1⅔ cups) whole milk
- 28g (2 tablespoons) unsalted butter, melted
- 42g (2 tablespoons) honey
- 4½ cups (500g) spelt flour
- 1½ teaspoons salt
- 36g (4 tablespoons) sesame seeds, divided

1. Make the Dough. In a large bowl, whisk together the starter, milk, melted butter, and honey. Add the flour and salt and mix to combine. Finish by hand, until a rough dough forms. Cover with a damp towel and let the dough rest for 30 minutes.
2. Add the Sesame Seeds. Mix in 3 tablespoons of sesame seeds until evenly distributed. Cover again and let the dough rest for 1 to 1½ hours.
3. Stretch and Fold. Begin by pulling up on one edge of the dough as high as you can stretch it without tearing and fold it in the middle of the dough. Give the bowl a quarter-turn and stretch and fold again. Repeat another two times, until you have made one complete rotation of the bowl. Repeat this step three more times, spacing them 30 minutes apart.
4. Bulk Ferment. Cover the bowl with a damp towel and let the dough rise at room temperature for 6 to 8 hours, until doubled in size and the top is domed.
5. Shape. Remove the dough from the bowl and place it on a lightly floured work surface. Roll the dough into an 8-by-4-inch rectangle, then roll up the rectangle into a log and tuck the ends underneath. Let it rest for 5 to 10 minutes. Place the log seam-side down in a lightly greased 8½-by-4½-inch loaf pan. Sprinkle the remaining 1 tablespoon of sesame seeds on top.
6. Proof. Cover the dough with a clean towel or shower cap and let rise for 1½ hours to 2 hours, until it has risen above the sides of the pan. Near the end of the rise, position a rack in the center of the oven and preheat the oven to 375°F.
7. Bake. Uncover the dough and bake for 40 to 45 minutes, until the crust is golden brown and the bread has reached an internal temperature of 190°F.
8. Cool. Let the bread cool in the pan for 10 minutes, then transfer the loaf to a wire rack to cool for at least 2 hours before slicing.

Oatmeal Sandwich Bread

Rich, tender sandwich loaf prepared with whole wheat flour, rolled oats, and molasses. Make avocado toast or grilled cheese with this hearty sourdough bread.

Prep time: 35 minutes | Cook time: 45 minutes | Serves One 9-inch loaf

- 100g (½ cup) active starter
- 240g (1 cup) water
- 240g (1 cup) whole milk
- 85g (¼ cup) molasses
- 28g (2 tablespoons) unsalted butter, melted
- 300g (2½ cups) whole wheat flour
- 240g (2 cups) bread flour
- 89g (1 cup) rolled oats, plus more for sprinkling on top
- 2 teaspoons salt
- Egg wash; 1 large egg white beaten with 1 tablespoon water

1. Make the Dough. In a large bowl, whisk together the starter, water, milk, molasses, and melted butter. Add both flours, the oats, and salt and mix to combine. Finish by hand, mixing until a rough dough forms. Cover the bowl and let the dough rest for 1½ to 2 hours.
2. Stretch and Fold. Begin by pulling up on one edge of the dough as high as you can stretch it without tearing and fold it in the middle of the dough. Give the bowl a quarter-turn and stretch and fold again. Repeat another two times, until you have made one complete rotation of the bowl. Repeat this step three more times, spacing them about 30 minutes apart.
3. Bulk Ferment. Cover the bowl with a damp towel and let the dough rise at room temperature for 8 to 12 hours, until it is doubled in size with a smooth, domed top.
4. Shape. Remove the dough from the bowl and place it on a lightly floured work surface. Roll the dough into a 9-by-5-inch rectangle, then roll up the rectangle into a log and tuck the ends underneath. Let it rest for 5 to 10 minutes. Place the log seam-side down in a lightly greased 9-by-5-inch loaf pan.
5. Proof. Cover the dough with a clean towel or shower cap and let rise for 1½ hours to 2 hours, until it has risen about 1 inch above the rim of the pan. Near the end of the rise, position a rack in the center of the oven and preheat the oven to 375°F.
6. Make the Topping. Uncover the dough and brush the risen loaf with the egg wash and sprinkle rolled oats on top.
7. Bake. Bake for 40 to 45 minutes, until the crust is golden brown and the bread has reached an internal temperature of 190°F.
8. Cool. Let the bread cool in the pan for 10 minutes, then transfer the loaf to a wire rack to cool for at least 2 hours before slicing.

Honey Kamut Sandwich Bread

Kamut flour is processed from Khorasan wheat, an ancient Egyptian grain. Like me, you'll enjoy the taste. Kamut makes soft, sweet sourdough with a delicate flavor. In this recipe, I blend Kamut flour with honey to bring out its natural sweetness, yielding a delicately nutty sandwich bread with a gorgeous golden color.

Prep time: 35 minutes | Cook time: 45 minutes | Serves One 8-inch loaf

- 100g (½ cup) active starter
- 210g (¾ cup + 2 tablespoons) water
- 42g (2 tablespoons) honey
- 28g (2 tablespoons) olive oil
- 152g (1¼ cups) bread flour
- 198g (1½ cups) Kamut flour
- 1 teaspoon salt

1. Make the Dough. In a large bowl, whisk together the starter, water, honey, and oil. Add both flours and the salt and mix to combine. Finish by hand, until a rough dough forms. Cover with a damp towel and let the dough rest for 30 minutes to 1 hour.
2. Stretch and Fold. Begin by pulling up on one edge of the dough as high as you can stretch it without tearing and fold it in the middle of the dough. Give the bowl a quarter-turn and stretch and fold again. Repeat another two times, until you have made one complete rotation of the bowl. Repeat this step three more times, spacing them about 30 minutes apart.
3. Bulk Ferment. Cover the bowl with a damp towel and let the dough rise at room temperature for 8 to 10 hours, until it is doubled in size and looks smooth and domed.
4. Shape. Remove the dough from the bowl and place it on a lightly floured work surface. Roll the dough into an 8-by-4-inch rectangle, then roll up the rectangle into a log and tuck the ends underneath. Let it rest for 5 to 10 minutes. Place the log seam-side down in a lightly greased 8½-by-4½-inch loaf pan.
5. Proof. Cover the dough with a clean towel or shower cap and let rise for 1½ to 2 hours, until the dough has risen about 1 inch above the rim of the pan. Near the end of the rise, position a rack in the center of the oven and preheat the oven to 375°F.
6. Bake. Uncover the dough and bake for 40 to 45 minutes, until the crust is lightly golden and the bread has an internal temperature of 190°F.
7. Cool. Let the bread cool in the pan for 10 minutes, then transfer the loaf to a wire rack to cool for at least 2 hours before slicing.

Muffaletta-Style Pizza

In 1906, Lupo Salvatore created the muffaletta sandwich, which is filled with Italian charcuterie and Creole olive salad. This is my pizza-inspired spin on the traditional recipe.

Prep time: 15 minutes | Cook time: 2 hours 15 minutes | Serves 2 (8½-inch) pizzas

- 1 pizza crust recipe (dough only)
- Sesame seeds, for sprinkling
- 60g (¼ cup) pimiento-stuffed olives, chopped
- 80g (¼ cup) jarred roasted red peppers, drained and chopped
- 65g (¼ cup) giardiniera, drained well and chopped
- 2½g (1 teaspoon) capers, rinsed and drained well
- 1 shallot, finely chopped (about 25g)
- 12g (1 tablespoon) olive oil, plus more for brushing
- 2½g (½ teaspoon) red wine vinegar
- Salt
- 34g (¼ cup) roughly chopped ham
- 34g (¼ cup) roughly chopped salami
- 34g (¼ cup) roughly chopped mortadella (optional)
- 112g (1 cup) shredded provolone

1. Make The Dough: Follow Pizza Crust recipe to create the pizza dough, using the measurements on that page.
2. Shape: Divide the dough into two equal pieces. Lightly dust a piece of parchment paper with High-Protein Flour and transfer one of the dough portions onto it. Sprinkle generously with sesame seeds and, using your fingertips or a rolling pin, press the dough into a circle about 8½ inches across and ¼ inch thick.
3. Proof: Cover loosely with plastic wrap and proof at room temperature until the dough is puffy, about 30 minutes.
4. Preheat: Place an inverted rimmed baking sheet on the bottom rack of the oven and preheat to 450°F.
5. Bake: Working one pizza at a time, slide the dough with its parchment paper onto the preheated baking sheet and bake until puffy, golden, and crisp on the bottom, about 8 minutes. Repeat with the remaining dough.
6. Make The Sauce: Meanwhile, in a medium bowl, combine the olives, red peppers, giardiniera, capers, shallots, olive oil, and vinegar. Season with salt to taste.
7. Bake The Muffaletta Pizzas: Brush each pizza crust with olive oil and spread with half of the sauce, leaving a ½-inch border. Top each with half of the ham, salami, mortadella (if using), and provolone. Place the pizzas directly on the preheated baking sheet and bake until the cheese is melted, 6 to 8 minutes.
8. Cool: Cool slightly, about 5 minutes, on a wire rack, then transfer each pizza to a cutting board and, using a pizza cutter or serrated knife, cut each round into four pieces.

Grilled Pizzas

Grilled pizzas are a great twist on an old favorite and can be made in the summer without turning on the oven.

Prep time: 55 minutes | Cook time: 2 to 3 minutes per pizza | Serves 8 small pizzas

FOR THE DOUGH
- 300 grams warm water, divided (1¼ cups plus 1 teaspoon)
- 2 grams instant yeast (½ teaspoon)
- 6 grams white cane sugar (1 teaspoon)
- 450 grams bread flour (3 cups plus 3½ tablespoons)
- 50 grams whole-wheat flour (⅓ cup)
- 10 grams sea salt (1½ teaspoons)

FOR THE GRILL
- ½ cup oil with high smoke point (e.g., avocado, ghee, vegetable)

FOR THE TOPPINGS
- ¼ to ½ cup pizza sauce
- 16 ounces low-moisture mozzarella cheese, shredded
- 4 ounces pepperoni
- 2 ounces Parmesan cheese, freshly grated
- 2 teaspoons oregano, dried

1. **Weigh the ingredients:** Making sure to tare your mixing bowl after each addition, combine 290 grams of water, the yeast, and the sugar. Allow the yeast to dissolve, then add the bread flour and whole-wheat flour.
2. **Mix:** Using a spoon or dough hook in a stand mixer, mix together until a shaggy dough forms.
3. **Add the salt:** Tare the bowl. Pour in the salt. Add the remaining 10 grams of water on top of the salt to dissolve. Mix to combine.
4. **Knead:** Knead the dough by hand for 8 to 12 minutes or with a dough hook in a stand mixer for 4 to 8 minutes, until the dough no longer sticks to the sides of the bowl and pulls away easily.
5. **Bulk ferment:** Cover the dough and leave it in a warm place to ferment for 1½ to 2 hours, until doubled in volume.
6. **Preheat the grill:** Preheat the grill until it is a steady 500°F. (Note: Once baking starts, the grill will not stay at 500°F and would be too hot if kept at that temperature. You will be aiming to maintain a range of 350°F to 400°F while baking—400°F is optimal.)
7. **Divide the dough:** Turn the dough out onto a work surface and divide into 8 pieces (about 100 grams each). Roll each piece into a ball. Cover the dough balls with a cloth.
8. **Prep the grill transfer tools:** Cut two large squares of parchment paper and place each on a baking sheet. Put the high-heat oil in a bowl and get a grill marinade brush ready (an alternative would be a spray bottle made for cooking oil).
9. **Roll the dough:** Lightly flour your work surface. Roll each ball of dough until it is a 7- to 8-inch-wide circle. Place the discs of rolled dough on the parchment sheets.
10. **Prebake the pizza crusts:** Once the grill is at temperature and the ingredients are all prepared, brush the oil (prepared in step 8) on the tops of the rolled-out pizza crusts and grill grates. Place 2 or 3 crusts on the grill, oil-side down. Close the grill lid and grill for 30 seconds. Open the lid, quickly brush the tops of the dough with the oil, and flip them using a metal spatula. Close the grill lid again and cook for 30 more seconds. Open the lid and transfer the pizza crusts back onto the parchment paper–lined baking sheet. Repeat with the rest of the pizza dough.
11. **Top the pizzas:** Once all the crusts have prebaked, top them with the pizza sauce and other toppings as desired. For a flavorful pepperoni pizza, top with about 1 tablespoon of pizza sauce, 2 to 3 tablespoons of mozzarella, 2 to 4 pepperoni slices, a generous sprinkling of Parmesan, and ¼ teaspoon of oregano.
12. **Bake:** Place 2 or 3 topped pizzas on the grill, close the lid, and bake for 1 minute. Keep an eye on the bottoms of the crusts to avoid burning. Open the lid, remove the pizzas, and repeat.
13. **Cool:** Allow the pizzas to cool for 5 to 15 minutes before slicing.

Chapter 10
Sweets and Treats for Leftover Starter

Coconut Sourdough Pancakes

Coconut is sweet for some. The sourdough starter makes this recipe unsweet. If you hate coconut, use normal milk instead. Vanilla can replace coconut extract. Adding sugar is optional.

Prep time: 15 minutes | Cook time: 2 minutes per batch | Serves 10 pancakes

FOR ACTIVATING THE STARTER
- 4¾ ounces (½ cup) sourdough starter
- 4 ounces (½ cup) lukewarm (90°F to 100°F) pure filtered or bottled water
- 4 ounces (1 cup) whole-wheat flour or buckwheat flour

FOR THE PANCAKE BATTER
- 4¼ ounces (1 cup) unbleached all-purpose flour
- 1 teaspoon baking soda
- ½ teaspoon fine sea salt
- 1 ounce (½ cup) flaked coconut
- 9½ ounces (1 cup) active sourdough starter
- 2 tablespoons butter, melted and cooled
- 1 egg
- 6 ounces (¾ cup) coconut milk
- ½ teaspoon coconut extract

TO ACTIVATE THE STARTER
- At least 6 to 12 hours before making the dough, in a medium bowl, combine the starter, lukewarm water, and flour, completely incorporating the ingredients into the starter. Loosely cover and let sit on the counter until ready to use.

TO MAKE THE PANCAKE BATTER
1. In a small bowl, stir together the flour, baking soda, salt, and coconut and set it aside.
2. In a large bowl, stir together the active starter, butter, egg, coconut milk, and coconut extract.
3. Add the dry ingredients to the wet ingredients and stir until just combined.
4. Preheat a cast iron skillet or a griddle over medium to medium-high heat. Sprinkle a couple drops of water onto the cooking surface. When the water sizzles, it's time to cook the pancakes. Pour in ½ cup of pancake batter for each pancake.
5. Cook until you see bubbles around the edges, then flip. Cook until the pancakes easily slide around the pan. You can lift one edge to peek and make sure they are not burning. Set the cooked pancakes on a plate and cover with paper towels to keep warm. If they do cool slightly, microwave them for about 10 seconds, or use a 250°F oven to keep them warm. Place an aluminum foil-covered baking sheet with an oven-safe dinner plate on it in the oven. Add the pancakes as needed and cover the plate with a clean kitchen towel.
6. Repeat with the remaining batter (it should make 10 pancakes, but if the coconut isn't used, there will be fewer). Serve these pancakes topped with a pat of butter and warm pure maple syrup.

Pecan Waffles

No more breakfast waffles! Pecan waffles with strawberries and whipped cream are a 24-hour breakfast staple. After a night out, have coffee and dessert. Adding vanilla ice cream at home won't hurt either.

Prep time: 10 minutes | Cook time: 5 minutes | Serves 4 to 6 belgian waffles

FOR ACTIVATING THE STARTER
- 4¾ ounces (½ cup) sourdough starter
- 4 ounces (½ cup) lukewarm (90°F to 100°F) pure filtered or bottled water
- 4 ounces (1 cup) whole-wheat, buckwheat, or (scant 1 cup) unbleached all-purpose flour

FOR THE WAFFLE BATTER
- 3⅓ ounces (¾ cup) chopped pecans (optional)
- 5⅓ ounces (1¼ cups) unbleached all-purpose flour, or whole-wheat flour, or a combination
- 1 tablespoon sugar
- 2 teaspoons baking powder
- ½ teaspoon baking soda
- ½ teaspoon fine sea salt
- 9½ ounces (1 cup) active sourdough starter
- 4 ounces (1 stick) butter, melted and slightly cooled, plus more for serving
- 4 ounces (½ cup) milk
- 2 eggs
- Nonstick cooking spray, for preparing the waffle iron
- Pure maple syrup, for serving

TO ACTIVATE THE STARTER
- At least 6 to 12 hours before making the dough, in a medium bowl, combine the starter, lukewarm water, and flour, completely incorporating the ingredients into the starter. Loosely cover and let sit on the counter until ready to use.

TO MAKE THE WAFFLE BATTER
1. Toast the pecans in the microwave on high power for 1 minute. Add 30 seconds if you can't smell them yet. Alternately, toast the pecans in a 350°F oven for 5 to 7 minutes. Let the pecans cool while you make the waffle batter.
2. In a small bowl, whisk the flour, sugar, baking powder, baking soda, and salt. Set aside.
3. In a large bowl, whisk the active starter, butter, milk, and eggs.
4. Heat the waffle iron according to the manufacturer's directions. Spray it with cooking spray.
5. Ladle ⅓ cup of batter onto the iron. Sprinkle 2 tablespoons of toasted pecans on top of the batter (if using). Close the lid and cook until golden brown. A good indication the waffle is almost done is when it stops steaming.
6. Repeat with the remaining batter.
7. Serve with butter and syrup. Peanut butter or other nut butters make tasty additions, too, plus they add a little protein to the meal.

Sourdough Chocolate Chip Cookies with Several Flavor Variations

The sourdough is a great addition because it balances out the sweetness and gives the dish a unique flavor.

Prep time: 30 minutes | Cook time: 15 minutes | Serves 36 Cookies

FOR ACTIVATING THE STARTER

- 4¾ ounces (½ cup) sourdough starter
- 4 ounces (½ cup) lukewarm (90°F to 100°F) pure filtered or bottled water
- 4 ounces (1 cup) whole-wheat flour or (scant 1 cup) unbleached all-purpose

FOR THE COOKIE DOUGH

- 8 ounces (1¾ cups) chopped pecans, lightly toasted and still warm
- 2 teaspoons fine sea salt, divided
- 19 ounces (4½ cups) unbleached all-purpose flour
- 2 teaspoons baking soda
- 1 pound (4 sticks) butter, at room temperature
- 14 ounces (2 cups) tightly packed brown sugar
- 5¼ ounces (¾ cup) granulated sugar
- 2 teaspoons vanilla extract
- 4 large eggs
- 9½ ounces (1 cup) active sourdough starter
- 24 ounces (4 cups) semisweet chocolate chips
- Nonstick cooking spray, for preparing the baking sheets

TO ACTIVATE THE STARTER

- At least 6 to 12 hours before making the dough, in a medium bowl, combine the starter, lukewarm water, and flour, completely incorporating the ingredients into the starter. Loosely cover and let sit on the counter until ready to use.

TO MAKE THE COOKIE DOUGH

1. While the toasted pecans are still warm, sprinkle with 1 teaspoon of salt and mix it in. Set the pecans aside.
2. In a medium bowl, whisk the flour, baking soda, and remaining 1 teaspoon of salt. Set aside.
3. In the bowl of a stand mixer fitted with the flat paddle attachment, or a large bowl and using a handheld electric mixer, cream together the butter, brown sugar, and granulated sugar.
4. Add the vanilla, then one at a time, add the eggs, mixing until each is incorporated before adding the next.
5. Add the active starter and mix until fully incorporated.
6. With your mixer running on low speed (so the flour stays in the bowl!), gradually add ½ cup of the flour mixture. Continue adding ½-cup portions of the flour mixture until it is all incorporated into the dough.
7. By hand, stir in the chocolate chips and pecans.
8. Preheat the oven to 375°F. Lightly coat two large baking sheets with cooking spray or cover them with parchment paper. Silicone mats are good, too—whatever works.
9. Scoop ⅛-cup (a coffee scoop) or heaping-tablespoon portions of dough onto the prepared baking sheets. The cookies will spread as they cook so don't put them too close together.
10. Place one sheet on the upper rack and one on the lower rack. Bake for 10 to 12 minutes, rotating the baking sheets halfway through the baking time from one shelf to the other and turning them 180 degrees (front to back). Use your nose—if the cookies are done, you'll smell them.
11. Transfer the baking sheets to wire racks to cool for 3 minutes. Remove the cookies from the sheets and cool completely on the racks. If stored in a cookie jar with a loose lid, the cookies will stay crispy. If stored in an airtight container, they will become softer.

Sourdough Tropical Carrot Cake

The inclusion of pineapple and coconut takes this cake to the next level, making it superior to standard carrot cakes. The sweetness is mitigated by the sourdough.

Prep time: 25 minutes| Cook time: 55 minutes| Serves 1 (9-by-13-inch) cake

FOR ACTIVATING THE STARTER

- 4¾ ounces (½ cup) sourdough starter
- 4 ounces (½ cup) lukewarm (90°F to 100°F) pure filtered or bottled water
- 4 ounces (1 cup) whole-wheat flour

FOR THE CAKE BATTER

- Nonstick cooking spray, for preparing the baking pan
- 8½ ounces (2 cups) unbleached all-purpose flour, plus more for preparing the baking pan
- 14 ounces (2 cups) sugar
- 1 teaspoon fine sea salt
- 1 teaspoon baking soda
- 9½ ounces (1 cup) active sourdough starter
- 8 ounces (1 cup) vegetable oil
- 4 eggs
- 8 ounces (2 cups) grated carrots
- 1 (20-ounce) can crushed pineapple, drained

FOR THE ICING

- 3 ounces (6 tablespoons) cream cheese, at room temperature
- 2 ounces (¼ cup) butter, at room temperature
- 9 ounces (2 cups) powdered sugar
- 1 teaspoon vanilla extract
- 2.2 ounces (½ cup) chopped pecans, lightly toasted (see Pecan Waffles)
- 1 ounce (½ cup) flaked coconut

TO ACTIVATE THE STARTER

- At least 6 to 12 hours before making the dough, in a medium bowl, combine the starter, lukewarm water, and flour, completely incorporating the ingredients into the starter. Loosely cover and let sit on the counter until ready to use.

TO MAKE THE CAKE BATTER

1. Preheat the oven to 325°F. Coat a 9-by-13-inch baking pan with cooking spray and flour the pan, knocking out any excess flour.
2. In a medium bowl, whisk the flour, sugar, salt, and baking soda.
3. In a large bowl, stir together the active starter, vegetable oil, and eggs.
4. Slowly add the dry ingredients to the wet ingredients, stirring until just mixed. There will be some lumps.
5. Stir in the carrots and pineapple. Pour the cake batter into the prepared pan and bake for 55 minutes, or until a toothpick inserted into the center comes out clean.
6. Transfer the pan to a wire rack and let the cake cool completely.

TO MAKE THE ICING

7. Once the cake is completely cool, make the icing: In a large bowl, using an electric handheld mixer, cream together the cream cheese and butter.
8. 2.A little at a time, add the powdered sugar, mixing until all is incorporated.
9. Add the vanilla and mix it in.
10. By hand, stir in the toasted pecans and coconut.
11. Frost the cake with the cream cheese icing. Keep the cake refrigerated until serving and refrigerate any leftovers.

Flavorful Focaccia Bread

Focaccia is Roman. Extra virgin olive oil covers the top. A plain version may just have salt on oil. You can buy fancier versions with many different additives today. Focaccia with cheese and herbs can be a meal in itself. I like fresh rosemary and Parmesan, red onion with salt and pepper, and grape tomatoes with feta. Choices abound.

Prep time: 1 hour and 25 minutes| Cook time: 35 minutes| Serves 12 pieces

FOR ACTIVATING THE STARTER
- 4¾ ounces (½ cup) sourdough starter
- 4 ounces (½ cup) lukewarm (90°F to 100°F) pure filtered or bottled water
- 4 ounces (1 cup) whole-wheat flour

FOR THE FOCACCIA DOUGH
- 2¼ teaspoons active dry yeast
- 12 ounces (1½ cups) warm (100°F to 125°F) pure filtered or bottled water
- 9½ ounces (1 cup) active sourdough starter
- 2 teaspoons fine sea salt
- 1 tablespoon sugar
- 12¾ ounces (3 cups) unbleached all-purpose flour, divided
- 2 tablespoons butter, at room temperature
- 2 tablespoons olive oil, plus more for your hands and the plastic wrap
- Freshly ground Himalayan salt, or other coarse salt
- Freshly ground black pepper

FOR THE TOPPINGS (ALL OPTIONAL DEPENDING ON TASTE)
- Crushed or roasted garlic
- Fresh or dried rosemary, oregano, basil, thyme, sage, marjoram, etc.
- Grated or shredded Parmesan, Romano, or Pecorino cheese
- Shredded sharp Cheddar, blue, feta, fresh mozzarella, or other cheese
- Sliced jalapeño peppers
- Thinly sliced baby portabella mushrooms
- Thinly sliced plum, cherry, or grape tomatoes
- Thinly sliced red onion

TO ACTIVATE THE STARTER
- At least 6 to 12 hours before making the dough, in a medium bowl, combine the starter, lukewarm water, and flour, completely incorporating the ingredients into the starter. Loosely cover and let sit on the counter until ready to use.

TO MAKE THE FOCACCIA DOUGH
1. Early in the day, in a small bowl, sprinkle the yeast over the warm water. Let the yeast bloom for 10 minutes.
2. In a large bowl, stir together the active starter, bloomed yeast, sea salt, sugar, and 2 cups of flour. Once the mixture is well incorporated, add the remaining 1 cup of flour and, in the bowl, knead it in. Cover the bowl with a clean kitchen towel and let rise for 1 hour.
3. Punch down the dough and let it rest for 10 minutes.
4. Generously coat a 9-by-13-inch baking pan or baking sheet with the butter and transfer the dough to it.
5. With well-oiled hands, press the dough down to fill the pan or into a rectangle on the baking sheet until it is about 1 inch thick.
6. Using your middle knuckle, dock (make indentations in) the dough.
7. Drizzle the olive oil over the top of the dough, covering the entire surface.
8. Season the entire top with a few grinds of Himalayan salt and pepper, or choose some of the optional ingredients—alone or in combination.
9. Lightly coat a piece of plastic wrap with olive oil and cover the focaccia with it. Let rise for 30 minutes.
10. Preheat the oven to 425°F.
11. Bake the focaccia for 15 minutes. Reduce the oven temperature to 375°F and bake for 15 minutes more.
12. Transfer the focaccia to a wire rack to cool for 10 minutes before serving.

Sourdough Breadstick Twists

Breadstick twists are popular. Soups, salads, and spaghetti & meatballs go nicely with them. They're a delicious afternoon snack. Try pesto or marinara. Imagine it with beer cheese dip. Yum.

Prep time: 1 hour and 25 minutes | Cook time: 25 minutes | Serves 8 twisted breadsticks

FOR ACTIVATING THE STARTER
- 9½ ounces (1 cup) sourdough starter
- 4 ounces (½ cup) lukewarm (90°F to 100°F) pure filtered or bottled water
- 4 ounces (1 cup) whole-wheat flour, (heaping 1 cup) rye flour, or (1 cup) pumpernickel

FOR THE BREAD DOUGH
- 6¾ ounces (scant 1¾ cups) whole-wheat flour, plus more for dusting
- 1 teaspoon sugar
- 1 teaspoon baking soda
- 1 teaspoon fine sea salt
- 9½ ounces (1 cup) active sourdough starter (refrigerate any remaining starter for future use)
- Nonstick cooking spray, for preparing the baking sheet
- 1 egg white, beaten
- Sesame seeds, for garnishing

TO ACTIVATE THE STARTER
- At least 6 to 12 hours before making the dough, in a medium bowl, combine the starter, lukewarm water, and flour, completely incorporating the ingredients into the starter. Loosely cover and let sit on the counter until ready to use.

TO MAKE THE BREAD DOUGH
1. In a large bowl, stir together the flour, sugar, baking soda, and salt until completely combined.
2. Stir in the active starter. When the dough becomes too difficult to stir, knead the dough, in the bowl, by hand. Cover with a clean kitchen towel and let sit for 1 hour.
3. Lightly flour a breadboard or clean work surface and turn the dough out on to it. Roll the dough around and knead it a few times to remove some of the stickiness. Flatten the dough into a rectangular shape about 10 by 8 inches.
4. Using a floured knife, cut the dough into eight (1-inch-wide) sticks.
5. Lightly coat a baking sheet with cooking spray.
6. Stretch each dough stick to about 1 foot long. Fold them in half, twist, and seal the ends together. Place the twists on the prepared baking sheet.
7. Cover the baking sheet with a clean kitchen towel and place in a warm, draft-free place for 20 minutes.
8. Preheat the oven to 375°F.
9. Brush the bread sticks with the egg white and generously sprinkle with sesame seeds.
10. Bake the bread sticks for 20 to 25 minutes, or until they are golden brown and not too hard.

Sourdough Pizza Dough

Average American eats 46 pizza pieces a year. If you make your own pizza crust, you can make some of those slices yourself. Sourdough starter adds flavor to pizza dough.

Prep time: 2 hours | Cook time: 15 minutes | Serves 1 (12-inch) pizza crust

FOR ACTIVATING THE STARTER
- 14¼ ounces (1½ cups) sourdough starter
- 4 ounces (½ cup) warm (100°F to 125°F) pure filtered or bottled water
- 4 ounces (1 cup) whole-wheat flour

FOR THE PIZZA CRUST DOUGH
- 1 tablespoon olive oil
- 1 teaspoon freshly ground Himalayan salt
- 6½ ounces (1½ cups) unbleached bread flour, divided, plus more for dusting
- Olive oil or nonstick cooking spray, for preparing the bowl
- Cornmeal, for dusting
- Pizza toppings, as desired, such as pizza sauce, grated or shredded cheese, pepperoni, sliced vegetables

TO ACTIVATE THE STARTER
- At least 6 to 12 hours before making the dough, in a medium bowl, combine the starter, lukewarm water, and flour, completely incorporating the ingredients into the starter. Loosely cover and let sit on the counter until ready to use.

TO MAKE THE PIZZA CRUST DOUGH
1. Two hours before making the pizza, in a large bowl, thoroughly mix together the entire amount of activated starter, olive oil, and salt. Add 1 cup of flour, stirring until it's completely incorporated.
2. Lightly flour a breadboard or a clean work surface and turn the dough out on to it. Begin kneading the dough, adding more flour if the dough is too wet. Knead for about 5 minutes. If the dough is still too wet, add a bit more flour. The dough should be soft and a little sticky. If it's really sticky, add more flour, 1 tablespoon at a time. If it's a bit too dry, add 1 tablespoon of water. Shape the dough into a ball.
3. Lightly coat a large bowl with olive oil and transfer the dough to it, turning to coat all sides. Cover the bowl with a plate or plastic wrap and let rest until it's time to make the pizza.
4. Sprinkle a baking stone with cornmeal and place the stone into the oven. Preheat the oven to 450°F.
5. If you don't have a pizza peel, sprinkle cornmeal on a rimless baking sheet or on an inverted sheet pan. Carefully slide the dressed pizza onto the prepared sheet. Very carefully, slide the pizza from the sheet onto the baking stone.
6. Bake the pizza for 10 to 15 minutes, depending on the toppings you've selected.
7. Using oven gloves and a heavy metal spatula, slide the pizza off the stone and back onto the baking sheet.
8. Slice and eat.

Double Piecrust

Adding sourdough starter to this pie dough adds tanginess that balances the pie's richness. For a stronger flavour in a quiche, skip the sugar.

Prep time: 8 hours | Cook time: varies, depending on the baked pie recipe | Serves enough for 2 piecrusts

FOR ACTIVATING THE STARTER
- 2.4 ounces (¼ cup) sourdough starter
- 4 ounces (½ cup) lukewarm (90°F to 100°F) pure filtered or bottled water
- 4 ounces (1 cup) whole-wheat flour

FOR THE PIECRUST DOUGH
- 9½ ounces (1 cup) active sourdough starter
- 8½ ounces (2 cups) unbleached all-purpose flour, or 8 ounces whole-wheat flour, plus more as needed
- 1 tablespoon sugar
- ½ teaspoon fine sea salt
- 12 ounces (3 sticks) cold butter

TO ACTIVATE THE STARTER
- At least 6 to 12 hours before making the dough, in a medium bowl, combine the starter, lukewarm water, and flour, completely incorporating the ingredients into the starter. Loosely cover and let sit on the counter until ready to use.

TO MAKE THE PIECRUST DOUGH
1. After 6 hours, place 9½ ounces (1 cup) of the fed starter into the refrigerator. If keeping the leftover starter, place it in another container.
2. In a medium bowl, stir together the flour, sugar, and salt. Cover the bowl with plastic wrap and place it in the refrigerator.
3. Cut the butter into chunks and place them in a bowl or resealable plastic bag and then back into the refrigerator.
4. Early the next day, place the flour mixture in the food processor. Process a couple of times to make sure it's well mixed.
5. Add the cold butter pieces and process until they're well incorporated and the mixture looks like small peas.
6. Spoon in the active starter, starting with half, and process. Add half of the remaining starter and process. If the mixture has come together into a ball that is not too wet, too sticky, or too dry, the remaining starter may not be needed. If it is too wet, sticky, or dry, add a bit more starter. If that doesn't work, and it's too dry or sticky, add 1 tablespoon or so of water. If it's too wet, add 1 tablespoon of flour.
7. Remove the dough from the bowl of the food processor and form it into a ball. Place the ball in a large bowl. Cover the bowl with plastic wrap and let sit on the kitchen counter for at least 7 hours. If need be, it can sit for up to 12 hours.
8. Divide the dough into two equal halves—eyeball it or use a scale. They don't have to be exact.
9. Flatten the pieces into disks and wrap them in plastic wrap or parchment paper. Refrigerate for at least 1 hour.
10. Roll out the dough and cook according to the filled pie recipe you've chosen.
11. This pie dough will last up to one week if the wrapped disks are put into an airtight container or freezer bag and kept in the refrigerator. They also can be frozen for up to three months in freezer-safe wrapping.

Southern Sourdough Biscuits

Biscuits with sausage gravy are a popular all-in-one dish. Each biscuit half in Eggs Benny is layered with sausage, a poached egg, and sausage gravy. Who needs English muffin ham and hollandaise? Biscuits are also in chicken and dumplings. Biscuits are used in sweets. Why create shortcake when you can use a fluffy biscuit?

Prep time: 15 minutes | Cook time: 10 minutes | Serves 8 biscuits

FOR ACTIVATING THE STARTER
- 2.4 ounces (¼ cup) sourdough starter
- 4 ounces (½ cup) lukewarm (90°F to 100°F) pure filtered or bottled water
- 4 ounces (1 cup) whole-wheat flour

FOR THE BISCUIT DOUGH
- 2½ ounces (5 tablespoons) plus 1 teaspoon cold butter
- 4¼ ounces (1 cup) unbleached all-purpose, or 4 ounces whole-wheat flour, plus more for dusting
- ¾ teaspoon baking soda
- ¼ teaspoon fine sea salt
- 9½ ounces (1 cup) active sourdough starter
- Nonstick cooking spray, for preparing the baking sheet
- Melted butter, for brushing (optional)

TO ACTIVATE THE STARTER
At least 6 to 12 hours before making the dough, in a medium bowl, combine the starter, lukewarm water, and flour, completely incorporating the ingredients into the starter. Loosely cover and let sit on the counter until ready to use.

TO MAKE THE BISCUIT DOUGH
1. Cut the butter into small cubes and place them in a bowl or resealable plastic bag and then back into the refrigerator.
2. In a large bowl, stir together the flour, baking soda, and salt until completely combined.
3. With a pastry cutter or two knives in scissors fashion, cut the cold butter cubes into the flour mixture until the mixture resembles small peas.
4. Stir in the active starter.
5. Flour a breadboard or clean work surface and turn the biscuit dough out on to it. With lightly floured hands, gently knead the biscuit dough five times by folding the dough from one side to the other and from the top to the bottom. Do not overwork the dough or the biscuits will be tough.
6. With floured hands or a floured rolling pin, pat or roll the dough into a rectangular shape ½ inch thick. Cut the dough into 8 squares or use a 2½-inch biscuit or cookie cutter to cut out the biscuit rounds, dipping the knife or cutter into flour before each cut. Do not twist the cutter, as it will seal the edges and the biscuits will not rise in the oven.
7. Preheat the oven to 425°F. Lightly coat a baking sheet with cooking spray, or line it with parchment paper or a silicone baking mat.
8. Place the biscuits on the prepared baking sheet. Bake for 8 to 10 minutes until slightly risen and golden brown on top.
9. Using a pastry brush, paint each warm biscuit with melted butter (if using) as soon as they come out of the oven. Serve warm.

Sourdough Pretzels

Homemade snacks are best. Having a modest party? Watch people fight over these pretzels. No mindless eating—they'll love every bite. This recipe uses unactivated sourdough starter, so it's quicker.

Prep time: 50 minutes | Cook time: 15 minutes | Serves 12 pretzels

- 12¾ ounces (3 cups) unbleached all-purpose flour, plus more for dusting
- 1 ounce (¼ cup) nonfat dry milk
- 1 tablespoon sugar
- 2 teaspoons instant yeast
- 1½ teaspoons fine sea salt
- 9½ ounces (1 cup) unfed sourdough starter
- 6 ounces (¾ cup) lukewarm (90°F to 100°F) pure filtered or bottled water
- 1 tablespoon butter, melted and slightly cooled
- Nonstick cooking spray, for preparing the baking sheets
- 2 tablespoons baking soda
- Freshly ground Himalayan salt

1. In a large bowl, whisk the flour, dry milk, sugar, yeast, and sea salt. Set aside.
2. In the bowl of a stand mixer fitted with the dough hook, or in a large bowl and using a handheld electric mixer, combine the unfed sourdough starter, lukewarm water, and butter. Turn the machine on low.
3. With the mixer running, slowly add the flour mixture. Continue to mix until the ingredients come together in a ball around the dough hook. If using a handheld mixer, mix as long as possible. When the dough becomes too stiff, use your hands or a rubber scraper to incorporate the rest of the flour into the dough. If the dough is too dry, add more water, 1 tablespoon at a time. If the dough is too wet, add flour, 1 tablespoon at a time.
4. Lightly sprinkle flour over the dough ball, cover with a clean kitchen towel, and set aside for 45 minutes in a warm, draft-free place.
5. Preheat the oven to 475°F. Coat two baking sheets with cooking spray.
6. Divide the dough into 12 pieces. The best way to do this is to weigh the dough and divide the weight by 12. Weigh each piece for the correct amount.
7. Roll each portion into a ball. Shape each ball into an 18-inch-long snake. Twist each piece into a pretzel shape, pressing the ends of the pretzels to make sure they stay in shape.
8. Place a wire rack on top of a clean kitchen towel.
9. Fill a medium pot halfway with water and bring to a boil over high heat. Stir in the baking soda.
10. Using tongs, place 2 or 3 pretzels (try not to overcrowd the pot) into the water and cook for 1 minute. Remove them from the water and place on the wire rack. Repeat with the remaining pretzels.
11. Place the boiled pretzels on the prepared baking sheets and sprinkle the pretzels with Himalayan salt.
12. Bake for 12 minutes and cool on wire racks before serving.

Sourdough Cinnamon-Sugar Doughnuts

This doughnut recipe includes sourdough starter. It cuts sugariness. Baking powder and soda also help. Extra leavening shortens rising time.

Prep time: 40 minutes | Cook time: 15 minutes | Serves 12 doughnuts

FOR ACTIVATING THE STARTER
- 2.4 ounces (¼ cup) sourdough starter
- 4 ounces (½ cup) lukewarm (90°F to 100°F) pure filtered or bottled water
- 4 ounces (1 cup) whole-wheat flour

FOR FRYING
- 2 quarts vegetable oil or peanut oil

FOR THE TOPPING
- 7 ounces (1 cup) sugar
- 2 teaspoons ground cinnamon

FOR THE DOUGHNUT DOUGH
- 9 ounces (2 cups) unbleached all-purpose flour, plus more for dusting
- 3½ ounces (½ cup) sugar
- 1 teaspoon baking powder
- ½ teaspoon baking soda
- ½ teaspoon fine sea salt
- 4¾ ounces (½ cup) active sourdough starter
- 1 egg
- 2½ ounces (⅓ cup) buttermilk
- 2 tablespoons vegetable oil
- 4 ounces (½ cup) butter, melted

TO ACTIVATE THE STARTER
- At least 6 to 12 hours before making the dough, in a medium bowl, combine the starter, lukewarm water, and flour, completely incorporating the ingredients into the starter. Loosely cover and let sit on the counter until ready to use.

TO PREPARE FOR FRYING THE DOUGHNUTS
- The morning of making the doughnuts, pour the vegetable oil into a large pot and place it on the stovetop. Don't heat it yet. Cover a wire rack with paper towels and set aside.

TO MAKE THE TOPPING
- In a wide, shallow bowl, stir together the sugar and cinnamon until well mixed. Place it near the prepared wire rack.

TO MAKE THE DOUGHNUT DOUGH
1. In a medium bowl, whisk the flour, sugar, baking powder, baking soda, and salt until combined. Set aside.
2. In a large bowl, stir together the active starter, egg, buttermilk, and vegetable oil.
3. Slowly add the dry ingredients to the wet ingredients, stirring to combine.
4. Turn the heat under the oil to high and let the oil heat to 350°F.
5. Flour a breadboard or clean work surface and turn the dough out on to it. Knead the dough a few times to make sure all the ingredients stay together.
6. With a floured rolling pin, roll the dough ¾ inch thick.
7. Using a doughnut cutter dipped in flour so the dough doesn't stick, cut the dough. Re-roll the dough scraps to cut out the remaining doughnuts. Save the doughnut holes to cook, too.
8. Working with only 2 or 3 doughnuts at a time, carefully place them in the hot oil and fry for 2 to 3 minutes per side. They should be golden brown and fluffy. The doughnut holes will cook a little faster.
9. Using tongs, lift the doughnuts from the oil and quickly dip them into the cinnamon-sugar mixture.
10. Place them on the prepared wire rack to drain.
11. Repeat until all the doughnuts are made.

Roasted Garlic and Cheddar Cheese Bialys

A bialy is the same size and form as a bagel, but they are different. A bialy's hole isn't through. This indentation frequently contains onion or garlic. Savory fillings dominate bialys. Bialys aren't boiled like bagels. Baked bialys are softer and less chewy.

Prep time: 9 hours and 40 minutes | Cook time: 15 minutes | Serves 12 bialys

FOR ACTIVATING THE STARTER
- 4¾ ounces (½ cup) sourdough starter
- 4 ounces (½ cup) lukewarm (90°F to 100°F) pure filtered or bottled water
- 4 ounces (1 cup) whole-wheat flour

FOR THE BIALY DOUGH
- 2.4 ounces (¼ cup) active sourdough starter
- 12 ounces (1½ cups) room temperature (75°F) pure filtered or bottled water
- 17 ounces (4 cups) unbleached all-purpose flour, unbleached bread flour, or whole-wheat flour, or a combination, plus more for dusting
- 1½ teaspoons fine sea salt
- 1 head garlic, roasted, cloves removed from their skins, mashed, and cooled
- 4 ounces (1 cup) grated extra-sharp white Cheddar cheese

TO ACTIVATE THE STARTER
- At least 6 to 12 hours before making the dough, in a medium bowl, combine the starter, lukewarm water, and flour, completely incorporating the ingredients into the starter. Loosely cover and let sit on the counter until ready to use.

TO MAKE THE BIALY DOUGH
1. In a large bowl, stir together the active starter and room temperature water until the starter completely dissolves into the water. Add the flour. Stir for as long as possible, then use your hands to get it to come together. Once the flour is incorporated, cover the bowl with a clean damp kitchen towel and let rest for 30 minutes.
2. Add the salt and, in the bowl, knead it in. Work the dough into a ball. Re-cover the bowl with the damp towel and let sit at room temperature overnight.
3. The next day, flour a breadboard or clean work surface and turn the dough out on to it. Press the dough into a log and shape. Cut the log into 12 even pieces. Roll each piece into a ball and sprinkle each ball with flour. Cover the balls with a clean kitchen towel and let them rest for 1 hour.
4. Preheat the oven to 450°F. Line a baking sheet with parchment paper.
5. Shape the balls into the size of a bagel, but without the hole. Working one at a time, dust the top of a bialy with flour and flip it over. Place it on the prepared baking sheet. Using 3 fingertips, make a deep indention in the top center of the bialy, but not so deep it goes all the way through. Stretch the indention a bit to widen the area. Repeat this with the remaining bialys.
6. Fill each of the indentions with roasted garlic and sprinkle the Cheddar cheese over the tops.
7. Bake for 10 to 12 minutes, or until the bialys are browned.
8. Transfer the bialys to a wire rack to cool. The bialys can be frozen to enjoy at a later time, if desired.

Holiday Fruited Loaf

Don't worry, this isn't a fruitcake. This candy-fruit bread is delicious. It's not a fruit-only cake. It tastes best when toasted and spread with real butter, like julekake.

Prep time: 2 hours and 40 minutes | Cook time: 45 minutes | Serves 1 loaf

FOR ACTIVATING THE STARTER
- 4¾ ounces (½ cup) sourdough starter
- 4 ounces (½ cup) lukewarm (90°F to 100°F) pure filtered or bottled water
- 4 ounces (scant 1 cup) unbleached all-purpose flour, or (1 cup) whole-wheat flour

FOR THE BREAD DOUGH
- 9½ ounces (2¼ cups) unbleached bread flour
- 1½ ounces (¼ cup) instant potato flakes
- 7 ounces (½ cup) sugar
- 2 teaspoons instant yeast, or bread machine yeast
- 1¼ teaspoons fine sea salt
- ½ teaspoon ground cardamom
- 6⅓ ounces (⅔ cup) active sourdough starter
- 6 ounces (¾ cup) lukewarm (90°F to 100°F) milk, plus more for coating the loaf (optional)
- 1 tablespoon butter, melted and cooled
- 1 pound (2 cups) mixed candied fruit
- 1¼ ounces (⅓ cup) old-fashioned rolled oats
- Olive oil or nonstick cooking spray, for preparing the bowl and bread pan

TO ACTIVATE THE STARTER
- At least 6 to 12 hours before making the dough, in a medium bowl, combine the starter, lukewarm water, and flour, completely incorporating the ingredients into the starter. Loosely cover and let sit on the counter until ready to use.

TO MAKE THE BREAD DOUGH
1. In a large bowl, whisk the flour, potato flakes, sugar, yeast, salt, and cardamom until combined. Set aside.
2. In the bowl of a stand mixer fitted with the dough hook, or in another large bowl and using a handheld electric mixer, mix the active starter, milk, and butter on low speed until combined.
3. Add the flour mixture to the sourdough mixture. Mix on low speed (you may have to use a sturdy spoon or spatula if mixing by hand) until combined. When the dough becomes too stiff, use your hands to knead it.
4. Add the candied fruit and oats. By hand, in the bowl (or turn it out onto a floured surface), knead them in until combined. Shape the dough into a ball.
5. Coat another large bowl with olive oil and transfer the dough to it, turning to coat all sides. Cover with a clean kitchen towel and let rise for 90 minutes.
6. Lightly coat an 8½-by-4½-inch bread pan with cooking spray and set aside.
7. Flour a breadboard or clean work surface and turn the dough out on to it. Shape the dough into a rectangle no wider than the prepared bread pan. Roll up the rectangle from one short side and place the dough, seam-side down, into the prepared pan. Re-cover the dough and let the bread rise for another hour.
8. Preheat the oven to 350°F.
9. For a shiny crust, if you like, use a pastry brush to paint the top of the loaf with milk.
10. Bake the bread for 40 to 45 minutes, or until it reaches an internal temperature of 200°F on a digital food thermometer.
11. Transfer the bread to a wire rack to cool in the pan for 5 minutes. Remove the bread from the pan and place it on the wire rack to cool completely before slicing into it.

Chapter 11
Cookies, Brownies, and Bars

Blondies

My kids don't like chocolate, so I needed a "brownie"-type dessert without chocolate. These blondies are as wonderful as brownies. Finish with ice cream. They're great for lunchboxes and traveling.

Prep time: 15 minutes | Cook time: 30 minutes | Serves 12 blondies

- 125 grams all-purpose flour blend
- 1 teaspoon ground cinnamon
- ½ teaspoon baking powder
- ½ teaspoon xanthan gum
- ¼ teaspoon salt
- ⅛ teaspoon baking soda
- 200 grams light brown sugar
- 5 tablespoons butter or nondairy alternative, melted
- 1 tablespoon vanilla extract
- 1 large egg

1. Preheat the oven to 350°F. Line a 9-by-9-inch baking pan with parchment paper, leaving some hanging over each side. This will make the cooked blondies easy to remove.
2. In a medium bowl, whisk the flour, cinnamon, baking powder, xanthan gum, salt, and baking soda.
3. In a large bowl, using a whisk or handheld electric mixer, mix the brown sugar, melted butter, and vanilla until well combined. Add the egg and mix again. Using a spatula, slowly add the flour mixture to the wet ingredients and stir just until combined. The batter will be very thick. Spread the batter evenly in the prepared pan, using the spatula and your fingertips to fill in the corners.
4. Bake for 25 minutes, or until a toothpick inserted into the center of the blondies comes out clean.
5. Let the blondies cool completely before cutting. Keep covered at room temperature for up to 5 days.

Chewy Fudgy Brownies

Make these delectable brownies to dump your gluten-free box mixes. These brownies are better than boxed ones. Ground espresso boosts their flavor.

Prep time: 15 minutes | Cook time: 35 minutes | Serves 16 brownies

- Gluten-free cooking spray
- 93 grams all-purpose flour blend
- 150 grams cane sugar or granulated sugar
- 50 grams light brown sugar
- 25 grams Dutch-process cocoa powder
- ½ teaspoon xanthan gum
- ¼ teaspoon ground espresso
- ¼ teaspoon salt
- 8 tablespoons (1 stick) butter or nondairy alternative, melted
- 180 grams semisweet chocolate chips or nondairy alternative
- 3 large eggs
- 1 teaspoon vanilla extract

1. Preheat the oven to 350°F. Coat a 9-by-9-inch baking pan with cooking spray or line it with parchment paper, leaving some hanging over the edges for easy removal from the pan.
2. In a medium bowl, whisk the flour, cane sugar, brown sugar, cocoa powder, xanthan gum, espresso, and salt to combine.
3. In a small saucepan, melt the butter over low heat. Remove the pan from the heat and stir in the chocolate chips until smooth and melted. Transfer the mixture to a medium bowl and let it cool for 10 minutes. Add the eggs and vanilla and whisk well. Using a spatula, fold the flour mixture into the chocolate mixture just until combined. Transfer the batter to the prepared baking pan and spread it evenly. This batter will be thick.
4. Bake for 30 to 32 minutes, or until a toothpick inserted into the center of the brownies comes out clean.
5. Let the brownies cool before cutting them into squares. Keep covered at room temperature for up to 4 days.

Salted Caramel Brownies

I love sweet-and-salty combinations. These fudgy brownies with caramel sauce are fantastic. Below are three additional fun topping possibilities.

Prep time: 35 minutes | Cook time: 50 minutes | Serves 16 brownies

FOR THE BROWNIES
- Gluten-free cooking spray
- 93 grams all-purpose flour blend
- 150 grams cane sugar or granulated sugar
- 50 grams light brown sugar
- 25 grams Dutch-process cocoa powder
- ½ teaspoon xanthan gum
- ¼ teaspoon salt
- 8 tablespoons (1 stick) butter or nondairy alternative
- 180 grams semisweet chocolate chips or nondairy alternative
- 3 large eggs
- 1 teaspoon vanilla extract

FOR THE SALTED CARAMEL SAUCE
- 200 grams cane sugar or granulated sugar
- 6 tablespoons butter or nondairy alternative
- ½ cup heavy cream or coconut cream
- 1 teaspoon salt

TO MAKE THE BROWNIES
1. Preheat the oven to 350°F. Coat a 9-by-9-inch baking pan with cooking spray or line it with parchment paper, leaving some hanging over the sides. This will make the brownies easy to remove.
2. In a small bowl, whisk the flour, cane sugar, brown sugar, cocoa powder, xanthan gum, and salt to combine.
3. In a small saucepan, melt the butter over low heat. Remove from the heat and stir in the chocolate chips until they are melted and smooth. Transfer the mixture to a large bowl and let it cool for 10 minutes.
4. Add the eggs and vanilla to the chocolate mixture and, using a whisk or handheld electric mixer, mix well to combine.
5. Using a spatula, fold in the flour mixture just until combined. This batter will be thick. Transfer the batter to the prepared baking pan and spread it evenly.
6. Bake for 30 to 32 minutes, or until a toothpick inserted into the center of the brownies comes out clean.
7. Let the brownies cool.
8. **TO MAKE THE SALTED CARAMEL SAUCE**
9. In a small saucepan, melt the cane sugar over medium heat, stirring constantly. If your sugar is not melting, increase the heat just a bit. Keep stirring so the sugar does not burn (this can happen quickly).
10. Once the sugar begins to melt, reduce the heat. Keep stirring until the sugar is completely melted. Remove the pan from the heat and slowly add the butter, being careful not to splatter hot sugar everywhere. Keep stirring as the butter melts.
11. Slowly stir in the cream. Place the pan over medium-low heat. When everything is melted together, increase the heat and bring the mixture to a boil. Boil for 1 to 2 minutes, until slightly thickened. Remove the saucepan from the heat giving it one or two more stirs. Stir in the salt.
12. Gently pour as much or as little of the caramel sauce as you want over the brownies. Let set for 5 minutes or more.
13. Slice and serve the brownies. Keep the brownies covered at room temperature for up to 2 days. If the caramel melts because of humidity, refrigerate the brownies. If there is caramel sauce left, let it cool (it will thicken as it cools), transfer to an airtight glass container, and refrigerate for up to 1 month.

Coconut Macaroons

Delicious and easy coconut macaroons. Choose almond or orange extract for delicious, chewy cookies. Better cookies have finer coconut flakes.

Prep time: 45 minutes | Cook time: 15 minutes per batch | Serves 18 macaroons

- 42 grams all-purpose flour blend
- ¼ teaspoon xanthan gum
- ¼ teaspoon salt
- 1 (7.4-ounce) can sweetened condensed coconut milk
- ½ teaspoon orange extract or almond extract
- 1 teaspoon vanilla extract
- 1 large egg white, beaten
- 100 grams unsweetened coconut flakes

1. In a small bowl, whisk the flour, xanthan gum, and salt to combine.
2. In a medium bowl, whisk the condensed milk and extracts. Add the beaten egg white and whisk to combine. Stir in the flour mixture and coconut flakes, mixing well. Cover the bowl with plastic wrap and refrigerate for 30 minutes.
3. Preheat the oven to 350°F. Line 2 baking sheets with parchment paper or silicone baking mats.
4. Using a 1-inch ice cream scoop, scoop the macaroons onto the prepared baking sheets. Smooth the bottom edges.
5. Baking one batch at a time, bake for 12 to 15 minutes, or until the coconut looks slightly toasted.
6. Let the cookies cool on the pan for at least 10 minutes, then gently transfer to a wire rack to cool completely. Keep covered and at room temperature for up to 5 days.

Pumpkin Everything Squares

Here's a new way to use pumpkins this fall. Pumpkin seeds produce a fantastic crust. Chilled and topped with whipped cream, these squares are creamy and delectable.

Prep time: 25 minutes | Cook time: 50 minutes | Serves 16 squares

FOR THE GRAHAM CRACKER CRUST
- 130 grams gluten-free graham cracker crumbs, store-bought or homemade
- 60 grams pumpkin seeds, chopped
- 2 tablespoons cane sugar or granulated sugar
- 8 tablespoons (1 stick) butter or nondairy alternative, melted and slightly cooled

FOR THE FILLING
- 32 grams all-purpose flour blend
- 1½ teaspoons pumpkin pie spice
- 1 teaspoon ground cinnamon
- ¼ teaspoon xanthan gum
- ¼ teaspoon salt
- 1 (8-ounce) package cream cheese or nondairy alternative
- 1 (15-ounce) can pumpkin puree
- 200 grams light brown sugar
- 2 large eggs
- 1¼ cups whole milk or coconut milk beverage
- 2 teaspoons vanilla extract

TO MAKE THE GRAHAM CRACKER CRUST
1. Preheat the oven to 350°F. Line a 9-by-9-inch baking pan with parchment paper, leaving some hanging over the sides. This will make the bars easy to remove.
2. In a food processor, combine the graham cracker crumbs, pumpkin seeds, and cane sugar. Pulse until a sandy consistency forms. With the processor running, slowly add the melted butter through the feed tube and watch the mixture thicken.
3. Press this crust mixture firmly into the bottom of the prepared pan.
4. Bake for 8 minutes. Remove the crust and leave the oven on.
5. TO MAKE THE FILLING
6. In a small bowl, whisk the flour, pumpkin pie spice, cinnamon, xanthan gum, and salt to combine.
7. In a large bowl, using a handheld electric mixer, beat the cream cheese until smooth and creamy. Add the pumpkin, brown sugar, eggs, milk, and vanilla and mix until combined. Add the flour mixture and mix until smooth. Do not overmix.
8. Pour the filling into the graham cracker crust.
9. Bake for 40 to 50 minutes, or until the center is set and doesn't jiggle.
10. Let the squares cool completely on a wire rack. Once cooled, cover the pan with aluminum foil and refrigerate for at least 1 hour before slicing and serving. Keep refrigerated, covered, for up to 5 days.

Zesty Lemon Squares

My son couldn't eat eggs but always wanted lemon squares. Making them egg-free was a letdown, so when he could have eggs again, I made these Zesty Lemon Squares. My favorite aspect of these lemon squares is the crust.

Prep time: 25 minutes | Cook time: 50 minutes | Serves 9 squares

FOR THE CRUST
- 190 grams all-purpose flour blend
- ½ teaspoon xanthan gum
- ½ teaspoon salt
- 12 tablespoons (1½ sticks) butter or nondairy alternative, melted and slightly cooled
- 100 grams cane sugar or granulated sugar
- 1 teaspoon vanilla extract

FOR THE FILLING
- 2 large eggs
- 200 grams cane sugar or granulated sugar
- 62 grams all-purpose flour blend
- ½ teaspoon baking powder
- ¼ teaspoon xanthan gum
- ¼ teaspoon salt
- 1 tablespoon grated lemon zest (about 1 large lemon)
- ½ cup fresh lemon juice (about 3 large lemons)
- 3 tablespoons powdered sugar

TO MAKE THE CRUST
1. Preheat the oven to 350°F. Line a 9-by-9-inch baking pan with parchment paper, leaving some hanging over the edges. This will make the bars easy to remove.
2. In a medium bowl, whisk the flour, xanthan gum, and salt to combine. Using a spatula, stir in the melted butter, sugar, and vanilla. Pour the crust into the prepared baking pan and spread it evenly.
3. Bake for 20 minutes. Remove and leave the oven on.

TO MAKE THE FILLING
4. While the crust bakes, in a small bowl, using a handheld electric mixer, beat the eggs.
5. In a medium bowl, whisk the sugar, flour, baking powder, xanthan gum, and salt to combine. Add the beaten eggs, lemon zest, and lemon juice and mix well.
6. Pour the filling evenly over the crust, then return to the oven and bake for 20 to 25 minutes, or until the middle is set and does not jiggle.
7. Let the bars cool for 10 to 20 minutes, then cover with aluminum foil and refrigerate at least 1 hour.
8. Dust the squares with the powdered sugar before serving. Refrigerate the bars, covered, for up to 5 days.

Red Velvet Whoopie Pies

These whoopie pies are delicious and adorable—perfect for Valentine's Day, Christmas, or anytime. Even dairy-free, the cream cheese filling in these sandwich cookies is delicious.

Prep time: 2 hours 35 minutes | Cook time: 20 minutes | Serves 14 sandwich cookies

FOR THE PIES
- 250 grams all-purpose flour blend
- 15 grams unsweetened natural cocoa powder
- 1 teaspoon baking soda
- ½ teaspoon xanthan gum
- ½ teaspoon salt
- 8 tablespoons (1 stick) butter or nondairy alternative
- 200 grams light brown sugar
- 1 large egg
- ⅔ cup whole milk or coconut milk beverage
- 2 teaspoons vanilla extract
- ½ teaspoon apple cider vinegar
- 1 teaspoon red gel food coloring

FOR THE FILLING
- 51 grams shortening
- 4 ounces cream cheese or nondairy alternative
- 1 tablespoon whole milk or coconut milk beverage
- 1 teaspoon vanilla extract
- 300 grams powdered sugar

TO MAKE THE PIES
1. In a medium bowl, whisk the flour, cocoa powder, baking soda, xanthan gum, and salt to combine.
2. In a large bowl, using a handheld electric mixer on medium speed, cream the butter. Add the brown sugar and mix until well combined.
3. Add half the flour mixture and mix to combine. Add the remaining flour mixture and mix again. Add the red food coloring and mix until completely incorporated.
4. Refrigerate for 2 hours to set, until the mixture looks like thick cupcake batter. During the last few minutes of chilling, preheat the oven to 350°F and line 2 baking sheets with parchment paper. (Don't use silicone mats because they might stain.)
5. Using a 1-inch ice cream scoop, transfer tablespoon-size mounds of the batter onto the prepared baking sheets about 3 inches apart.
6. Bake for 10 to 12 minutes until the centers appear set but the cookies are still soft.

TO MAKE THE FILLING
7. In a medium bowl, using a handheld electric mixer on medium speed, cream together the shortening and cream cheese until smooth and creamy. Add the milk and vanilla. Mix, then add the powdered sugar and mix well until smooth.
8. Pair the red velvet cookies by size. Spread a generous layer of filling on the inside of one cookie and top it with the other to form a sandwich. Repeat with the remaining cookies.
9. Keep in an airtight container at room temperature for up to 3 days, or refrigerate for up to 5 days.

S'mores Cookies

The pleasures of s'mores, a classic treat from your youth, can now be enjoyed in the simplest possible method. There's no need to light up a fire.

Prep time: 35 minutes | Cook time: 18 minutes per batch | Serves 12 cookies

- 50 grams mini marshmallows
- 250 grams all-purpose flour blend
- 52 grams finely crushed Homemade Graham Crackers or gluten-free graham cracker crumbs
- 2 teaspoons arrowroot
- 1 teaspoon baking soda
- ½ teaspoon xanthan gum
- ½ teaspoon salt
- 8 tablespoons (1 stick) butter or nondairy alternative
- 150 grams light brown sugar
- 50 grams cane sugar or granulated sugar
- 1 large egg
- 2 teaspoons vanilla extract
- 180 grams semisweet chocolate chips or nondairy alternative

1. Preheat the oven to 375°F. Line 2 baking sheets with parchment paper or silicone baking mats.
2. Cut the mini marshmallows in half using kitchen shears.
3. In a medium bowl, whisk the flour, graham cracker crumbs, arrowroot, baking soda, xanthan gum, and salt to combine.
4. In a large bowl, using a handheld electric mixer on medium speed, cream together the butter, brown sugar, and cane sugar. Add the egg and vanilla. Mix well to combine. Beat in the flour mixture in two additions and mix to form a dough. Using a spatula, fold in half the marshmallows and half the chocolate chips. The batter will be thick and sticky.
5. Using tablespoon-size portions, roll the dough into balls and place them on the prepared baking sheets 3 inches apart.
6. Bake one batch at a time. Transfer to the oven and bake for 8 minutes. The cookies will still be very soft. Remove from the oven and top each cookie with some of the remaining marshmallows and chocolate chips.
7. Return to the oven and bake for 7 to 10 minutes more, or until the cookies are golden on the edges and soft in the middle.
8. Let the cookies cool on the baking sheet for 10 minutes, then gently transfer them to a wire rack to cool completely.
9. Keep the cookies in an airtight container at room temperature for up to 5 days or freeze for up to 1 month.

The Softest Peanut Butter Cookies

I like chocolate and banana with peanut butter. When I first went gluten-free, I couldn't find a nice gluten-free cookie to satisfy my sweet taste. Today I get to eat cookies (and get some protein, right?).

Prep time: 1 hour 15 minutes | Cook time: 12 minutes per batch | Serves 24 cookies

- 156 grams all-purpose flour blend
- ½ teaspoon baking soda
- ½ teaspoon xanthan gum
- 8 tablespoons (1 stick) butter or nondairy alternative
- 100 grams light brown sugar
- 50 grams cane sugar or granulated sugar, plus 2 tablespoons
- 180 grams creamy gluten-free peanut butter
- 1 large egg
- 1 teaspoon vanilla extract

1. In a small bowl, whisk the flour, baking soda, and xanthan gum to combine.
2. In a large bowl, using a handheld electric mixer on medium speed, cream together the butter, brown sugar, and 50 grams of cane sugar. Add the peanut butter and mix until smooth and creamy. Add the egg and vanilla. Mix until combined.
3. Slowly add the flour mixture and mix until combined. Do not overmix. Cover the bowl with plastic wrap and refrigerate for at least 1 hour.
4. Preheat the oven to 350°F. Line 2 baking sheets with parchment paper or silicone baking mats.
5. Place the remaining 2 tablespoons of cane sugar in a small bowl.
6. Using a 1-inch ice cream scoop, scoop the cookies and gently roll them in the cane sugar to coat lightly. Place the cookies on the prepared baking sheets 3 inches apart. Using the tines of a fork, make a crisscross imprint on each one.
7. Baking one batch at a time, bake for 10 to 12 minutes, or until the edges are slightly browned. The cookies will still be very soft and may have small cracks.
8. Let the cookies cool on the baking sheet to continue baking without becoming overdone. Gently transfer to a wire rack. Keep in an airtight container at room temperature for up to 7 days.

Dunkable Chocolate Chip Cookies

This is a classic dunking chocolate chip cookie. Make smaller or bigger cookies. After-school snack with milk. These chocolate chip cookies are flavored with brown sugar and maple syrup.

Prep time: 45 minutes | Cook time: 12 minutes per batch | Serves 34 cookies

- 210 grams all-purpose flour blend
- 1 teaspoon baking soda
- ½ teaspoon xanthan gum
- ½ teaspoon salt
- 51 grams shortening
- 133 grams light brown sugar
- 1 large egg
- 2 tablespoons maple syrup
- 2 teaspoons vanilla extract
- ½ teaspoon apple cider vinegar
- 225 grams semisweet chocolate chips or nondairy alternative

1. Line 2 baking sheets with parchment paper or silicone baking mats.
2. In a small bowl, whisk the flour, baking soda, xanthan gum, and salt to combine.
3. In a medium bowl, using a handheld electric mixer on medium speed, cream together the shortening and brown sugar. Add the egg, maple syrup, vanilla, and apple cider vinegar. Mix again until combined. Add the flour mixture and mix to form a dough. Using a spatula, fold in the chocolate chips.
4. Using a 1-inch ice cream scoop, scoop the cookies onto one of the prepared baking sheets. It's okay if they are close together. Refrigerate for 30 minutes.
5. Preheat the oven to 375°F.
6. Transfer half of the chilled cookies onto the second prepared baking sheet, placing them 3 inches apart. Leave the remaining cookies in the refrigerator.
7. Bake the first batch for 10 to 12 minutes, or until lightly browned on the sides.
8. Let the cookies cool on the baking sheet for 10 minutes, then transfer to a wire rack to cool completely.
9. Refill the baking sheet with the chilled cookies from the fridge and bake as directed.

Thin Mint Copycat Cookies

Former Girl Scout me had to make Thin Mints. We still order Girl Scout cookies to contribute to firefighters, but you can make your own with this recipe. Who can resist chocolate peppermint?

Prep time: 15 minutes, plus 30 minutes to chill | Cook time: 10 minutes per batch | Serves 28 cookies

FOR THE COOKIES
- 190 grams all-purpose flour blend
- 75 grams Dutch-process cocoa powder
- 1 teaspoon baking powder
- ½ teaspoon xanthan gum
- ¼ teaspoon salt
- 179 grams shortening
- 200 grams cane sugar or granulated sugar
- 1 large egg
- 1 teaspoon vanilla extract
- ¼ teaspoon peppermint extract

FOR THE COATING
- 360 grams semisweet chocolate chips or nondairy alternative
- ½ teaspoon coconut oil, melted
- ¼ teaspoon peppermint extract

TO MAKE THE COOKIES

1. Preheat the oven to 350°F. Line 2 baking sheets with parchment paper. Cut two additional large sheets of parchment for rolling the dough.
2. In a medium bowl, whisk the flour, cocoa powder, baking powder, xanthan gum, and salt to combine.
3. In a large bowl, using a handheld electric mixer on medium speed, cream together the shortening and sugar, stopping to scrape down the bowl as needed. Add the egg, vanilla, and peppermint extract and mix until combined. Add the flour mixture and mix until combined. The dough will look slightly sticky.
4. Transfer the dough to one sheet of parchment paper and place the other on top. Roll the dough to a large round about ¼ inch thick. Using a 2-inch round cookie cutter, cut out the cookies and place them on the baking sheets. Reroll the remaining dough and repeat until no dough is left.
5. Baking one sheet at a time, bake for 8 to 10 minutes.
6. Let the cookies cool on the pan for 10 minutes, then transfer to a wire rack. They will be soft at first but will crisp as they cool.
7. TO MAKE THE COATING
8. In a medium saucepan, melt the chocolate over medium-low heat, stirring constantly so it does not burn. Stir in the coconut oil and peppermint extract.
9. Dip each cookie in the melted chocolate and coat completely. Using a fork, lift them out of the chocolate, letting any excess fall back into the pan. Place the dipped cookies back on the parchment-lined baking sheets. Refrigerate for 30 minutes to help the chocolate set.
10. Just like traditional Thin Mints, these cookies are best eaten cold. Refrigerate leftovers in an airtight container for up to 1 week or freeze for up to 1 month.

Blackberry Shortbread Thumbprints

You'll know my favorite fruit, pizza topping, and cookie extract after reading this book. Both are here. Before eating, ensure sure the cookies are cool and the icing is set.

Prep time: 20 minutes, plus 30 minutes to chill | Cook time: 14 minutes per batch | Serves 24 cookies

- 250 grams all-purpose flour blend
- 1 teaspoon xanthan gum
- ½ teaspoon baking powder
- 136 grams shortening
- 133 grams cane sugar or granulated sugar
- 1 teaspoon vanilla extract
- ½ teaspoon orange extract
- ½ cup blackberry jam

1. Line 2 baking sheets with parchment paper or silicone baking mats.
2. In a small bowl, whisk the flour, xanthan gum, and baking powder to combine.
3. In a large bowl, using a handheld electric mixer on medium speed, cream together the shortening and sugar. Add the vanilla and orange extract and mix to combine. Add flour mixture and mix to form a dough.
4. Using 1-tablespoon portions, roll the dough into balls and place them on the prepared baking sheets. Gently make a thumbprint in the center of each cookie. Smooth any cracks along the outer edges with your fingers. Fill each thumbprint with about ½ teaspoon of jam. Refrigerate for 30 minutes.
5. Preheat the oven to 350°F.
6. Baking one batch at a time, bake for 12 to 14 minutes, or until the edges are slightly browned.
7. Let the cookies cool on the pan for 5 to 10 minutes, then gently transfer to a wire rack to cool completely.
8. Using a fork, drizzle the glaze over the cookies. Let set and dry for about 1 hour. Keep in an airtight container at room temperature for up to 5 days, or freeze for up to 1 month.

Easy Frosted Sugar Cookies

I'll never forget when I made a gluten-free sugar biscuit with shape. I blame shortening vs. butter. Nonna used shortening to make cookies, so I tried it and they were excellent. I love almond in my cookies, but orange extract is amazing.

Prep time: 1 hour 20 minutes | Cook time: 13 minutes per batch | Serves 16 cookies

FOR THE COOKIES
- 312 grams all-purpose flour blend, plus more for dusting
- ½ teaspoon xanthan gum
- ½ teaspoon baking powder
- ¼ teaspoon salt
- 102 grams shortening
- 150 grams cane sugar or granulated sugar
- 1 large egg
- 2 teaspoons vanilla extract
- ¼ teaspoon orange extract
- ¼ cup plus 1 tablespoon cold water

FOR THE FROSTING
- 240 grams powdered sugar
- ¼ cup whole milk or coconut milk beverage
- ½ teaspoon vanilla extract

TO MAKE THE COOKIES
1. In a small bowl, whisk the flour, xanthan gum, baking powder, and salt to combine.
2. In a large bowl, using a handheld electric mixer on medium speed, cream together the shortening and sugar. Add the egg, vanilla, and orange extract and mix to combine. Slowly add the flour mixture and cold water. Stir until coarse crumbs form. Continue to form the dough by hand. The warmth of your hands will help the dough come together.
3. Divide the dough into 4 equal portions, wrap each in plastic wrap, and chill for 30 minutes to 1 hour. Any longer and your dough will be too hard to work with and you will need to let it sit on the counter for 5 to 10 minutes so it is easier to work with.
4. Preheat the oven to 350°F. Line 2 baking sheets with parchment paper or silicone baking mats.
5. Place two sheets of parchment paper on a work surface and dust them with flour. Place one dough portion between the two sheets of parchment and roll it to ¼-inch thickness. Using cookie cutters, cut the dough into desired shapes and transfer them to the prepared baking sheets. Gather the scraps and repeat the steps with the remaining 3 dough portions.
6. Bake for 11 to 13 minutes. The cookies will be soft but very lightly browned around the edges.
7. Let the cookies cool on the baking sheet for 10 minutes, then use a spatula to gently transfer them to a wire rack to cool completely.

TO MAKE THE FROSTING
8. In a medium bowl, stir together the powdered sugar, milk, and vanilla until smooth.
9. Dip each cookie top into the icing, then transfer to a wire rack. Allow the icing to set for about 1 hour.
10. Keep the cookies in an airtight container at room temperature for up to 4 days. They can be frozen without icing for up to 1 month in a freezer bag. Separating the cookies with parchment paper before freezing helps keep them fresh.

Cranberry Oatmeal Cookies

These gluten-free oatmeal raisin cookies with cranberries are delicious and safe to eat. Alternatively, use raisins.

Prep time: 15 minutes | Cook time: 10 minutes per batch | Serves 24 cookies

- 300 grams certified gluten-free rolled oats
- 156 grams all-purpose flour blend
- 1 teaspoon baking soda
- 1 teaspoon ground cinnamon
- ¼ teaspoon ground nutmeg
- ¼ teaspoon xanthan gum
- ¼ teaspoon salt
- 16 tablespoons (2 sticks) butter or nondairy alternative
- 200 grams light brown sugar
- 2 large eggs
- 1 teaspoon vanilla extract
- 150 grams dried cranberries

1. Preheat the oven to 350°F. Line 2 baking sheets with parchment paper or silicone baking mats.
2. In a food processor, pulse the oats 5 or 6 times to break them down.
3. In a medium bowl, whisk the flour, baking soda, cinnamon, nutmeg, xanthan gum, and salt to combine. Whisk in the oats and set aside.
4. In a large bowl, using a handheld electric mixer on medium speed, cream together the butter and brown sugar. Add the eggs and vanilla. Mix well to combine. Beat in the flour mixture in two additions and mix to form the dough. Using a spatula, fold in the cranberries.
5. Using tablespoon-size portions, roll the dough into balls and place them on the prepared baking sheets 3 inches apart.
6. Baking one batch at a time, bake for 10 minutes, or until the edges are crispy.
7. Let cookies cool on the baking sheets for 10 minutes, then gently transfer them to a wire rack to cool completely. Keep in an airtight container at room temperature for up to 5 days.

Sensational Snickerdoodles

These cookies remind me of a gluten-free bakery we found early on. I'm glad I figured out how to make these cookies for my kids. I love cream cheese. It makes cookies tastier. Better to chill dough longer. Chill it overnight.

Prep time: 1 hour 15 minutes | Cook time: 15 minutes | Serves 24 cookies

- 190 grams all-purpose flour blend
- 1 teaspoon xanthan gum
- 1 teaspoon cream of tartar
- 2 teaspoons ground cinnamon, divided
- ½ teaspoon baking soda
- ½ teaspoon salt
- 8 tablespoons (1 stick) butter or nondairy alternative
- 2 ounces cream cheese or nondairy alternative
- 150 grams cane sugar or granulated sugar, plus 2 tablespoons
- 1 large egg
- 2 teaspoons vanilla extract

1. In a small bowl, whisk the flour, xanthan gum, cream of tartar, 1 teaspoon of cinnamon, the baking soda, and salt to combine.
2. In a large bowl, using a handheld electric mixer on medium speed, cream together the butter and cream cheese until smooth. Mix in 150 grams of sugar until well combined. Add the egg and vanilla and mix to combine, stopping to scrape down the bowl as needed.
3. Beat the flour mixture into the cream cheese mixture in two additions, mixing to form a dough. This dough will be thick and pasty. Transfer the dough to an airtight container and refrigerate for at least 1 hour, or overnight for best results.
4. Preheat the oven to 350°F. Line 2 baking sheets with parchment paper. (I recommend parchment because these cookies are so soft that the silicone mats will grip the edges but leave a hollow middle.)
5. In a small bowl, stir together the remaining 1 teaspoon of cinnamon and the remaining 2 tablespoons of sugar.
6. Using tablespoon-size portions, roll the chilled dough into balls. Roll the balls in the cinnamon sugar and place them on the prepared baking sheet 3 inches apart. Fill both baking sheets. While one sheet is in the oven, place the other in the refrigerator.
7. Bake for 11 to 13 minutes, or until the edges are set. The cookies will still be soft. Do not overbake.
8. Let the cookies cool completely on the baking sheet, where they will continue baking without becoming overdone. Bake the second batch as directed. Keep in an airtight container at room temperature for up to 5 days.

Biscotti

My family loves biscotti. Nonna made them and stored them in a huge container in her pantry; Nonno would slip me a couple when I visited. This gluten-free version brought back childhood memories. The true test of biscotti is how they taste dunked in coffee.

Prep time: 15 minutes | Cook time: 50 minutes | Serves 16 biscotti

- 190 grams all-purpose flour blend
- 60 grams brown rice flour
- 1 teaspoon baking powder
- ½ teaspoon xanthan gum
- ½ teaspoon salt
- 4 tablespoons butter or nondairy alternative
- 150 grams cane sugar or granulated sugar
- 3 large eggs, divided
- 1½ teaspoons vanilla extract
- ½ teaspoon orange extract

1. Preheat the oven to 350°F. Line 2 baking sheets with parchment paper or silicone baking mats.
2. In a medium bowl, whisk the all-purpose flour, brown rice flour, baking powder, xanthan gum, and salt to combine.
3. In a large bowl, using a handheld electric mixer on medium speed, cream together the butter and sugar. Add 2 of the eggs and the vanilla and orange extracts, and mix until combined. Add the flour mixture and mix until combined, stopping to scrape down the bowl as needed. Your dough will resemble a very thick batter.
4. Add about 1 tablespoon of water to a piping bag and rub the bag from the outside to spread the water inside the bag. This will help the dough slide through the bag. Fill the piping bag with the biscotti dough. Cut the tip of the bag a little bit bigger than 1 inch wide. Squeeze the dough into two equal-size logs onto one baking sheet. With wet fingertips, flatten the logs until they are about 1 inch in height.
5. In a small bowl, whisk the remaining egg and 1 tablespoon water to create an egg wash. Using a pastry brush, lightly brush the egg wash over the top of each log.
6. Bake for 20 to 25 minutes. Remove from the oven, but leave the oven on.
7. With a sharp nonserrated knife, cut each log on the diagonal into ¾-inch-thick slices. Push down on the knife rather than saw, to prevent the cookies from breaking. Place each cookie on the second prepared baking sheet, cut-side up.
8. Return to the oven and bake for 12 to 14 minutes, or until golden, with crisp edges.
9. Let the biscotti cool on the pan for about 10 minutes, then transfer to a wire rack to cool completely. They will continue to crisp as they cool. Keep in an airtight container at room temperature for 1 to 2 weeks or freeze for up to 3 months.

Chapter 12
Cakes and Cupcakes

Vanilla Cupcakes

This is a keeper. These sweet, fluffy cupcakes are quick and great with frosting. Whipping egg whites makes these cupcakes unique. Get creative since these gluten-free cupcakes will look and taste store-bought.

Prep time: 15 minutes | Cook time: 30 minutes | Serves 12 cupcakes

FOR THE CUPCAKES
- 190 grams all-purpose flour blend
- 1 teaspoon baking powder
- ½ teaspoon xanthan gum
- ¼ teaspoon baking soda
- ¼ teaspoon salt
- 3 large egg whites
- 200 grams cane sugar or granulated sugar
- ½ cup avocado oil or canola oil
- ¼ cup whole milk or coconut milk beverage
- 1 tablespoon vanilla extract

FOR THE FROSTING
- 134 grams shortening
- 1 teaspoon vanilla extract
- 480 grams powdered sugar, plus more as needed

TO MAKE THE CUPCAKES
1. Preheat the oven to 350°F. Line a 12-cup muffin tin with cupcake liners.
2. In a small bowl, whisk the flour, baking powder, xanthan gum, baking soda, and salt to combine.
3. In a large bowl, using a handheld electric mixer, whip the egg whites until they form a soft peak. Add the cane sugar, oil, milk, and vanilla. Mix well. Add the flour mixture and mix until combined.
4. Evenly divide the batter between the prepared muffin cups, filling them three-quarters full.
5. Bake for 18 to 20 minutes, or until a toothpick inserted into the center of a cupcake comes out clean.
6. Let the cupcakes cool in the pan for 10 minutes, then transfer them to a wire rack to cool completely.

TO MAKE THE FROSTING
7. While the cupcakes are cooling, in a large bowl, using a handheld electric mixer on medium speed, cream together the shortening and vanilla until smooth.
8. Add the powdered sugar and mix on low speed until smooth and creamy, adding 1 tablespoon of water at a time until you get the desired consistency. If the frosting is too thick, add 1 tablespoon more of water; if it is too thin, add 1 tablespoon of powdered sugar.
9. Fill a piping bag fitted your desired tip with the frosting and decorate each cupcake as desired. Keep covered at room temperature for up to 4 days.

Pumpkin Pie Cupcakes

If you want to forego Thanksgiving pie, serve them instead. Perfect for small fingers. No leftovers with coconut whipped cream on top. For optimal results, chill the coconut cream overnight.

Prep time: 15 minutes | Cook time: 30 minutes | Serves 12 cupcakes

FOR THE CUPCAKES
- 125 grams all-purpose flour blend
- 2 teaspoons pumpkin pie spice
- 1 teaspoon ground cinnamon
- ½ teaspoon xanthan gum
- ¼ teaspoon ground cloves
- ¼ teaspoon baking powder
- ¼ teaspoon baking soda
- ¼ teaspoon salt
- 1 (7.4-ounce) can sweetened condensed coconut milk
- 150 grams cane sugar or granulated sugar
- 2 large eggs
- 1 (15-ounce) can pumpkin puree

FOR THE COCONUT WHIPPED CREAM
- 1 (14-ounce) can coconut cream, chilled overnight
- 2 tablespoons powdered sugar

TO MAKE THE CUPCAKES
1. Preheat the oven to 350°F. Line a 12-cup muffin tin with cupcake liners.
2. In a small bowl, whisk the flour, pumpkin pie spice, cinnamon, xanthan gum, cloves, baking powder, baking soda, and salt to combine.
3. In a large bowl, using a spatula, mix the condensed coconut milk and cane sugar. Stir all the clumps out of the milk. Add the eggs and mix well. Add the pumpkin puree and the flour mixture. Stir just until combined. Do not overmix.
4. Scoop the batter evenly into the prepared muffin cups.
5. Bake for 28 to 30 minutes, or until a toothpick inserted into the center of a cupcake comes out clean.
6. Let the cupcakes cool in the pan for 30 minutes.

TO MAKE THE COCONUT WHIPPED CREAM
1. Open the chilled can of coconut cream and pour off the watery liquid. Scoop only the solid part into a large bowl and add the powdered sugar. Using a handheld electric mixer, beat until smooth and creamy.
2. Transfer to a piping bag with a 1A tip and apply some to each cupcake. Refrigerate leftovers, covered, for up to 5 days.

Thin Mint Cupcakes

I can't take credit for putting cookie dough in a cupcake, but this was the first time I tried it—and wow. Make my Thin Mint Copycat Cookies dough first for best results. These chocolate cupcakes are delicious and minty. Definitely.

Prep time: 65 minutes | Cook time: 30 minutes | Serves 12 cupcakes

FOR THE CUPCAKES
- 95 grams all-purpose flour blend
- 50 grams Dutch-process cocoa powder
- 1 tablespoon arrowroot
- ¾ teaspoon baking powder
- ½ teaspoon baking soda
- ½ teaspoon xanthan gum
- ¼ teaspoon salt
- 150 grams cane sugar or granulated sugar
- 50 grams light brown sugar
- 2 large eggs
- ⅓ cup avocado oil or canola oil
- ½ cup whole milk or coconut milk beverage
- 2 teaspoons vanilla extract
- ½ teaspoon apple cider vinegar
- ½ recipe Thin Mint Copycat Cookies, prepared through step 4 and rolled into 12 balls
- FOR THE MINT FROSTING
- 136 grams shortening
- ¼ teaspoon peppermint extract
- 2 drops green food coloring
- 480 grams powdered sugar
- 4 tablespoons whole milk or coconut milk beverage

TO MAKE THE CUPCAKES
1. Preheat the oven to 350°F. Line a 12-cup muffin tin with cupcake liners.
2. In a medium bowl, whisk the flour, cocoa powder, arrowroot, baking powder, baking soda, xanthan gum, and salt to combine.
3. In a large bowl, using a whisk or handheld electric mixer, mix the cane sugar, brown sugar, eggs, oil, milk, vanilla, and vinegar. Beat in the flour mixture in two additions, mixing on low speed to blend and stopping to scrape down the bowl as needed, and making sure there are no brown sugar clumps. The batter should be thick.
4. Place 1 cookie dough ball into each prepared muffin cup. Evenly divide the batter over each, filling each cup no more than two-thirds full.
5. Bake for 18 to 20 minutes, or until a toothpick inserted in the side of a cupcake comes out clean. (Be careful to avoid the cookie dough center when testing for doneness.)
6. Let the cupcakes cool in the pan for at least 10 minutes, then transfer to a wire rack to cool completely.

TO MAKE THE MINT FROSTING
7. In a large bowl, using a handheld electric mixer on medium speed, cream the shortening.
8. Add the mint extract, food coloring, and powdered sugar and mix to combine. While mixing, add the milk by the tablespoon and mix until smooth and creamy.
9. Frost the cupcakes. Keep leftovers in an airtight container at room temperature for up to 4 days.

Super Moist Cream Cheese Pound Cake

Bundt cake vs. pound cake: Density. This heavy cake is incredibly moist, though. Cool this cake thoroughly before slicing so you can grab a slice like bread, but better.

Prep time: 25 minutes | Cook time: 1 hour 30 minutes | Serves 1 tube cake

- Shortening, for preparing the pan
- 375 grams all-purpose flour blend
- 3 tablespoons arrowroot
- 1 teaspoon xanthan gum
- ½ teaspoon baking powder
- ¼ teaspoon salt
- 24 tablespoons (3 sticks) butter or nondairy alternative
- 1 (8-ounce) package cream cheese or nondairy alternative
- 500 grams cane sugar or granulated sugar
- 80 grams vanilla Greek yogurt or nondairy alternative
- 6 large eggs, beaten
- 2 teaspoons vanilla extract

1. Preheat the oven to 325°F. Grease a 10- to 12-cup Bundt pan with shortening.
2. In a medium bowl, whisk the flour, arrowroot, xanthan gum, baking powder, and salt to combine.
3. In a large bowl, using a handheld electric mixer on medium speed, cream together the butter and cream cheese, stopping to scrape down the bowl as needed. Add the sugar and mix well. Add the yogurt, beaten eggs, and vanilla. Mix until combined.
4. Add the flour mixture to the wet ingredients and mix just until combined. Do not overmix.
5. Pour the batter into the prepared Bundt pan and tap the pan on the counter to remove any air bubbles.
6. Bake for 1 hour 15 minutes to 1 hour 20 minutes, or until a toothpick inserted into the center of the pound cake comes out clean.
7. Let the cake cool completely in the pan. This may take 1 to 2 hours. Invert the cake over a wire rack and remove it from the pan. Keep covered at room temperature, or refrigerate, for up to 5 days.

Gingerbread Cupcakes

Because I have a lovely gingerbread cookie on my blog, I made cupcakes. These cupcakes topped with cream cheese frosting make Christmas feel like year-round.

Prep time: 25 minutes | Cook time: 30 minutes | Serves 12 cupcakes

FOR THE CUPCAKES
- 167 grams all-purpose flour blend
- 2 tablespoons arrowroot
- 1½ teaspoons ground cinnamon
- ½ teaspoon xanthan gum
- ½ teaspoon baking powder
- ½ teaspoon baking soda
- ½ teaspoon ground ginger
- ½ teaspoon ground nutmeg
- ½ teaspoon ground cloves
- ¼ teaspoon salt
- ½ cup avocado oil or canola oil
- 100 grams light brown sugar
- ½ cup whole milk or coconut milk beverage
- ½ cup maple syrup
- 1 large egg
- 1 teaspoon vanilla extract
- ½ teaspoon apple cider vinegar

FOR THE CREAM CHEESE FROSTING
- 102 grams shortening
- 4 ounces cream cheese or nondairy alternative
- 480 grams powdered sugar
- 1 teaspoon vanilla extract
- 4 tablespoons whole milk or coconut milk beverage

TO MAKE THE CUPCAKES
1. Preheat the oven to 350°F. Line a 12-cup muffin tin with cupcake liners.
2. In a medium bowl, whisk the flour, arrowroot, cinnamon, xanthan gum, baking powder, baking soda, ginger, nutmeg, cloves, and salt to combine.
3. In a large bowl, using a handheld electric mixer, beat the oil and brown sugar to blend. Add the milk, maple syrup, egg, vanilla, and vinegar. Mix well. Beat in the flour mixture in two additions, mixing to combine, and stopping to scrape down the bowl as needed.
4. Evenly divide the batter between the prepared muffin cups, filling them two-thirds full.
5. Bake for 20 to 22 minutes, or until a toothpick inserted into the center of a cupcake comes out clean.
6. Let the cupcakes cool in the pan for at least 10 minutes, then transfer to a wire rack to cool completely.

TO MAKE THE CREAM CHEESE FROSTING
7. In a large bowl, using a handheld electric mixer on medium speed, cream together the shortening and cream cheese. Add the powdered sugar and vanilla. Mix as you add the milk by the tablespoon until smooth and creamy.
8. Frost the cupcakes. Refrigerate leftovers, covered, for up to 5 days.

Gooey Butter Cake

You must try toasted ravioli, Provel cheese (on pizza), and gooey butter cake in St. Louis. This "I can't believe it's gluten-free" Gooey Butter Cake might make me a lifelong St. Louisan. Warm or cold, you'll love this cake.

Prep time: 15 minutes | Cook time: 50 minutes | Serves 1 (9-by-13-inch) cake

FOR THE BOTTOM CAKE LAYER
- Shortening, for preparing the pan
- 250 grams all-purpose flour blend
- 150 grams cane sugar or granulated sugar
- 1 tablespoon baking powder
- 1 teaspoon xanthan gum
- 8 tablespoons (1 stick) butter or nondairy alternative, melted
- 2 large eggs
- 1 teaspoon vanilla extract

FOR THE TOP CREAMY LAYER
- 1 (8-ounce) package cream cheese or nondairy alternative
- 2 large eggs
- 1 teaspoon vanilla extract
- 480 grams powdered sugar

TO MAKE THE BOTTOM CAKE LAYER
1. Preheat the oven to 350°F. Grease a 9-by-13-inch pan with shortening.
2. In a medium bowl, whisk the flour, sugar, baking powder, and xanthan gum to combine. Add the melted butter, eggs, and vanilla. Using a spatula, stir to combine.
3. Using your clean hands, continue to mix, forming a dough. Press it firmly into the prepared pan.

TO MAKE THE TOP CREAMY LAYER
4. In a large bowl, using a handheld electric mixer, beat the cream cheese until smooth. Add the eggs and vanilla. Mix for 2 minutes until well combined.
5. With the mixer on low speed, slowly add the powdered sugar, 120 grams (1 cup) at a time. Mix until a batter forms. Pour the batter over the bottom layer.
6. Bake for 40 to 45 minutes, or until the top becomes golden.
7. Let the cake cool before slicing. Refrigerate leftovers, covered, for up to 1 week.

Very Strawberry Cupcakes

These strawberry cupcakes are amazing. This thick strawberry filling makes it seem like a strawberry is in every bite. If you prepare and refrigerate the filling the day before, making these cupcakes will be faster. These cupcakes' strawberry-frosting makes them enticing. Natural, no dyes. It's perfect.

Prep time: 1 hour 45 minutes | Cook time: 50 minutes | Serves 12 cupcakes

FOR THE STRAWBERRY FILLING
- 250 grams sliced fresh strawberries
- 2 tablespoons cane sugar or granulated sugar
- FOR THE CUPCAKES
- 207 grams all-purpose flour blend
- 2 tablespoons arrowroot
- 1 teaspoon xanthan gum
- 1 teaspoon baking soda
- ¼ teaspoon salt
- 8 tablespoons (1 stick) butter or nondairy alternative
- 200 grams cane sugar or granulated sugar
- 3 large egg whites
- 60 grams vanilla Greek yogurt or nondairy alternative
- 2 teaspoons vanilla extract
- ⅓ cup whole milk or coconut milk beverage
- FOR THE STRAWBERRY FROSTING
- 34 grams freeze-dried strawberries
- 240 grams powdered sugar
- 68 grams shortening
- 2 to 3 tablespoons whole milk or coconut milk beverage
- 1 teaspoon vanilla extract

TO MAKE THE STRAWBERRY FILLING

1. In a small saucepan, combine the strawberries and sugar. Bring to a simmer over medium heat and cook for about 20 minutes, stirring occasionally to prevent burning. The strawberries will reduce and thicken. Transfer to a bowl, cover with plastic wrap, and refrigerate for at least 1 hour.

TO MAKE THE CUPCAKES

2. Preheat the oven to 350°F. Line a 12-cup muffin tin with cupcake liners.
3. In a small bowl, whisk the flour, arrowroot, xanthan gum, baking soda, and salt to combine.
4. In a large bowl, using a handheld electric mixer on medium speed, cream together the butter and cane sugar. Add the egg whites and mix until combined, stopping to scrape down the bowl as needed. Add the yogurt, vanilla, and milk. Mix again.
5. Using a spatula, scrape the sides and the bottom of the bowl to make sure all ingredients at the bottom are mixed in. With the mixer on low speed, slowly add the flour mixture. The batter will look curdled. That's okay.
6. Using a spatula, fold in ½ cup of the strawberry filling (you may have a bit extra leftover) until it is evenly spread through the batter. Evenly divide the batter between the prepared muffin cups, filling each two-thirds full. Do not overfill.
7. Bake for 20 to 22 minutes, or until a toothpick inserted into the center of a cupcake comes out clean.
8. Let the cupcakes cool completely before frosting.

TO MAKE THE STRAWBERRY FROSTING

9. In a food processor, pulse the freeze-dried strawberries to form a fine powder.
10. In a large bowl, using a handheld electric mixer, beat together the powdered sugar, shortening, strawberry powder, milk, and vanilla until smooth.
11. Transfer the frosting to a piping bag with your choice of tip. Frost the cupcakes. Refrigerate leftovers, covered, for up to 5 days.

Angel Food Cake

When I started baking with eggs, I was determined to make a handmade angel food cake better than store-bought. Here it is... usually it asks for almond extract, but don't disregard what orange extract can accomplish for baked goods.

Prep time: 25 minutes | Cook time: 60 minutes | Serves 1 (10-inch) cake

- 156 grams all-purpose flour blend
- 350 grams cane sugar or granulated sugar
- 2 tablespoons arrowroot
- ½ teaspoon xanthan gum
- ¼ teaspoon salt
- 1½ cups egg whites (about 12 large eggs)
- 1 teaspoon cream of tartar
- ½ teaspoon vanilla extract
- ½ teaspoon orange extract

1. Position an oven rack to the third lowest position and preheat the oven to 325°F.
2. In a food processor, combine the flour, sugar, arrowroot, xanthan gum, and salt. Process to a fine powdery texture.
3. In a large bowl, using a handheld electric mixer, beat the egg whites until they form stiff peaks. Be careful not to overmix. Add the cream of tartar, vanilla, and orange extract and give a quick stir with a spatula.
4. Using the spatula, fold the flour mixture into the egg whites. Do not overmix.
5. Pour the batter into an ungreased 10-inch tube pan.
6. Bake for 50 to 60 minutes, or until a toothpick inserted into the center of the cake comes out clean.
7. On a wire rack, invert the cake and let it cool in the pan. When completely cooled, remove the cake from the pan. Keep leftovers covered at room temperature for up to 3 days, or refrigerate for up to 5 days.

Fudgy Chocolate Cupcakes

These fudgy cupcakes may remind you of Hostess. They're a chocoholic's dream. Chocolate ganache is divine. (Make these dairy-free and soy-free by using Enjoy Life chocolate.)

Prep time: 35 minutes | Cook time: 30 minutes | Serves 12 cupcakes

FOR THE CUPCAKES
- 190 grams all-purpose flour blend
- 25 grams Dutch-process cocoa powder
- 1 teaspoon baking powder
- ½ teaspoon xanthan gum
- ¼ teaspoon salt
- 155 grams dark chocolate chips or nondairy alternative
- 6 tablespoons butter or nondairy alternative
- 200 grams cane sugar or granulated sugar
- 160 grams vanilla Greek yogurt or nondairy alternative
- 2 large eggs
- 2 teaspoons vanilla extract

FOR THE GANACHE
- 270 grams semisweet chocolate chips or nondairy alternative
- ¼ cup coconut oil, melted

TO MAKE THE CUPCAKES
1. Preheat the oven to 350°F. Line a 12-cup muffin tin with cupcake liners.
2. In a medium bowl, whisk the flour, cocoa powder, baking powder, xanthan gum, and salt to combine.
3. In a small saucepan, combine the chocolate chips and butter. Melt over low heat, stirring constantly until smooth. Set aside.
4. In a large bowl, using a handheld electric mixer, beat the sugar, yogurt, eggs, and vanilla until well mixed. Add the chocolate mixture and continue beating. Beat in the flour mixture in two additions. Mix until combined. The batter will be very thick.
5. Evenly divide the batter between the prepared muffin cups. With a slightly damp finger, smooth the top of each.
6. Bake for 18 to 20 minutes, or until a toothpick inserted into a cupcake comes out clean.
7. Let the cupcakes cool completely before frosting.

TO MAKE THE GANACHE
8. In a small saucepan, combine the chocolate chips and coconut oil. Melt over low heat, stirring until smooth.
9. Dip the top of each cupcake in the chocolate ganache. Once you have dipped all 12 cupcakes, dip them again. Set aside to let the chocolate ganache set and solidify.
10. Keep leftovers covered at room temperature for up to 3 days.

Death-by-Chocolate Cake

This chocolate cake is delicious. Espresso and chocolate enhance taste. It's double-delicious. Even without coffee, this cake will satisfy your chocolate desire.

Prep time: 35 minutes | Cook time: 30 minutes | Serves 1 (9-inch) two-layer frosted cake

FOR THE CAKE
- Shortening, for preparing the pans
- 157 grams all-purpose flour blend, plus more for dusting
- 75 grams unsweetened natural cocoa powder
- 62 grams arrowroot
- 2 teaspoons ground espresso
- 2 teaspoons baking soda
- 1 teaspoon baking powder
- 1 teaspoon xanthan gum
- 1 teaspoon salt
- 350 grams cane sugar or granulated sugar
- 1 cup avocado oil or canola oil
- 2 large eggs
- 1 teaspoon apple cider vinegar

FOR THE CHOCOLATE BUTTERCREAM FROSTING
- 136 grams shortening
- 720 grams powdered sugar
- 75 grams unsweetened natural cocoa powder
- 2 teaspoons vanilla extract
- 6 tablespoons whole milk or coconut milk beverage

TO MAKE THE CAKE
1. Preheat the oven to 350°F. Grease two 9-inch springform pans with shortening. Sprinkle a little flour inside and tap the pans to spread the flour evenly around each pan.
2. In a medium bowl, whisk the flour, cocoa powder, arrowroot, ground espresso, baking soda, baking powder, xanthan gum, and salt to combine.
3. In a large bowl, using a whisk or handheld electric mixer, beat the sugar, oil, eggs, milk, yogurt, brewed espresso (if using), vanilla, and vinegar until well mixed, stopping to scrape down the bowl as needed.
4. Evenly divide the batter between the prepared pans.
5. Bake for 25 to 28 minutes, or until a toothpick inserted into the center of a cake comes out clean.
6. Let the cakes cool in the pans for at least 15 minutes.
7. Using a large serrated knife, cut off the thin domed layer from the top of each cake. Creating a flat surface will help the cakes stack well.

TO MAKE THE CHOCOLATE BUTTERCREAM FROSTING
8. In a large bowl, using a handheld electric mixer, beat the shortening until smooth and creamy. Add the powdered sugar, cocoa powder, and vanilla.
9. Frost the cake layers and outside of the cake as desired. Refrigerate leftovers, covered, for up to 5 days.

Carrot Cake

Don't be deterred by this cake's large ingredient list. They're all needed for that fall blend. This cake is a must-bake whether you add pineapple, almonds, or coconut.

Prep time: 35 minutes | Cook time: 40 minutes | Serves 1 (9-inch) two-layer frosted cake

FOR THE CAKE

- Shortening, for preparing the pan
- 250 grams all-purpose flour blend, plus more for dusting
- 62 grams arrowroot
- 2 teaspoons baking powder
- 2 teaspoons ground cinnamon
- 1 teaspoon xanthan gum
- 1 teaspoon baking soda
- 1 teaspoon ground ginger
- ½ teaspoon salt
- ¼ teaspoon ground nutmeg
- ¼ teaspoon ground cloves
- 300 grams light brown sugar
- 100 grams cane sugar or granulated sugar
- 1 cup avocado oil or canola oil
- 4 large eggs
- 180 grams unsweetened applesauce
- 1 teaspoon vanilla extract
- 1 teaspoon apple cider vinegar
- 220 grams grated carrot (about 6 small carrots)
- 55 grams canned crushed pineapple, drained (optional)
- 50 grams shredded coconut (optional)
- 62 grams chopped nuts (optional)
- FOR THE CREAM CHEESE FROSTING
- 2 (8-ounce) packages cream cheese or nondairy alternative
- 8 tablespoons (1 stick) butter or nondairy alternative
- 2 to 3 tablespoons whole milk or coconut milk beverage
- 1 teaspoon vanilla extract
- ⅛ teaspoon salt
- 720 grams powdered sugar

TO MAKE THE CAKE

1. Preheat the oven to 350°F. Grease two 9-inch springform pans with shortening. Sprinkle a little flour inside and tap the pans to spread the flour evenly around each pan.
2. In a medium bowl, whisk the flour, arrowroot, baking powder, cinnamon, xanthan gum, baking soda, ginger, salt, nutmeg, and cloves to combine.
3. In a large bowl, using a whisk or handheld electric mixer, beat together the brown sugar, cane sugar, oil, eggs, applesauce, vanilla, and vinegar until combined, making sure there are no clumps of brown sugar remaining.
4. Using a spatula, fold the flour mixture into the wet ingredients in two parts, mixing between each. Fold until just combined. Gently fold in the carrots. If using, fold in the pineapple, coconut, and nuts.
5. Evenly divide the batter between the prepared cake pans.
6. Bake for 30 to 35 minutes, or until a toothpick inserted in the center of a cake comes out clean.
7. Let the cakes cool in the pans for 15 minutes. Release the clamp from each pan and remove the sides. Transfer the cakes and plates to a wire rack to cool completely.

TO MAKE THE CREAM CHEESE FROSTING

8. In a large bowl, using a handheld electric mixer on medium speed, cream together the cream cheese and butter until smooth.
9. Reduce the speed to low and add the milk, vanilla, salt, and powdered sugar. Mix until smooth and creamy.
10. Frost the cake as desired. Refrigerate leftovers, covered, for up to 4 days.

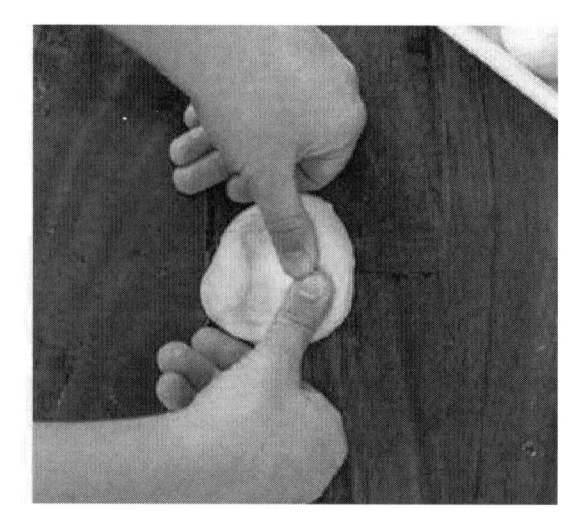

Lemon Lover's Bundt Cake

If you like lemon, you'll enjoy this Bundt cake. You can't find a more refreshing summertime treat than this one, thanks to its tangy lemon flavor. The glaze and lemon syrup add just the right amount of sourness to counteract the sweetness.

Prep time: 45 minutes | Cook time: 50 minutes | Serves 1 bundt cake

FOR THE CAKE
- Shortening, for preparing the pan
- 375 grams all-purpose flour blend
- 1 teaspoon xanthan gum
- 1 teaspoon salt
- ½ teaspoon baking powder
- ½ teaspoon baking soda
- 16 tablespoons (2 sticks) butter or nondairy alternative
- 400 grams cane sugar or granulated sugar
- 4 large eggs
- ½ teaspoon vanilla extract
- 30 grams grated lemon zest (about 8 lemons)
- ½ cup fresh lemon juice (about 4 lemons)
- 1 cup buttermilk, or 1 cup coconut milk beverage plus 1 tablespoon apple cider vinegar
- FOR THE LEMON SYRUP
- 100 grams cane sugar or granulated sugar
- ½ cup fresh lemon juice (about 4 lemons)

FOR THE GLAZE
- 120 grams powdered sugar
- 2 tablespoons whole milk or coconut milk beverage
- ¼ teaspoon vanilla extract
- ¼ teaspoon lemon extract

TO MAKE THE CAKE
1. Preheat the oven to 350°F. Grease a 10- to 12-cup Bundt pan with shortening.
2. In a medium bowl, whisk the flour, xanthan gum, salt, baking powder, and baking soda to combine.
3. In a small bowl, using a handheld electric mixer on medium speed, cream together the butter and sugar.
4. In a third bowl, whisk the eggs, vanilla, lemon zest, and lemon juice to blend. Add this to the creamed butter and sugar. Mix well to combine. It will look curdled, but that's okay.
5. Add half the flour mixture and ½ cup of buttermilk to the egg mixture and mix on low speed to blend. Add the remaining ½ cup of buttermilk and then the remaining flour mixture and mix just until everything is combined. Do not overmix.
6. Pour the batter into the prepared Bundt pan.
7. Bake for 40 to 45 minutes, or until a toothpick inserted into the center of the cake comes out clean.
8. Let the cake cool in the pan for 15 minutes while you prepare the lemon syrup.
9. TO MAKE THE LEMON SYRUP
10. In a small saucepan, combine the sugar and lemon juice. Cook over medium heat, stirring, until the sugar is completely dissolved. Bring the syrup to a boil and boil for 2 to 3 minutes. Remove from the heat and let the syrup cool. It will thicken a little as it cools.
11. Line a baking sheet with parchment paper and set a wire rack in the pan. Remove the cake from the Bundt pan and flip it over onto the wire rack. Slowly pour the cooled syrup over the cake and allow the cake to soak it up.
12. Let the cake cool completely.
13. TO MAKE THE GLAZE
14. In a small bowl, whisk the powdered sugar, milk, vanilla, and lemon extract until smooth. Drizzle the glaze over the cake top and serve.
15. Keep covered at room temperature, or refrigerate, for up to 5 days.

Classic Cheesecake

This cheesecake recipe captures that flavor. The recipe is time-consuming, however it may be split into two sessions. For optimal results, refrigerate the cheesecake overnight. So you can have cheesecake for morning.

Prep time: 65 minutes | Cook time: about 3 hours, plus overnight chilling | Serves 1 (9-inch) cheesecake

FOR THE CRUST
- 95 grams all-purpose flour blend, plus more for dusting
- ¼ teaspoon xanthan gum
- ¼ teaspoon salt
- 8 tablespoons (1 stick) butter or nondairy alternative
- 50 grams cane sugar or granulated sugar
- 1 large egg yolk
- 1 teaspoon vanilla extract
- FOR THE CHEESECAKE FILLING
- 4 (8-ounce) packages cream cheese or nondairy alternative, room temperature
- 300 grams cane sugar or granulated sugar
- 80 grams vanilla Greek yogurt or nondairy alternative
- 1 tablespoon vanilla extract
- 2 large egg yolks
- 4 large eggs

TO MAKE THE CRUST
1. Line the bottom of a 9-inch springform pan with aluminum foil and dust with a bit of flour. The foil should wrap around the entire bottom portion of the pan, including the outside.
2. In a small bowl, whisk the flour, xanthan gum, and salt to combine.
3. In a large bowl, using a whisk or handheld electric mixer, mix the butter, sugar, egg yolk, and vanilla until combined. Add the flour mixture and mix until a sticky dough forms.
4. Transfer the dough to the prepared pan and dust a bit more flour on top so it doesn't stick to your fingers. Flatten the dough into a 6-inch-diameter disk, cover with plastic wrap, and chill for 30 minutes.
5. Position an oven rack in the third lowest position and preheat the oven to 350°F.
6. Release the clamp from the pan and remove the sides. Place a small piece of parchment paper over the chilled dough and use a rolling pin to stretch the dough to reach the edges of the pan. Work the edges so the dough fits well. Replace the sides of the pan, and tighten the clamp. Use your fingertips to push the dough up the sides just a little.
7. Bake for 10 minutes. Remove from the oven but leave the oven on. Leave the oven rack where it is, but increase the oven temperature to 500°F.
8. Let the crust cool for at least 10 minutes before preparing the cheesecake filling.
9. TO MAKE THE CHEESECAKE FILLING
10. In a large bowl, using a whisk or handheld electric mixer, beat the cream cheese until smooth and creamy. Add the sugar, yogurt, and vanilla and mix again to combine. Add the egg yolks only and mix again.
11. Add the whole eggs, 2 at a time, mixing after each set and stopping to scrape down the bowl as needed, also giving the bottom of the bowl a stir to make sure all the cream cheese is incorporated. Pour the batter over the cooled crust.
12. Bake for 10 minutes, then (without opening the oven) reduce the oven temperature to 200°F and bake for 2 hours 30 minutes. The edges will be golden but the center may not be quite set. If you have an instant-read thermometer, the internal temperature should read 165°F.
13. Let the cake sit in the pan at room temperature for 2 hours. Cover it with plastic wrap and refrigerate overnight.
14. To remove the cake from the pan, run a butter knife along the outside of the cake to detach it from the sides. Release the clamp and remove the sides. Refrigerate, covered, for up to 4 days.

Triple-Layer Birthday Cake with Buttercream Frosting

A triple-layer birthday cake suggests "Let's celebrate." They're popular. I started making triple-layer cakes because gluten-free layers tend to be flatter than my old layers. Not this cake. This juicy and tasty dish bakes all three layers at once. Springform pans work well.

Prep time: 35 minutes | Cook time: 30 minutes | Serves 1 (9-inch) three-layer frosted cake

FOR THE CAKE

- Shortening, for preparing the pans
- 375 grams all-purpose flour blend, plus more for dusting
- 62 grams arrowroot
- 1 tablespoon baking powder
- 1½ teaspoons xanthan gum
- 1 teaspoon baking soda
- ½ teaspoon salt
- 3 large eggs
- 2 large egg whites
- 400 grams cane sugar or granulated sugar
- 1½ cups whole milk or coconut milk beverage
- 1 cup avocado oil or canola oil
- 1 tablespoon vanilla extract
- 1 teaspoon apple cider vinegar

FOR THE BUTTERCREAM FROSTING

- 205 grams shortening
- 8 tablespoons (1 stick) butter or nondairy alternative
- 720 grams powdered sugar
- 2 teaspoons vanilla extract
- ¼ cup heavy cream or coconut cream

TO MAKE THE CAKE

1. Preheat the oven to 350°F. Grease three 9-inch springform pans with shortening. Sprinkle a little flour inside and tap the pans to spread the flour evenly around each pan.
2. In a medium bowl, whisk the flour, arrowroot, baking powder, xanthan gum, baking soda, and salt to combine.
3. In a small bowl, whisk the whole eggs to combine.
4. In a large bowl, using a handheld electric mixer, whip the egg whites until soft peak forms. Add the cane sugar and beaten eggs to the egg whites and mix for 1 minute.
5. Add the milk, oil, vanilla, and vinegar. Mix well. With the mixer on low speed, mix in the flour in 3 additions, stopping to scrape down the bowl, as needed.
6. Evenly divide the batter between the prepared pans.
7. Bake for 25 to 30 minutes, or until a toothpick inserted into the center of a cake comes out clean.
8. Let the cakes cool in the pans for at least 15 minutes. Release the clamp from each pan and remove the sides. Transfer the cakes and plates to a wire rack to cool completely.
9. Using a large serrated knife, cut off the thin domed layer from the top of each cake. Creating a flat surface will help the cakes stack well.

TO MAKE THE BUTTERCREAM FROSTING

10. In a large bowl, using a handheld electric mixer on medium speed, cream together the shortening and butter. Add the powdered sugar and vanilla. Mix, while slowly adding the heavy cream, until smooth and creamy.
11. Frost the cake layers and outside of the cake as desired. Refrigerate leftovers, covered, for up to 5 days.

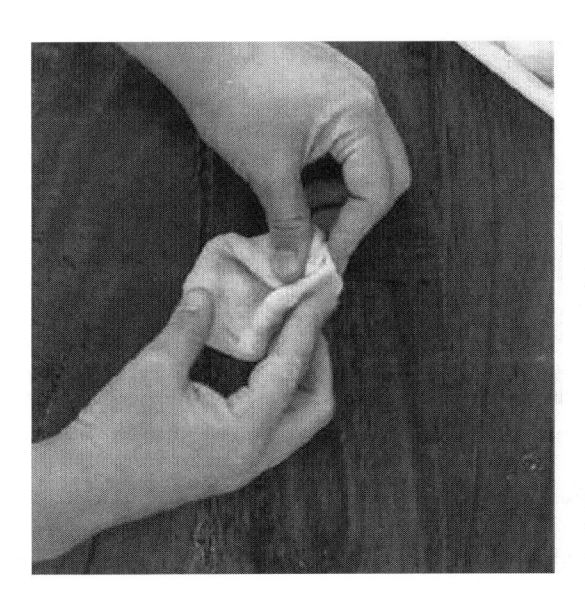

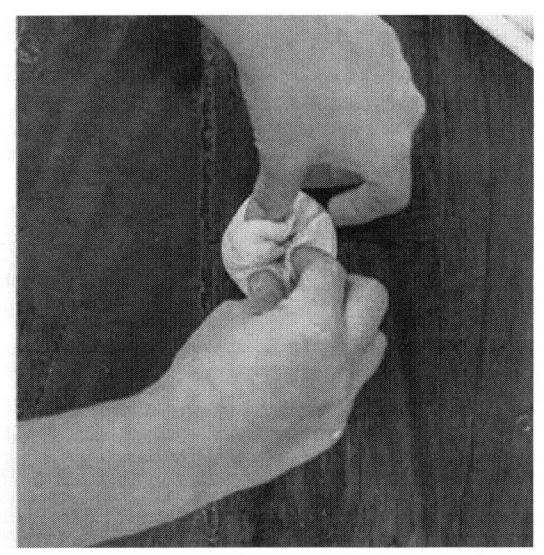

Chapter 13
Holidays

Sweet Levain Rolls Master Recipe

This master recipe makes sweet levain breads that rise higher and are fluffier. This recipe's delicate, buttery richness reminds me of childhood family gatherings. My family devours these rolls rapidly. They're perfect for a holiday meal or Friday night supper. This book's master recipe generates a range of celebratory breads with simple procedures and superb outcomes.

Prep time: 45 minutes | Cook time: 35 minutes | Serves 12 dinner rolls

FOR THE SWEET LEVAIN
- 30 grams active starter
- 15 grams sugar
- 50 grams water
- 100 grams all-purpose or bread flour
- For the dough
- 200 grams milk, warmed
- 42 grams unsalted butter, at room temperature or melted
- 180 grams of the activated sweet levain
- 380 grams bread flour
- 7 grams sea salt
- 1 large egg yolk
- For the glaze
- 2 tablespoons unsalted butter, melted
- 1½ tablespoons honey
- 1 tablespoon water

1. Make the sweet levain: 6 to 10 hours before mixing your dough, combine the ingredients for sweet levain in a clean container. The mixture will be very stiff so you may need to use your hands to make sure all the ingredients mix together. Cover and let activate until it increases in volume and becomes a very thick, aerated dough.
2. Warm the milk: Measure the milk into a saucepan and cook over medium heat until you begin to see steam rising off it or until it reaches a temperature of 130° to 140°F.
3. Scale: Place a mixing bowl on the scale, tare the weight of the scale, and pour in 200 grams of the warm milk. Add 42 grams of butter and 180 grams of the sweet levain, using a spoon to gently stir and break it apart. Add the flour. (When using the scale to measure ingredients, use the tare function to remove the weight of the mixing bowl and other previous ingredients so you can weigh each individual ingredient easily as you add each one to the bowl.)
4. Mix: Stir together with a spoon until partially combined. Add the egg yolk and salt and continue mixing the dough, using a dough scraper to scrape the sides of the bowl. (if you have a stand mixer and a dough hook, use it to mix and knead the dough).
5. Knead: Knead the mixture with your hands and using a dough scraper, either in the bowl or on a clean work surface (or in the stand mixer) for 5 to 10 minutes, until the dough is smooth and releases easily from the bowl or work surface.
6. Bulk fermentation: Cover the dough and leave it at room temperature to ferment for 2 to 3 hours.
7. Stretch and fold: At least 30 minutes into the bulk fermentation, to further strengthen the dough, pull one-quarter of the dough upwards and fold it over the middle. Repeat this process with the other three-quarters of the dough. Re-cover the dough. This step can be done every 30 minutes, up to 3 times, during bulk fermentation for maximum development of dough strength.
8. Divide: Lightly flour a clean work surface and transfer the dough from the bowl to the work surface. Divide the dough into 12 equal pieces, either visually or by weighing the dough on the scale.
9. Prepare the baking dish: Rub 1 teaspoon of butter into a pie dish or a square baking dish.
10. Shape: Take one piece of the dough and flatten it. Gather the edges into the middle and press them together to form a ball. Place the sealed side down and roll or rotate the ball to create friction. You'll eventually create a smooth, taut, round roll. Place the ball into the prepared baking dish and repeat with the remaining 11 balls of dough.
11. Proof: Cover the shaped rolls and let proof at room temperature for 4 to 5 hours, until the dough is 1½ times its original size and the impression from a finger lightly pressed into the dough slowly rises back.
12. Preheat: Preheat the oven to 375°F.
13. Prepare the glaze: In a small saucepan over medium heat, mix together the butter, honey, and water until combined. If you like your bread a little sweeter, feel free to add a little more honey. Brush the glaze generously over the tops of the rolls, reserving some of the glaze to brush on the rolls after baking.
14. Bake: Place the baking dish into oven and bake for 22 to 26 minutes, until the rolls expand, have a golden-brown color on top, and the internal temperature of the outside edge rolls are 190°F. Brush the reserved glaze over the baked rolls while they are still warm.
15. Cool: Allow the dish to cool for about 30 minutes. These are best enjoyed warm.

Red, White, and Blueberry Bread

This bread is perfect for Memorial Day, Independence Day, or Bastille Day (if you're French). The jams in the filling add sweetness and flavor. In the summer, use homemade strawberry and blueberry jam to boost the flavor. Layers of jam can make shaping messy, but the end result is a beautiful centerpiece.

Prep time: 47 to 52 minutes | Cook time: 30 to 35 minutes | Serves 1 large loaf

FOR THE SWEET LEVAIN
- 30 grams active sourdough starter
- 15 grams sugar
- 50 grams water
- 100 grams all-purpose or bread flour
- For the dough
- 200 grams warm milk
- 42 grams unsalted butter, at room temperature or melted
- 180 grams of the activated sweet levain
- 380 grams bread flour (all-purpose flour may be substituted)
- 7 grams sea salt
- 1 large egg yolk
- For the filling
- ⅓ to ½ cup strawberry jam
- ⅓ to ½ cup blueberry jam
- For the vanilla icing
- ½ cup sifted confectioners' sugar
- 1 to 3 teaspoons milk
- ¼ teaspoon vanilla extract

1. Make the dough: Follow the Sweet Levain Rolls Master Recipe through step 7, using the ingredients listed.
2. Prepare the filling: The jam should be smooth and spreadable. If it is chunky, use an immersion blender or food processor to create a smoother texture.
3. Prepare the baking sheet: Line a baking sheet with parchment paper.
4. Divide and preshape: Divide the dough into 2 equal pieces. Lightly flour the work surface and, using a rolling pin, roll out each piece to a 6-by-14-inch rectangle. Spread the blueberry jam over one piece of dough, leaving a 1-inch margin on the long sides. Spread the strawberry jam over the other piece of rolled dough, leaving a 1-inch margin on the long sides. Starting at a long side, roll up each piece of dough and pinch the seam to seal it.
5. Shape: Using a serrated bread knife or a sharp knife, cut halfway through the roll lengthwise, about to the center of the dough, and pull open to expose the layers of dough and jam. This is a messy process and jam will spill out; the sharper your knife, the easier this will go. Clean the knife after cutting through the first section of dough and repeat the process with the other rolled dough. Loosely twist the two pieces together and transfer the dough to the parchment paper-lined baking sheet.
6. Proof: Cover the dough with a kitchen towel and proof at room temperature for 3 to 5 hours or until the impression made by a finger lightly pressed into the dough slowly rises back.
7. Preheat: 30 to 60 minutes before proofing is done, preheat the oven to 375°F.
8. Bake: Place the baking sheet into the oven and bake for 30 to 35 minutes until golden brown on the edges. The jam can burn sometimes so check frequently. Test the internal temperature to see if it's 190°F. If it is not done, tent the bread with aluminum foil until finished baking.
9. Cool: Transfer to a cooling rack to cool for at least 30 minutes and up to 60 minutes.
10. Prepare the icing: In a medium bowl, whisk together the confectioners' sugar, milk, and vanilla until it is smooth and thick. It should be a drizzling consistency.
11. Serve: Place the cooled loaf on a serving plate and drizzle with the vanilla icing. Cut into slices and serve.

Sourdough Rustic Bread Master Recipe

It's wonderful for any meal and gatherings. My family eats it for breakfast, sandwiches, and other meals multiple times a week. With a sourdough starter, you can prepare this bread with common ingredients and tools.

Prep time: 35 minutes | Cook time: 45 minutes | Serves 1 loaf

- For the starter
- 15 grams starter
- 60 grams all-purpose or bread flour
- 60 grams water
- For the dough
- 370 grams water, divided
- 100 grams active starter
- 100 grams whole-wheat flour
- 400 grams all-purpose or bread flour
- 10 grams sea salt
- For dusting the proofing bowl
- Rice flour or cornmeal

1. Refresh the starter: 6 to 8 hours before mixing your dough, take your sourdough starter out of the refrigerator and place 15 grams of the starter into a clean, empty jar. Discard any starter left in the original jar. Add the 60 grams of flour and 60 grams of water to the jar and stir well. Leave the refreshed starter out at room temperature for 6 to 8 hours until it doubles in volume and becomes bubbly. (After using what's needed for the recipe, keep the remainder for your next refresh.)
2. Scale: Place a mixing bowl on the scale, tare the weight of the scale, and pour in 360 grams of water. Add 100 grams of the active starter and the whole-wheat and all-purpose flour. (When using the scale to measure ingredients, use the tare function to remove the weight of the mixing bowl and other previous ingredients so you can weigh each individual ingredient easily as you add each one to the bowl.)
3. Mix: Using a spoon, mix the ingredients together (if you have a stand mixer and a dough hook, mix until the dough starts to pull away from the sides of the bowl) and knead for about 5 minutes. There should be no dry spots of flour. After the initial mixing, it can be helpful to mix the dough with your hands or with a plastic dough scraper to make sure that all the water is incorporated into the flour. Be sure to scrape the sides of the bowl so no dry pieces of dough stick to it.
4. Autolyse: Cover the bowl and rest the dough for at least 20 minutes and up to 60 minutes.
5. Add salt: Tare the mixture and add the 10 grams of salt and the final 10 grams of water to dissolve the salt. Continue folding the dough, rotating and folding it to make sure it is fully mixed, at least 5 minutes.
6. Rest: Cover the bowl and let rest at room temperature for 30 minutes.
7. Stretch and fold: To further strengthen dough, pull up one-quarter of the dough and fold it over the middle. Repeat this process with the other three-quarters of the dough. Re-cover the dough. This step can be done up to 4 times for maximum development of dough strength during the bulk fermentation.
8. Bulk fermentation: Let the dough ferment at room temperature for at least 2 hours, and up to 4 hours, until the dough is 1½ times its original size and has a smooth texture.
9. Preshape and bench rest: Transfer the dough from the bowl onto an unfloured clean work surface. Quickly push the dough scraper under one half of the dough and fold the dough over itself. Push the scraper under one side of the dough and rotate it in a circle 3 to 5 times until it forms a rough ball. Leave the dough to rest for 20 minutes.
10. Prepare the proofing bowl: Dust a proofing bowl or an 8-inch-wide colander lined with a kitchen towel generously with rice flour or cornmeal so that the sides and bottom have a thick, even coating.
11. Final shape: Lightly flour the work surface and the top of the preshaped dough round. Using the dough scraper, push under the entire piece of dough and, using your opposite hand to guide the dough, lift it off the work surface, and flip it onto its floured side. The sticky, unfloured side of the dough should be facing up. Take two opposite edges of dough and gently pull them up creating some length without tearing the dough (if the dough tears, stop stretching and continue with the steps). Fold the edges into the middle of the dough, one on top of the other, using the sticky edges to help them adhere to each other. The dough will look a bit like a burrito. Taking the end of the dough below the seam, gently lengthen with a slight stretching motion and roll the dough onto itself in a spiral until it seals at the opposite end. The floured side of the dough should be facing up, and from the side the rolled dough should look like a baby's bottom. The dough has structure but still needs tension. Using a bench scraper, pull the dough across the work surface or rotate it in a circle, without flipping the dough over, until it tightens into a taut ball. Quickly push the scraper under the dough, lift it off the work surface, guiding it with the opposite hand, and flip the dough upside down into the prepared proofing bowl. The floured side should be down.
12. Final shaping step-by-step
13. Proof: Cover the dough and proof for 1 to 2 hours at room temperature, until the impression made by a finger lightly pressed into the dough slowly rises back.
14. Preheat: 30 to 60 minutes before the proofing is done, preheat the oven to 500°F. Place a Dutch oven or cloche inside the oven on the center rack to preheat. If you don't have a Dutch oven or cloche, use the manual steaming technique directions.
15. Bake: Cut a large piece of parchment paper that is approximately twice as wide as the dough. Center

the parchment paper over the proofing bowl and flip the bowl upside down to release the dough onto the paper. Using a serrated bread knife or a bread lame, cut a slit all the way across the top of the dough, about ¼-inch deep. Carefully transfer the dough from the parchment paper into the preheated Dutch oven or cloche (or onto a cookie sheet, if using the manual steam method) and cover it with the lid. Place the bread in the oven. Reduce the oven temperature to 460°F and bake for 20 minutes. Carefully remove the bread from the Dutch oven and place it directly onto the oven rack (remove the steam tray if using manual steam). Reduce the heat to 450°F and bake for an additional 20 minutes to create a golden-brown crust.
16. Cool: Transfer the bread to a cooling rack and allow it to cool for at least 60 minutes before slicing.

Olive Oil Rolls

These bread rolls have a tender crumb and would work wonderfully both as dinner rolls and as buns for sandwiches.

Prep time: 15 minutes plus 4 hours for the dough to rise | Cook time: 15 minutes| Serves 1 bread roll (12 servings), makes 12 rolls

- 2 cups (250 g) flour, bread or all-purpose
- ½ tsp (1.4 g) active dry yeast
- ½ tsp (2.85 g) salt
- ½ cup plus 3 tbsp (162 g) lukewarm water
- 3 tbsp (40 g) olive oil
- ¾ tsp (5.3 g) honey

1. Put the water and honey in a small bowl and sprinkle the dry yeast into the water mixture. Set aside for 5 minutes and then stir to combine.
2. Place the flour and salt into the bowl of a stand mixer and whisk to mix the salt through the flour evenly. Switch to the dough hook and make a well in the middle of the bowl and add the yeast mixture.
3. Knead the dough with the dough hook for about 10-12 minutes, until the dough forms a ball. Stop a few times during the kneading to scrape the sides of the bowl clean and remove dough from the hook.
4. Lightly dust a work surface with flour and knead it by hand for 2-3 minutes. Then place the dough ball into a greased mixing bowl and roll the ball around to coat the surface with oil.
5. Cover the bowl and leave in a warm area in the kitchen to rise for 2 hours until the dough has doubled in size.
6. Remove the dough and place it on the floured work surface again and punch it down.
7. Make 12 evenly sized balls of dough or alternatively you can roll out the dough in a rectangular shape and roll up, and then cut into 12 rolled up balls. Keep the dough covered while you make the balls to prevent it from drying out.
8. Place the dough balls into a baking sheet that has been lined with parchment paper. Cover the rolls with a damp cloth and leave to rise until rolls have doubled in size again, about 1 hour.
9. Preheat the oven during the second rising time to 400 degrees F (200 degrees C).
10. Brush the dough balls with olive oil using a pastry brush, before placing the rolls into the oven.
11. Bake the rolls until they are golden brown, for 10-15 minutes. Test to see if they are done by knocking on the bottom to hear the hollow sound that means it is done.
12. Place on a cooling rack to cool down for about 10 minutes before serving.

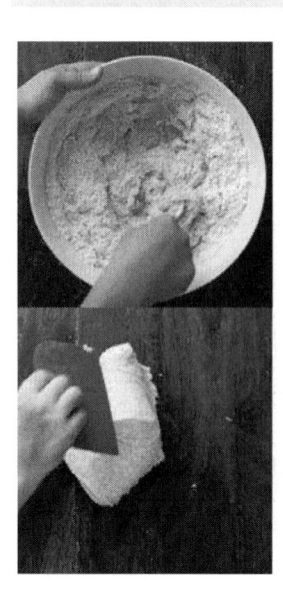

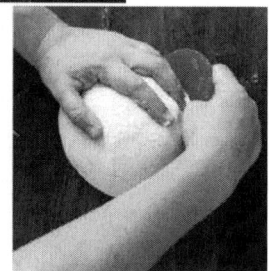

Brioche Cinnamon Rolls

Brioche produces delicious cinnamon rolls. The cinnamon filling is soft, fluffy, and tender. When the rolls are baked and inverted onto a tray, they will have a sweet, caramelized glaze. These are a family tradition for Christmas morning, birthdays, and other important occasions.

Prep time: 25 minutes | Cook time: 35 minutes | Serves 12 rolls

FOR THE DOUGH
- 156 grams whole milk
- 256 grams whole eggs
- 72 grams sugar
- 6 grams yeast
- 180 grams very soft butter
- 600 grams all-purpose flour
- 12 grams salt
- For the filling
- 110 grams soft butter
- 250 grams brown sugar
- 15 grams cinnamon
- 1 tablespoon vanilla extract
- Flaky sea salt for topping (optional)

1. Create the dough: Follow the Master Recipe for Enriched Bread through step 6, using the ingredient amounts listed. After the rise, the dough can be chilled in the refrigerator for 2 hours to overnight, to make it easier to roll out.
2. Make the filling: In a medium bowl, combine the butter, sugar, cinnamon, and vanilla with a spatula and set aside.
3. Roll out: Flour your work surface. Take the dough from the refrigerator, if chilled, and roll it out with a rolling pin to a rectangle about 24 inches by 8 inches. The longer side should be horizontal.
4. Shape: Using a rubber spatula, spread about ¾ of the filling over the dough, covering the surface but leaving a small strip of dough uncovered on the long side farthest from you; you will use this to seal the edge of the dough. Gently roll up the dough, pushing the edge of the dough away from you and rolling it up like a yoga mat. Seal the seam by pressing the dough together. Using a metal dough scraper, cut the spiral into 12 (2-inch) rolls. If your roasting pan doesn't have a nonstick surface, line it with parchment paper or aluminum foil. Spread the remaining cinnamon-sugar filling over the bottom of the pan, then place the rolls into the pan cut-side up, spacing them evenly apart so that they have room to rise.
5. Proof: At this point, you have two options: You can proof and bake the rolls, or you can refrigerate them from 2 hours to overnight and then proof and bake them. Whichever option you choose, proof for 1 hour 30 minutes to 2 hours, until they are puffy and full of air and feel like a marshmallow. When pressed with a finger, it should leave an indent instead of springing back up.
6. Preheat: While the dough is proofing, preheat your oven to 375°F.

Red Velvet Chocolate Chip Bread

Red Velvet Chocolate Chip Bread is a Valentine's Day favorite. It's rich without being overbearing and goes well with butter, fruit, or nut butter. Beets provide the red hue. My kids were fascinated by the magenta-colored dough, which became a dark reddish color after baking. If you don't have little chips, use regular-sized ones. To avoid staining wood or marble, shape dough on a big baking sheet.

Prep time: 60 to 70 minutes | Cook time: 40 minutes | Serves 1 loaf

FOR THE STARTER
- 15 grams starter
- 60 grams all-purpose or bread flour
- 60 grams water
- For the red dye
- 473 grams water
- 500 grams red beets, root and stem trimmed
- For the dough
- 250 grams red beet dye
- 110 grams water, divided
- 100 grams active starter
- 100 grams whole-wheat flour
- 400 grams all-purpose or bread flour
- 10 grams sea salt
- 25 grams maple syrup or honey
- 15 grams raw cacao powder or unsweetened cocoa powder
- 35 grams mini semi-sweet chocolate chips
- For dusting the proofing bowl
- Rice flour or cornmeal

1. Make the red beet dye: This step can be done up to a week ahead of time. Bring 2 cups of water to boil in a medium-size pot over high heat. Add the beets, cover the pot, reduce the heat to medium-low, and simmer for 15 minutes. Turn off the heat and leave the lid on the pot. Let sit for 30 to 60 minutes or until the liquid is room temperature. Strain the liquid into a jar with a lid and store it in the refrigerator until you're ready to make the dough. The cooked beets can be eaten right away or frozen for up to 8 months and used in smoothies.
2. Make the dough: Follow the Sourdough Rustic Bread Master Recipe through step 6, using the ingredients listed. Add the red beet dye to the dough in step 2 when mixing the dough.
3. Stretch and fold: Add the maple syrup, cacao powder, and chocolate chips to the dough. Pull up one-quarter of the dough and fold it over the middle. Repeat this process with the other three-quarters of the dough, or until the ingredients are incorporated into the dough. Re-cover the dough and continue the fermentation for 2 to 3 more hours.
4. Shape, proof, and bake: Follow the Sourdough Rustic Bread Master Recipe from steps 9 through 15. When shaping the dough, use an alternate surface like a large baking sheet to avoid staining a wood or marble surface.

Cranberry Orange Hot Cross Buns

I love the orange, cranberry, spice, and delicate, airy texture. Sometimes I double the recipe. Buns expand while baking, so check the internal temperature to see if they're done.

Prep time: 47 to 52 minutes | Cook time: 47 to 52 minutes | Serves 9 large buns or 12 medium buns

FOR THE SWEET LEVAIN
- 30 grams active sourdough starter
- 15 grams sugar
- 50 grams water
- 100 grams all-purpose or bread flour
- For the dough
- 50 grams dried sweetened cranberries, roughly chopped
- 85 grams freshly squeezed orange juice (about 1 medium orange)
- 200 grams warm milk
- 70 grams unsalted butter, melted and divided
- 30 grams brown sugar
- 180 grams of the activated sweet levain
- 380 grams bread flour
- 7 grams sea salt
- 1 large egg
- ½ teaspoon cinnamon
- ¼ teaspoon nutmeg
- ½ teaspoon ground cloves
- Zest of 1 orange
- 2 tablespoons unsalted butter, melted
- For the vanilla icing
- ½ cup sifted confectioners' sugar
- 1 to 3 teaspoons milk or orange juice
- ¼ teaspoon vanilla extract

1. **Soak the cranberries:** In a small bowl combine the cranberries and orange juice and let soak for at least 1 hour before using.
2. **Make the dough:** Follow the Sweet Levain Rolls Master Recipe through step 5, using the ingredients listed. The brown sugar is added along with the milk, 42 grams of butter, and the sweet levain. The spices are mixed in with the salt and the egg.
3. **Fold:** Drain the cranberries and press out any excess juice. Add the cranberries and orange zest to the dough and fold them in until the orange zest is evenly distributed. It's okay if some cranberries are not fully incorporated; this will resolve later. The dough will be softer at this point.
4. **Bulk fermentation:** Cover the dough and ferment for 2 to 3 hours until the dough expands to 1½ times its original size.
5. **Stretch and fold:** During bulk fermentation, to further strengthen dough, pull up one-quarter of the dough and fold it over the middle. Repeat this process with the other three-quarters of the dough. Re-cover the dough. This step can be done every 30 minutes, up to 3 times, during bulk fermentation for maximum development of dough strength.
6. **Divide:** Transfer the dough from the bowl to a clean, unfloured work surface. Divide the dough into 9 equal pieces for large buns or 12 equal pieces for medium buns, either visually or by weighing the dough on the scale.
7. **Prepare the baking dish:** Grease an 8-inch square baking dish with butter for 9 buns or a 9-by-13-inch baking dish for 12 buns.
8. **Shape:** Flatten 1 piece of dough with your hand and gather the edges into the middle. Turn the dough over and roll it against the work surface to tighten the dough into a smooth ball. If the dough is sticking, use a light dusting of flour and/or a dough scraper to shape the dough. Transfer the shaped bun to the prepared baking dish. Repeat with the remaining pieces dough. Arrange the buns and space them out evenly in the baking dish.
9. **Proof:** Cover the shaped buns with a kitchen towel and proof for 3 to 5 hours at room temperature until nearly doubled in size and the impression made by a finger lightly pressed into the dough slowly rises back.
10. **Preheat:** Preheat the oven to 375°F.
11. **Brush with butter:** Using a pastry brush, brush the tops of the buns with the remaining melted butter.
12. **Bake:** Place the baking dish into the oven and generously spray the walls of the oven with water. Bake for 20 to 24 minutes, until the rolls expand and turn golden brown.
13. **Cool:** Transfer to a cooling rack and let cool for about 30 minutes. Serve warm or to ice them with vanilla icing, continue with step 14.
14. **Prepare the vanilla icing:** In a medium bowl, whisk together the confectioners' sugar, milk, and vanilla until it is smooth and thick. Spoon the icing into a pastry bag fitted with a small round tip (or fill a resealable plastic bag with a very small corner snipped off) and pipe crosses on the tops of the buns with vertical and horizontal lines going through the middle of the buns.

Apple Spice Sourdough Bread

When fall arrives, apples are in season and bakeries and grocery shops smell of warming spices. This sourdough bread is not overly sweet and has lots of baked apple, cinnamon, nutmeg, ginger, and cloves. It's perfect for breakfast, a wonderful sandwich at lunch, or a mildly sweet slice after supper. Make this on a cozy October evening and enjoy the fragrances.

Prep time: 45 minutes | Cook time: 45 minutes | Serves 1 loaf

FOR THE STARTER

- 15 grams sourdough starter
- 60 grams all-purpose or bread flour
- 60 grams water
- For the dough
- 360 grams water, divided
- 100 grams of the active starter
- 100 grams whole-wheat flour
- 400 grams all-purpose or bread flour
- 10 grams sea salt
- 75 grams green apples, peeled, cored, and diced into ¼-inch pieces
- 15 grams brown sugar or granulated maple sugar
- 1 tablespoon pumpkin pie spice (or mix together 1½ teaspoons cinnamon, 1 teaspoon ground ginger, ½ teaspoon nutmeg, ½ teaspoon ground cloves)
- For dusting the proofing bowl
- Rice flour or cornmeal

1. **Make the dough:** Follow the Sourdough Rustic Bread Master Recipe through step 6 using the ingredients listed.
2. **Stretch and fold:** Add the diced apples, sugar, and spices to the dough. To further strengthen the dough, pull up one-quarter of the dough and fold it over the middle. Repeat this process with the other three-quarters of the dough, making sure to incorporate all the ingredients. Re-cover the dough and continue fermentation for 2 to 3 more hours, until the dough expands to 1½ times its original size.
3. **Shape, proof, and bake:** Follow the Sourdough Rustic Bread Master Recipe from steps 9 through 15.

Ciabatta Sandwich Rolls

Soft, chewy Ciabatta is the perfect sandwich base. Serve these ciabatta sandwich rolls at a summer build-your-own-sandwich buffet.

Prep time: 35 minutes | Cook time: 15 minutes | Serves 8 rolls

400 grams warm water, divided (1⅔ cups plus ½ tablespoon)
2 grams instant yeast (½ teaspoon)
500 grams bread flour (3½ cups)
10 grams sea salt (1½ teaspoons)

1. **Weigh the ingredients:** Making sure to tare your mixing bowl after each addition, combine 390 grams of warm water and the yeast and allow it to dissolve. Add the bread flour.
2. **Mix:** Using a spoon or dough hook in a stand mixer, mix all the ingredients together until a shaggy dough is formed. Be sure to scrape the sides of the bowl so that no dry pieces of dough stick to it.
3. **Add salt:** Tare the bowl. Pour in the salt, then add the remaining 10 grams of water to dissolve the salt.
4. **Stretch and fold:** Fold the dough by hand for 8 to 12 minutes or with a dough hook in a stand mixer for 4 to 8 minutes, until the dough no longer sticks to the sides of the bowl and pulls away easily.
5. **Bulk ferment:** Cover the dough and leave it in a warm place to ferment for 1½ to 2 hours, until doubled in volume.
6. **Divide the dough:** Cut an extra-long sheet of parchment (if using pre-cut sheets, slightly overlap two sheets) and generously flour them. Pour the ciabatta dough onto the floured surface. Doing your best not to release any of the built-up air, use the sharp edge of a dough scraper coated in flour to divide the dough. This dough is difficult to weigh due to its high hydration, so to divide, cut the dough in half, then cut each piece in half again. Finally, cut each piece in half again, resulting in eight pieces. Gently push the pieces of dough so that they are evenly spaced from each other, 3 to 4 inches apart.
7. **Shape the dough:** Flour your hands and the dough scraper. With the scraper, gently push a piece of dough by the edges to move it into position on the parchment and shape. Alternate which sides you push, gently forming a rough rectangle that measures 3½-by-4½ inches. Repeat with the remaining dough. The rolls will not look identical, but aim for them all to be a similar size. Dust the tops with flour and cover them with a clean, dry kitchen cloth.
8. **Proof:** Proof the rolls for 45 minutes to 1½ hours.
9. **Preheat:** About 30 minutes before the proofing is finished, place a baking stone on the center rack of the oven (bake directly on a baking sheet if you do not have a baking stone) with a steam pan filled with water on the bottom rack and preheat the oven to 500°F.
10. **Bake:** Cut the parchment sheet in the middle to bake the ciabatta in two batches. Transfer one sheet of parchment with four proofed ciabatta rolls into the hot oven. Spray a generous mist of water on the oven walls and close the door. Reduce the heat to 460°F and bake for 10 minutes, then remove the steam pan and bake for 5 to 10 more minutes, until the crust is crisp and golden brown. Return the steam pan to the oven and repeat this step with the other batch of ciabatta rolls.
11. **Cool:** Cool the rolls on a cooling rack for at least 30 minutes.

Bavarian-Inspired Pretzel Rolls

Bavarian-style pretzel buns remind us of family vacations. Now, making them at home signals a special supper, even if it's simply another summer night. Butter or as a hot dog bun, they're excellent.

Prep time: 50 minutes | Cook time: 15 minutes | Serves 8 rolls

FOR THE DOUGH
- 330 grams warm water, divided (1½ cups plus 2 tablespoons)
- 15 grams honey (1 tablespoon)
- 4 grams instant yeast (1 teaspoon)
- 550 grams bread flour (3⅔ cups)
- 50 grams whole-wheat flour (⅓ cup)
- 42 grams unsalted butter, at room temperature (3 tablespoons)
- 10 grams salt (1½ teaspoons)

FOR POACHING
- 6 to 8 cups water
- 3 tablespoons baking soda

FOR THE EGG WASH
- 1 large egg
- ½ teaspoon water
- 1 to 3 teaspoons coarse salt, for topping

1. Weigh the ingredients: Making sure to tare your mixing bowl after each addition, combine 320 grams of warm water, the honey, instant yeast, bread flour, and whole-wheat flour in a mixing bowl.
2. Mix: Mix the ingredients until a shaggy dough forms, then add the butter, salt, and remaining 10 grams of water. Mix to combine.
3. Knead: Knead the dough for 10 to 15 minutes by hand or 3 to 8 minutes with a dough hook in an electric stand mixer, until the dough is smooth, is no longer sticky, and releases easily from the bowl or work surface.
4. Bulk ferment: Cover the dough and ferment for 1½ to 2 hours, until it has doubled in volume.
5. Prepare the baking sheet: Place a large piece of parchment paper on a flat baking sheet.
6. Shape: On an unfloured work surface, divide the dough into 8 pieces (about 120 grams each). Shape the dough pieces into round balls. Flip a ball upside down and press down gently to flatten and form it into a rough square shape. Fold the top two corners into the middle at right angles to create a triangle shape. Fold the triangle top down, then fold the left and right sides of the dough to meet the triangle sides in the center. Fold the top edge of the dough to meet the bottom edge nearest you. Pinch the seam, then roll the dough back and forth to tighten and lengthen until it's about 5 to 6 inches long. Set the shaped dough, seam-side down, on the parchment paper-lined baking sheet. Repeat with the remaining balls of dough.
7. Proof: Cover and proof for 30 to 60 minutes, until the dough is about 1½ times larger in volume. Touching the dough with a fingertip should leave an indentation.
8. Preheat: Preheat the oven to 400°F.
9. Poach: Bring the water to a boil in a large pot and add the baking soda. Add 1 or 2 of the proofed rolls. Boil for 30 seconds, then flip with a slotted spoon and boil for 30 more seconds. Put the poached rolls back on the parchment paper-lined baking sheet. Repeat with the remaining rolls.
10. Make the egg wash: Beat the egg and water together and brush the mixture over the pretzel rolls.
11. Score: With a bread lame, slice 3 diagonal lines across the top of each roll of dough about ¼ inch deep. Top with the coarse salt.
12. Bake: Place the rolls in the oven and bake for 15 to 18 minutes, until the outsides are a molasses brown color.
13. Cool: Place the rolls on a cooling rack and cool for 20 to 30 minutes before serving.

Pumpkin Rolls

These pumpkin rolls are perfect for Thanksgiving or other fall events. My kids enjoy the little pumpkins' shape and taste. Ultra-moist pumpkin and comforting spices make the perfect dinner roll. Because these rolls are so wet, they don't solidify after baking, and their dark hue makes it hard to tell when they're done. Measure the interior temperature till it reaches 180°F. Use pumpkin purée, not pumpkin pie filling, which includes extra additives.

Prep time: 45 minutes | Cook time: 25 minutes | Serves 12 rolls

FOR THE SWEET LEVAIN
- 30 grams active sourdough starter
- 15 grams sugar
- 50 grams water
- 100 grams all-purpose or bread flour
- For the dough
- 150 grams warm milk
- 150 grams pure pumpkin purée
- 50 grams brown sugar
- 42 grams unsalted butter, at room temperature or melted
- 180 grams of the activated sweet levain
- 300 grams bread flour or all-purpose flour
- 80 grams whole-wheat flour
- 7 grams sea salt
- 1 large egg
- 1 tablespoon pumpkin pie spice (or mix together 1½ teaspoons cinnamon, 1 teaspoon ground ginger, ½ teaspoon nutmeg, ½ teaspoon ground cloves)
- For the egg wash
- 1 large egg
- 2 teaspoons water
- Pinch sea salt
- For the topping
- 6 pecans, halved lengthwise

1. Make the dough: Follow the Sweet Levain Rolls Master Recipe through step 7, using the ingredients listed.
2. Prepare the baking sheet: Line a baking sheet with parchment paper.
3. Divide: Transfer the dough from the bowl to a clean, floured work surface. Divide the dough into 12 equal pieces, either visually or by weighing the dough on the scale.
4. Shape: Flour the work surface. Take 1 piece of dough and roll it with your hands into a 16-inch rope. Make a loop, about 2 inches in diameter, in the middle of the rope leaving a short 2- to 3-inch short section on one side and a long 5- to 6-inch section on the other. Take the long section and wrap it around the loop 2 or 3 times and tuck the end under the roll. Take the short section and wrap it around the loop once, tuck it under the roll with the other end, and press the ends to seal the shape. Place the shaped dough onto the prepared baking sheet. Repeat this with the rest of the dough. The rolls should be spaced at least 3 inches apart. Line another baking sheet with parchment paper if you run out of room.
5. Shaping Pumpkin Rolls
6. Proof: Cover the dough with a kitchen towel and proof at room temperature for 3 to 5 hours.
7. Preheat: 30 to 60 minutes before the end of proofing, preheat the oven to 375°F.
8. Make the egg wash: Whisk the egg, water, and salt together and brush the egg wash over the surface of the pumpkin rolls.
9. Bake: Place the baking pan in the oven and spray the walls of the oven with water. Bake for 18 to 20 minutes, until they reach an inner temperature of 180°F. The color will darken slightly.
10. Top the rolls: Transfer to a cooling rack. Place a pecan half upright in the center of each roll to serve as a decorative "stems."
11. Cool: Let cool for at least 30 minutes. Enjoy them plain, with butter, with pumpkin butter, or topped with a slice of apple.

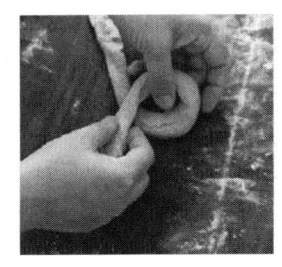

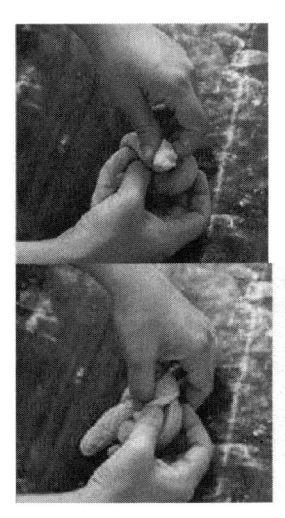

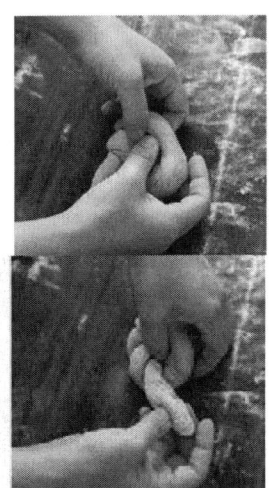

Molasses Spice Cinnamon Swirl Bread

Ginger, cinnamon, nutmeg, and clove were supposed to warm the body in the Middle Ages. Because of tradition and taste, these spices remain in wintertime cuisine. This bread is spicy and molasses-rich. Whole-wheat flour adds flavor and chewiness.

Prep time: 55 minutes | Cook time: 35 minutes | Serves 1 loaf

FOR THE SWEET LEVAIN

- 30 grams active sourdough starter
- 15 grams sugar
- 50 grams water
- 100 grams all-purpose or bread flour
- For the dough
- 180 grams of the activated sweet levain
- 380 grams high-protein whole-wheat flour (such as hard red wheat)
- 200 grams warm milk
- 42 grams unsalted butter, at room temperature or melted
- 30 grams dark molasses
- 7 grams sea salt
- 1 large egg yolk
- 2 teaspoons ground ginger
- 1 teaspoon cinnamon
- ¼ teaspoon nutmeg
- ⅛ teaspoon ground cloves
- For the filling
- 1 large egg white
- 3½ tablespoons brown sugar
- 2 teaspoons cinnamon
- For the topping
- 2 tablespoons unsalted butter, melted

1. Make the dough: Follow the Sweet Levain Rolls Master Recipe through step 7, using the ingredients listed. Add the molasses with the butter in step 3 and the ginger, cinnamon, nutmeg, and cloves in step 4.
2. Prepare the pan: Lightly grease a loaf pan with coconut oil, avocado oil, or ghee, or line the pan with parchment paper trimmed to fit.
3. Make the filling: In a small bowl, whisk the egg white until it is foamy and set aside. In another small bowl, mix together the brown sugar and cinnamon.
4. Shape: Transfer the dough to a floured work surface. Flour a rolling pin and roll out the dough until it is about 16 inches long, as wide as your loaf pan, and ½-inch thick. Brush the egg white over the dough and sprinkle with the sugar mixture, leaving a ½-inch margin at one of the short ends. Starting from the short end covered with filling to the edge, roll up the dough and pinch the seam together to seal. Fold the ends of the dough under the seam and transfer the shaped loaf to the pan.
5. Proof: Cover the pan with a kitchen towel and proof for 2½ to 4 hours at room temperature, until the impression made by a finger lightly pressed into the dough slowly rises back.
6. Preheat: 30 minutes before the proofing is done, roll up kitchen towels and line a metal oven-safe pan with the towels. Fill the pan with water until the towels are saturated and just covered. Place the prepared steam tray on the lowest rack in the oven. Preheat the oven to 500°F.
7. Bake: Brush the top of the loaf with melted butter. Place the loaf into the oven, reduce the temperature to 450°F, and bake for 15 minutes. Remove the steam tray, reduce the temperature to 425°F, and bake for an additional 15 to 20 minutes, until golden brown.
8. Cool: Remove the bread from the loaf pan and place it on a cooling rack. Let it cool for at least 1 hour before slicing.

Caramel Pecan Sticky Buns

Sticky buns are enticing. Gooey caramel melts in your mouth, and toasted nuts give crunch and sweet savoriness. If you proof them overnight in the fridge, you may bake them for Christmas morning brunch. Pecans can burn quickly, making you start over. The caramel pecan topping must thicken without overcooking.

Prep time: 65 minutes | Cook time: 35 minutes | Serves 12 sticky buns

FOR THE TOASTED PECANS
- 1¼ cups whole pecans
- 2 tablespoons unsalted butter
- For the sweet levain
- 30 grams active sourdough starter
- 15 grams sugar
- 50 grams water
- 100 grams all-purpose or bread flour
- For the dough
- 200 grams warm milk
- 84 grams unsalted butter, at room temperature or melted
- 180 grams of the activated sweet levain
- 380 grams bread flour or all-purpose flour
- 7 grams sea salt
- 1 large egg yolk
- For the filling
- ¼ cup unsalted butter, at room temperature
- ¼ cup plus 3 tablespoons brown sugar
- 1 tablespoon cinnamon
- ½ teaspoon nutmeg
- ⅔ cup toasted pecans, finely chopped
- For the caramel pecan topping
- 3½ tablespoons unsalted butter
- ⅔ cup maple syrup
- 2 tablespoons brown sugar
- ½ teaspoon vanilla extract
- Pinch sea salt
- ⅔ cup toasted pecans, roughly chopped

1. Toast the pecans: In a large skillet, melt the butter over medium heat. Add the pecans and cook, stirring frequently, until the pecans start to brown and become aromatic, about 5 minutes. Transfer the pecans to a plate to cool. You can toast the pecans up to 1 week ahead of time and store them in a sealed jar or airtight container at room temperature until ready to use.
2. Make the dough: Follow the Sweet Levain Rolls Master Recipe through step 7, using the ingredients listed.
3. Chop pecans: Divide the pecans in half and place them in separate bowls. Using a sharp knife or a food processor with a pulse function, finely chop half of the pecans leaving some of the pecans in roughly ¼-inch pieces. Return to the bowl and set aside for the filling. Using the knife, roughly chop the other half of the pecans into large halves or quarter pieces and several smaller pieces. These will decorate the top of the sticky buns.
4. Prepare the caramel pecan topping: In a medium-size saucepan, melt the butter over medium heat. Add the maple syrup and cook, stirring often, until the mixture forms lots of foamy bubbles, 3 to 5 minutes. Reduce the heat to medium-low and add the brown sugar, vanilla, salt, and the roughly chopped pecans and mix together into a thick caramel texture. Pour the caramel into the baking dish and spread it out as evenly as you can with a spatula.
5. Prepare the filling: In a small bowl, mix together the softened butter, brown sugar, cinnamon, and nutmeg until it becomes a creamy, spreadable mixture.
6. Shape: Transfer the dough to a floured work surface. Using a floured rolling pin, roll the dough into a 12-by-18-inch rectangle. Spread the butter filling across the dough with a spatula, leaving a ½-inch margin along one of the long edges. Sprinkle the finely chopped pecans evenly over the butter filling. Starting from the longest side that is fully covered in filling, roll up the dough tightly and pinch the seam to seal. Cut the rolled dough into 12 equal rounds that are about 1½ inches thick. Arrange the rounds, cut-side down, over the caramel pecan topping.
7. Proof: Cover the pan with a kitchen towel and proof for 3 to 5 hours at room temperature until dough nearly doubles in size and the impression made by a finger lightly pressed into the dough slowly rises back.
8. Preheat: 30 to 60 minutes before the proofing is done, preheat the oven to 375°F.
9. Bake: Place the baking dish in the oven and reduce the heat to 350°F. Bake for 28 to 32 minutes, until the buns are golden brown and register a temperature of 190°F.
10. Cool: Transfer the pan to a cooling rack and let cool in the baking dish for 2 to 3 minutes. Line a baking sheet with parchment paper and invert it over the baking dish of sticky buns. Using pot holders to protect your hands from the still-hot baking dish, carefully and quickly invert the baking dish and baking sheet onto the cooling rack. Remove the baking pan. Use a fork or a spatula to scrape any remaining caramel or pecans onto the sticky buns. Serve the buns warm.

Appendix 1 Measurement Conversion Chart

Volume Equivalents (Dry)	
US STANDARD	METRIC (APPROXIMATE)
1/8 teaspoon	0.5 mL
1/4 teaspoon	1 mL
1/2 teaspoon	2 mL
3/4 teaspoon	4 mL
1 teaspoon	5 mL
1 tablespoon	15 mL
1/4 cup	59 mL
1/2 cup	118 mL
3/4 cup	177 mL
1 cup	235 mL
2 cups	475 mL
3 cups	700 mL
4 cups	1 L

Weight Equivalents	
US STANDARD	METRIC (APPROXIMATE)
1 ounce	28 g
2 ounces	57 g
5 ounces	142 g
10 ounces	284 g
15 ounces	425 g
16 ounces (1 pound)	455 g
1.5 pounds	680 g
2 pounds	907 g

Volume Equivalents (Liquid)		
US STANDARD	US STANDARD (OUNCES)	METRIC (APPROXIMATE)
2 tablespoons	1 fl.oz.	30 mL
1/4 cup	2 fl.oz.	60 mL
1/2 cup	4 fl.oz.	120 mL
1 cup	8 fl.oz.	240 mL
1 1/2 cup	12 fl.oz.	355 mL
2 cups or 1 pint	16 fl.oz.	475 mL
4 cups or 1 quart	32 fl.oz.	1 L
1 gallon	128 fl.oz.	4 L

Temperatures Equivalents	
FAHRENHEIT(F)	CELSIUS(C) APPROXIMATE)
225 °F	107 °C
250 °F	120 ° °C
275 °F	135 °C
300 °F	150 °C
325 °F	160 °C
350 °F	180 °C
375 °F	190 °C
400 °F	205 °C
425 °F	220 °C
450 °F	235 °C
475 °F	245 °C
500 °F	260 °C

Appendix 2 The Dirty Dozen and Clean Fifteen

The Environmental Working Group (EWG) is a nonprofit, nonpartisan organization dedicated to protecting human health and the environment Its mission is to empower people to live healthier lives in a healthier environment. This organization publishes an annual list of the twelve kinds of produce, in sequence, that have the highest amount of pesticide residue-the Dirty Dozen-as well as a list of the fifteen kinds of produce that have the least amount of pesticide residue-the Clean Fifteen.

THE DIRTY DOZEN	
The 2016 Dirty Dozen includes the following produce. These are considered among the year's most important produce to buy organic:	
Strawberries	Spinach
Apples	Tomatoes
Nectarines	Bell peppers
Peaches	Cherry tomatoes
Celery	Cucumbers
Grapes	Kale/collard greens
Cherries	Hot peppers
The Dirty Dozen list contains two additional items kale/collard greens and hot peppers-because they tend to contain trace levels of highly hazardous pesticides.	

THE CLEAN FIFTEEN	
The least critical to buy organically are the Clean Fifteen list. The following are on the 2016 list:	
Avocados	Papayas
Corn	Kiw
Pineapples	Eggplant
Cabbage	Honeydew
Sweet peas	Grapefruit
Onions	Cantaloupe
Asparagus	Cauliflower
Mangos	
Some of the sweet corn sold in the United States are made from genetically engineered (GE) seedstock. Buy organic varieties of these crops to avoid GE produce.	

Appendix 3 Index

A

activated sweet levain 41, 43, 113, 114, 118, 121, 122, 123
active sourdough starter 41, 43
active starter 29, 59, 67, 68, 69, 79, 84, 85, 90, 113, 115, 119
all-purpose flour 14, 29, 31, 32, 33, 34, 35, 36, 38, 39, 40, 42, 44, 46, 47, 57, 58, 59, 60, 63, 64, 66, 71, 72, 76, 77, 82, 83, 84, 85, 87, 89, 90, 91, 92, 101, 114, 115, 117, 121, 123
all-purpose flour blend 94, 95, 96, 97, 98, 99, 100, 101, 103, 104, 105, 106, 107, 108, 109, 110, 111
all-purpose or bread flour 43
almond 49, 50, 51, 52
almond extract 95
almond flour 49, 50, 51, 52
anise extract 50
apple cider vinegar 52, 67, 97, 98, 104, 105, 107, 108, 109, 111
arrowroot 97, 104, 105, 106, 107, 108, 111
artichoke hearts 12
avocado oil 46, 47, 76, 103, 104, 105, 107, 108, 111, 122

B

baking powder 36, 42, 44, 49, 50, 52, 82, 90, 94, 96, 99, 100, 101, 103, 104, 105, 107, 108, 109, 111
baking soda 42, 49, 50, 51, 82, 83, 84, 86, 88, 89, 90, 94, 97, 98, 100, 101, 103, 104, 105, 106, 107, 108, 109, 111, 120
balsamic vinegar 11
barley malt flour 13, 15, 22, 28
basil 35, 85
bay leaves 59
bell pepper 71
berry jam 43, 114
biga 4, 13
bittersweet chocolate 67
blackberries 44
blackberry jam 99
blueberries 29, 44, 49
blueberry jam 114
bolted hard wheat flour 9, 10, 13, 14, 15, 16, 17, 20, 21, 22, 23, 25, 26, 27, 28
bread flour 29, 41, 43, 45, 46, 54, 55, 56, 59, 62, 63, 64, 65, 66, 67, 68, 69, 78, 79, 80, 86, 91, 92, 113, 114, 115, 117, 118, 119, 120, 121, 122, 123
briny olive 16
brown rice flour 101
brown sugar 41, 42, 45, 68, 72, 83, 94, 95, 96, 97, 98, 100, 104, 108, 117, 119, 121, 122, 123
buckwheat flour 59, 66, 82
butter 3, 4, 7, 11, 25, 31, 35, 36, 38, 39, 41, 42, 43, 44, 45, 49, 50, 51, 52, 55, 56, 58, 60, 62, 63, 67, 68, 69, 72, 73, 78, 82, 83, 84, 85, 87, 88, 89, 90, 92, 94, 95, 96, 97, 98, 100, 101, 104, 105, 106, 107, 108, 109, 110, 111, 113, 117, 118, 120, 121, 122, 123
buttermilk 25, 90, 109

C

cacao powder 77, 117
canola oil 35, 103, 104, 105, 107, 108, 111
canola oil spray 35
capers 79
caraway seeds 64, 69, 77
cardamom 43, 92
carrot 59, 84, 108
cashews 50
chai masala mix 50
chia seeds 64
chicken stock 59
cinnamon 4, 39, 41, 42, 43, 51, 63, 67, 68, 72, 90, 94, 96, 100, 101, 103, 105, 108, 117, 118, 119, 121, 122, 123
clove 42, 91, 103, 105, 108, 118, 119, 121, 122
cocoa powder 39, 94, 95, 97, 99, 104, 107, 117
coconut 49, 50, 51, 52, 82, 84, 95, 103, 108, 122
coconut cream 50, 95, 103, 111
coconut extract 82
coconut flour 49, 52
coconut milk 49, 82
coconut milk beverage 96, 97, 100, 103, 104, 105, 106, 107, 108, 109, 111
coconut oil 49, 50, 51, 99, 107, 122
cold butter 44, 87, 88
combination 33, 44, 82, 91
cornmeal 20, 36, 86, 115, 117, 119
Cornmeal 36, 86
cream 39, 41, 43, 49, 50, 51, 52, 83, 95, 96, 97, 98, 99, 100, 101, 103, 104, 105, 106, 108, 109, 110, 111, 123
cream cheese 51, 64, 84, 96, 97, 101, 104, 105, 108, 110
creamy gluten-free peanut butter 98

D

dark chocolate chips 107
dark molasses 122
dark raisins 56
dried cranberries 51, 100
dried herbs 32, 35
dried sweetened cranberries 118
dry yeast 3, 9, 10, 13, 14, 15, 16, 17, 31, 42, 57, 85, 116
Dutch-process cocoa 67

E

egg 4, 7, 32, 36, 38, 39, 40, 41, 42, 43, 45, 46, 49, 50, 51, 52, 56, 58, 60, 67, 68, 69, 71, 72, 73, 74, 78, 82, 83, 84, 86, 90, 94, 95, 96, 97, 98, 99, 100, 101, 103, 104, 105, 106, 107, 108, 109, 110, 111, 113, 114, 117, 118, 120, 121, 122, 123
egg white protein 49, 50
egg white protein powder 49, 50
einkorn wheat flour 66
Emmenthaler cheese 60
espresso 94, 107
extra-virgin olive oil 9, 11, 12, 13, 14, 16, 17

F

fennel seeds 65
Flaxseed 40
flaxseed meal 67
flax seeds 26, 50
food-grade lye 13
freeze-dried strawberries 106
fresh blueberries 29
fresh oysters 60
fresh strawberries 106
full fat milk 49

G

garlic 59, 73, 74, 85, 91
garlic powder 73, 74
giardiniera 79
ginger 42, 105, 108, 119, 121, 122
gluten-free oat bran 73
graham cracker crumbs 96, 97
granulated sugar 67, 68, 71, 72, 83, 94, 95, 96, 97, 98, 99, 100, 101, 103, 104, 105, 106, 107, 108, 109, 110, 111
granulated sweetener 49
green apple 119
green food coloring 104

H

ham 45, 60, 79, 96, 97
hazelnut 50
heavy cream 95, 111
hemp seeds 64
high-protein flour 71, 72, 73, 74
Homemade Graham Crackers 97
honey 15, 32, 40, 46, 47, 55, 62, 63, 64, 65, 66, 69, 73, 75, 76, 78, 79, 113, 116, 117, 120

I

instant potato flakes 92
instant yeast 45, 46, 47, 54, 55, 56, 57, 58, 71, 72, 76, 77, 80, 89, 92, 119, 120
Italian seasoning blend 74

J

jalapeño pepper 85

K

Kamut flour 68, 79

L

lemon 29, 43, 44, 49, 96, 109
lemon extract 109
lemon juice 44, 96, 109
lemon zest 29, 49, 96, 109
light rye flour 69
liquid stevia 52

M

malt syrup 15
maple syrup 32, 82, 98, 105, 117, 123
marinara sauce 74
marjoram 85
milk 3, 7, 25, 38, 43, 44, 45, 46, 49, 51, 56, 58, 60, 62, 63, 66, 67, 68, 69, 75, 77, 78, 82, 89, 92, 95, 103, 104, 105, 107, 108, 109, 111, 113, 114, 118
mini marshmallows 97
mixed candied fruit 92
molasses 77, 78, 120, 122
mortadella 79
mozzarella 46, 71, 74, 80, 85
mozzarella cheese 46, 76, 80
mushroom 38, 59, 71, 85

N

no calorie sweetener 51
nonfat dry milk 89
nutmeg 42, 60, 100, 105, 108, 118, 119, 121, 122, 123

O

old-fashioned rolled oats 73, 92
old starter 19
olive 9, 11, 12, 13, 14, 16, 17, 21, 32, 33, 34, 35, 36, 46, 47, 54, 59, 62, 64, 65, 71, 72, 73, 79, 86
olive oil 11, 17, 21, 32, 33, 34, 35, 36, 46, 47, 54, 59, 62, 64, 65, 71, 72, 73, 74, 76, 79, 85, 86, 116
onion 11, 59, 71, 85
orange 75, 95, 99, 100, 101, 106, 118
orange extract 95, 99, 100, 101, 106
orange juice 75, 118
oregano 35, 80, 85

P

Pain de Mie 60
Parmesan cheese 46, 71, 74, 80
peanut oil 90
pearl sugar 56
pecan 73, 82, 83, 84, 121, 123
Pecorino cheese 85
peppermint extract 99, 104
pepperoni 71, 74, 80, 86
pesto 76
pineapple 51, 84, 108
pineapple chunks 51
pistachio 43
pizza crust recipe 79
pizza sauce 71, 74, 80, 86
polenta 26
poolish 4, 10, 11, 12, 17, 55
poppy seeds 15, 40, 45

The Complete Cosori Air Fryer Cookbook | 127

pork shoulder roast 59
potato 21, 45, 59, 92
powdered sugar 44, 67, 84, 96, 97, 100, 103, 104, 105, 106, 107, 108, 109
probiotic capsules 50
provolone 79
psyllium husk 52
pumpkin pie spice 51, 96, 103, 119, 121
pumpkin puree 50, 96, 103
pumpkin seeds 26, 96
pure pumpkin purée 121

R
raisins 56, 63, 68, 72
raw sunflower seeds 25
red gel food coloring 97
red wine 59
red wine vinegar 60, 79
Rice flour 29, 31, 33, 34, 115, 117, 119
ripe bolted wheat Sourdough Starter 28
ripe rye sourdough starter 26, 27
ripe rye Sourdough Starter 22
ripe Sonora Sourdough Starter 24
ripe spelt Sourdough Starter 23
ripe whole durum Sourdough Starter 21
ripe whole-wheat sourdough starter 25
roasted red pepper 79
rolled oats 73, 78, 100
rosemary 36, 46, 47, 85
rye flour 19, 20, 22, 64, 77, 86

S
sage 29, 85
salami 79
sausage 52, 55, 71
semisweet chocolate chips 83, 94, 95, 97, 98, 99, 107
semolina 29, 33, 36
semolina flour 36
Semolina flour 33
sesame seeds 15, 21, 26, 33, 45, 49, 52, 69, 72, 78, 79
shallot 60, 79
shortening 97, 98, 99, 100, 103, 104, 105, 106, 107, 108, 109, 111
shredded cheese 52, 86
sifted confectioners' sugar 43, 114, 118
soaker 25, 26, 27
sorghum flour 42
sourdough starter 19, 29, 46, 47, 62, 63, 64, 65, 66, 67, 76, 77, 82, 83, 84, 85, 86, 87, 88, 89, 90, 91, 92, 114, 115, 118, 119, 121, 122, 123
spelt bran 23
spelt flour 13, 23, 59, 78
starter 19, 20, 21, 22, 23, 24, 25, 26, 27, 28, 29, 46, 47, 59, 62, 63, 64, 65, 66, 67, 68, 69, 75, 76, 77, 78, 79, 82, 83, 85, 86, 87, 88, 89, 91, 92, 115, 117
stevia drop 50
strawberry jam 43, 114
sugar 3, 5, 6, 38, 39, 41, 42, 43, 44, 45, 46, 47, 56, 57, 58, 62, 67, 68, 69, 71, 72, 76, 77, 80, 82, 83, 84, 85, 86, 87, 89, 90, 92, 94, 95, 96, 97, 98, 99, 100, 101, 103, 104, 105, 106, 107, 108, 109, 110, 111, 113, 114, 117, 118, 119, 121, 122, 123
sunflower seed oil 71, 72, 73
sunflower seeds 26, 40, 64
sweetened condensed coconut milk 95, 103
swerve 50, 51

T
thyme 35, 59, 85
tomato 17, 47, 76, 85
tomato guts 17
turmeric 65

U
unsalted butter 42, 43, 44, 45, 56, 58, 60, 62, 63, 67, 68, 69, 72, 73, 78, 113, 114, 118, 120, 121, 122, 123
unsweetened almond milk 51
unsweetened apple sauce 51
unsweetened applesauce 108
unsweetened coconut flakes 95
unsweetened natural cocoa powder 107
ursa baguette dough 11, 12

V
vanilla 39, 42, 43, 49, 50, 51, 67, 83, 94, 95, 96, 97, 98, 99, 100, 101, 103, 104, 105, 106, 107, 108, 109, 110, 111, 117, 118, 123
vanilla extract 42, 43, 49, 50, 51, 67, 83, 84, 94, 95, 96, 97, 98, 99, 100, 101, 103, 104, 105, 106, 107, 108, 109, 110, 111, 114, 117, 118, 123
vanilla Greek yogurt 104, 106, 107, 110
vanilla stevia 49
vegetable oil 40, 57, 59, 84, 90

W
warm milk 41, 43, 45, 77, 113, 114, 118, 121, 122, 123
wheat 3, 6, 9, 10, 12, 13, 14, 15, 16, 17, 20, 21, 22, 23, 25, 26, 27, 28, 29, 42, 45, 47, 55, 66, 67, 80, 115, 117, 120
wheat bran 22, 25, 26
whey protein 51
white cane sugar 42, 44, 46, 47, 76, 77, 80
white Cheddar cheese 91
white sugar 57
white whole wheat flour 67
whole buckwheat groats 25
whole einkorn berries 27
whole-grain durum flour 21
whole-grain einkorn flour 27, 75
whole grain flour 62, 63, 64
whole grain rye flour 64
whole-grain Sonora flour 24
whole-grain spelt flour 13, 23, 26
whole milk 38, 39, 40, 44, 56, 58, 60, 67, 68, 69, 75, 78, 96, 97, 100, 103, 104, 105, 106, 107, 108, 109, 111, 117
whole rye flour 22

whole-wheat 20, 25, 29, 42, 45, 47, 76, 80, 82
whole-wheat flour 29, 42, 45, 47, 76, 80, 82, 83, 84, 85, 86, 87, 88, 90, 91, 92, 115, 119, 120, 121, 122

X
xanthan gum 94, 95, 96, 97, 98, 99, 100, 101, 103, 104, 105, 106, 107, 108, 109, 110, 111

Y
yeast 3, 4, 5, 6, 7, 9, 10, 13, 14, 15, 16, 17, 19, 28, 29, 31, 32, 33, 34, 35, 36, 38, 39, 40, 42, 45, 46, 47, 54, 55, 56, 57, 58, 71, 72, 76, 77, 80, 85, 89, 92, 116, 117, 119, 120
yogurt 9, 19, 66, 104, 107, 110

Z
zucchini 42

MARIAN D. BENNETT

Printed in Great Britain
by Amazon